The Occult in Mediaeval Europe, 500

Related titles from Palgrave Macmillan

Stuart Clark (ed.), *Languages of Witchcraft: Narative, Ideology and Meaning in Early Modern Culture*

P. G. Maxwell-Stuart, *Witchcraft in Europe and the New World, 1400–1800*

P. G. Maxwell-Stuart (ed.), *The Occult in Early Modern Europe: A Documentary History*

Geoffrey Scarre and John Callow, *Witchcraft and Magic in Sixteenth- and Seventeenth-Century Europe*, 2nd edition

Gary K. Waite, *Heresy, Magic and Witchcraft in Early Modern Europe*

The Occult in Mediaeval Europe, 500–1500

A Documentary History

Edited and translated by
P. G. Maxwell-Stuart

palgrave
macmillan

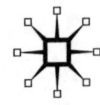

Selection, translation and editorial matter
© P. G. Maxwell-Stuart 2005

All rights reserved. No reproduction, copy or transmission of this publication may be made without written permission.

No paragraph of this publication may be reproduced, copied or transmitted save with written permission or in accordance with the provisions of the Copyright, Designs and Patents Act 1988, or under the terms of any licence permitting limited copying issued by the Copyright Licensing Agency, 90 Tottenham Court Road, London W1T 4LP.

Any person who does any unauthorised act in relation to this publication may be liable to criminal prosecution and civil claims for damages.

The author has asserted his right to be identified as the author of this work in accordance with the Copyright, Designs and Patents Act 1988.

First published 2005 by
PALGRAVE MACMILLAN
Houndmills, Basingstoke, Hampshire RG21 6XS and
175 Fifth Avenue, New York, N.Y. 10010
Companies and representatives throughout the world

PALGRAVE MACMILLAN is the global academic imprint of the Palgrave Macmillan division of St. Martin's Press, LLC and of Palgrave Macmillan Ltd. Macmillan® is a registered trademark in the United States, United Kingdom and other countries. Palgrave is a registered trademark in the European Union and other countries.

ISBN-13: 978 1–4039–0290–0 hardback
ISBN-10: 1–4039–0290–9 hardback
ISBN-13: 978 1–4039–0289–4 paperback
ISBN-10: 1–4039–0289–5 paperback

This book is printed on paper suitable for recycling and made from fully managed and sustained forest sources.

A catalogue record for this book is available from the British Library.

Library of Congress Cataloging-in-Publication Data

    The occult in Mediaeval Europe, 500–1500 / edited and translated by P. G. Maxwell-Stuart.
      p. cm.
    Includes bibliographical references and index.
      ISBN 1–4039–0290–9 (hardcover) – ISBN 1–4039–0289–5 (pbk.)
        1. Occultism–Europe–History–To 1500–Sources. I. Maxwell-Stuart, P. G.

BF1434.E85O25 2005
130'.94'0902–dc22   2004058394

10 9 8 7 6 5 4 3 2 1
14 13 12 11 10 09 08 07 06 05

Printed in China

For David Stewart

Contents

List of Illustrations   xvi
Acknowledgements   xvii

Introduction   1

The Created Universe   11

1. The constituent parts of the world. St Isidore of Seville: *De natura rerum* (612/13)   13
2. A journey through the cosmos. Bernardus Silvestris: *Cosmographia* (1141)   15
3. The elements and the humours. Pseudo-Bede: *De mundi celestis terrestrisque constitutione* (second half 12th century)   19

Portents and prodigies   20

4. A travelling star. *Acta et processus canonizacionis beate Birgitte* (c.1391)   20
5. Two suns. *Chronicum Scotorum* (12th century)   21
6. Eclipses. *Anglo-Saxon Chronicle*   21
7. Eclipse. William of Malmesbury: *Historia Novella* (1142–7)   21
8. Eclipse. Rodulfus Glaber: *Historiae* (late 1020s–1045/6)   22
9. A rain of blood. André de Fleury: *Vita Gauzlini* (c.1042)   22
10. A Storm. *Annales Fuldenses*, referring to the year 857   25
11. A globe of fire. *The Myracles of Oure Lady* (1496)   25
12. Various portents. Sigebert of Gembloux: *Chronica*, on the year 1000   26
13. Various signs. *Annales Fuldenses*, referring to the year 870   26
14. Portents. *Chronicum Scotorum* (12th century)   27
15. A mysterious voice. Georgios Kedrenos: *Compendium historiarum* (late 12th century)   27
16. Portents. *Annales Fuldenses*, referring to the year 878   28

17	Expectations of the end of the world. Abbo of Fleury: *Apologeticus ad Hugonem et Rodbertum, reges Francorum* (c.994/6)	29
18	Doubts about how to compute the arrival of the end of the world. Anon.: *Blickling Homily on Holy Thursday* (971)	29
19	Evil portents at Emperor Alexios's coronation. Niketas Choniates: *Historia* (early 13th century)	30
20	A monster. Georgios Kedrenos: *Compendium historiarum* (late 12th century)	31
21	The meaning of monsters. Sebastian Brant: *De monstroso ansere atque porcellis in villa Gugenheim* (1496). Adapted	31
22	Why the original inhabitants of Britain were giants. Anon.: *De origine gigantum* (mid 1330s)	32

Occult properties of the natural world — 33

23	The meaning of stones. Marbodus: *Liber lapidum* (c.1090)	33

Signs on the human body — 36

24	Physiognomy. James Yonge: *The Governance of Princes* (1422)	36
25	The evil eye. Robert Grosseteste: *Expositio in epistolam Sancti Pauli ad Galatas* (c.1225)	38
26	The evil eye. Alfonso de Tostado: *Las catorze questiones* (mid 15th century)	39

Non-human entities — 40

27	Orders of angels. Nicholas of Cusa: *Dialogi de ludo globi*, Book 2 (1463)	40
28	Angels and demons. St John of Damascus: *De fide orthodoxa* (early 8th century)	41
29	The use of demons. John Barbour: *The Brus* (1370s)	42
30	Fairies. *The Trial of St Joan of Arc* (1431)	43
31	A werewolf. Giraldus Cambrensis: *Topographia Hiberniae* (c.1187)	43
32	Unearthly visitants. *De gestis Herwardi Saxonis* (late 11th/early 12th century)	47

33	The dead. Peter Damian: *Letter to Pope Nicholas II*, (written between December 1059 and July 1061)	48
34	Dead monks. Trithemius: *Beati Rabani Mauri Vita* (refers to 837)	49
35	A disturbing vision. Thomas of Cantimpré: *Bonum universale de apibus* (1256–61)	50
36	An evil spirit. *Vita Sancti Roberti Abbatis* (11th century)	51
37	A mysterious transvection. Peter Damian: *Letter to Abbot Desiderius and the Abbey of Monte Cassino* (c.1065)	52
38	A political use of demoniacs. Niketas Choniates: *Historia* (early 13th century)	53
39	Torments inflicted by demons. Blessed Angela of Foligno: *Vita* (late 13th century)	54
40	Exorcism. Hieronymus Radiolensis: *Miracula Sancti Joannis Gualberti* (late 11th century)	56

Miracles 59

41	Curing the sick. Andrew of Strumi: *Vita Sancti Joannis Gualbert* (referring to end of 12th/beginning of 13th century)	59
42	Blood in the chalice. Giovanni Villani: *Croniche Fiorentine* (early 14th century)	59
43	An anointed King's ability to cure the sick. Robert Fitzhugh: *Memorandum*, 31 May 1435	60
44	A false miracle. Giovanni di m. Pedrino Depintore: *Cronica del suo tempo* (mid 15th century)	60

Methods of divination and discovering truth 61

45	How to cast lots. *Sortes XII Patriarcharum* (second half of 11th century)	61
46	Imperial patronage of divination. Niketas Choniates: *Historia* (early 13th century). Adapted	62
47	How to uncover a murderer. *Lex Frisionum* (late 8th/early 9th century)	63
48	Organising an ordeal. Eberhard of Bamberg: *Breviarium* (12th century)	64
49	Championing a witch. Adémar of Chabannes: *Chronicon* (late 1020s)	65

Contents

The Parallel Universe of Magic — 69

Popular practices — 71

1. The various kinds of magic. Hugh of St Victor: *Didascalion* (late 1120s) — 71
2. Magic as part of everyday life. David of Ganjak: *Penitential* (c.1130s) — 73
3. Advice to beware of using divination and magic. Aelfric: *Homily on the Octaves and Circumcision of Our Lord* (1020s–40s) — 74
4. Mixing religion and magic. Etienne de Bourbon: *Anecdotes historiques* (early 13th century) — 75
5. Heretics and magic. Heribert: *Epistola de haereticis Petragoricis* (c.1147) — 76
6. Magic by means of a pact. Heinrich von Gorkum: *De superstitionibus quibusdam casibus* (early 15th century) — 76
7. The dangers of divination. Nicholas of Cusa: *Sermon, 'Ibant Magi'* (6 January 1431) — 77
8. Days regarded as unlucky. Jean Gerson: *De superstitiosa dierum observantia* (1421) — 82
9. Finding a thief by divination. Etienne de Bourbon: *Anecdotes historiques* (early 13th century) — 83
10. Geomancy. Rolandino da Padova: *Cronica in factis et circa facta Marchie Trivixane* (1262) — 84
11. Magic at the Papal Court. Pope John XXII: *Letter* (27 February 1318) — 84
12. Magic at the Imperial Court. Theodore Balsamon: *In epistolam Sancti Basilii canonicam III* (1170s) — 86
13. How to investigate workers of magic. Bernardo Gui: *Practica inquisitionis heretice pravitatis* (1323/4) — 87
14. Image magic. Athelwold: *Record of an exchange of lands* (late 10th century) — 89
15. Maleficent images. Niketas Choniates: *Historia* (late 12th/early 13th century) — 90

Ritual magic — 90

16. Conjuration of Spirits. Pietro d'Abano: *Heptameron seu elementa magica* (late 13th century) — 90

17	Types of magical procedure. Moses Maimonides: *Dalalat al'Ha'rin* [A Guide of the Perplexed] (1190)	98
18	Making amulets. Alexander of Tralles: *De arte medicina* (late 6th century)	99
19	Making magical seals. Arnald of Villanova: *De sigillis* (c.1301)	100
20	German weather magic. *Adjuration against a hailstorm* (11th century)	103
21	Christ as a sorcerer.: Anon.: *Christ Before Pilate: The Dream of Pilate's Wife* (1463–77)	103

Hostile magic, demons, and witchcraft — 104

22	Necromancy. *The Trial of Gilles de Rais* (1440)	104
23	Politically inspired necromancy. Enguerrand de Monstrelet: *Chroniques* (referring to 1407)	110
24	Demons cause illness. Guibert de Nogent: *Monodiae* (c.1115)	112
25	Witches' acts of harmful magic. Johannes Nider: *Preceptorium divine legis* (c.1437)	113
26	Witchcraft and marriage. *Summa Parisiensis* [Commentary on the *Decreta* of Gratian, Causa 33, question 1] (c.1154–9)	114
27	A lying witch. Marie de France: *Les Fables* (1189–1208)	115
28	An incubus and the use of apotropaic magic. *Acta et processus canonizacionis beate Birgitte* (c.1391)	116
29	The witch as vampire. Etienne de Bourbon: *Anecdotes historiques* (early 13th century)	117
30	A witch in battle. *De gestis Herwardi Saxonis* (late 11th/early 12th century)	118
31	The witch as a subject for humour. Etienne de Bourbon: *Anecdotes historiques* (early 13th century)	119
32	Blackening people's reputations. Etienne de Bourbon: *Anecdotes historiques* (early 13th century)	120
33	Flying to the Sabbat. Martin le France: *Le Champion des Dames* (1440)	120
34	The Sabbat described during a witch-trial. Jacques du Clercq: *Mémoires* [adapted], relating to 1460	122

35	A lawyer's reservations about the Sabbat. Ambrosius de Vignate: *Tractatus de hereticis* (c.1468). Adapted	129

Prohibition, reservation, and scepticism — 134

36	*Pactus legis Salicae* (6th century)	135
37	King Rothair: *Edictus* (643)	135
38	*Leges Visigothorum*: King Flavius Chindasvind (c.644)	136
39	Harmful magic. *Lex Ribuaria de maleficio* (c.7th century)	139
40	King Liutprand: *Laws* (727)	139
41	King Childeric III: *Capitularia* (742)	140
42	Charlemagne: *Capitularia* (873)	140
43	Early English Laws (9th and 10th centuries)	141
44	Dionysius Exiguus: *Canones* (6th century)	142
45	*Council of Orléans* (511)	142
46	*Council of Auxerre* (c.573–c.603)	143
47	*Council of Paris* (829). Adapted	143
48	Pope Leo IV: *Letter to the Bishops of Britain* (848/9)	144
49	Herard, Archbishop of Tournois: *Capitularia* (858)	145
50	*Council of Worms* (May 868)	145
51	Instructions about the punishment of workers of magic. Pope Benedict XII: *Letter*, 7 April 1338	145
52	*Synod of Salamanca*, 2 May 1451	146
53	Condemnation of magicians in Lombardy. Pope Alexander VI: *Decretal* (1501)	148
54	Qualified scepticism. Michael Italikos: *Letters* (mid 12th century)	148
55	Reservations about magic. Barsanuphios: *Letters* (6th century)	150
56	Types of magical operation. Guillaume d'Auvergne: *De universo* (first half 13th century)	150
57	Reservations about the worth of evidence relating to witchcraft. Ulrich Molitor: *De laniis et phitonicis mulieribus* (1489)	153
58	Proposed punishments for those found guilty of practising harmful magic in Catalonia. Anthoni de Balcebre: *Document relating to witches in the Àneu Valley* (1424)	158

Interpreting and Manipulating the Universe   161

Astrology   163

1. The planets and their houses at the creation. Pseudo-Bede: *De mundi celestis terrestrisque constitutione* (second half 12th century)   165
2. Interpreting celestial phenomena. Giovanni Villani: *Croniche Fiorentine* (early 14th century)   166
3. Astrology and free will. Albertus Magnus: *Speculum astronomiae* (c.1260)   166
4. Astrology and religion. Albertus Magnus: *Speculum astronomiae* (c.1260)   168
5. Jesus in the stars. Hermann of Carinthia: *De Essentiis* (1143)   170
6. Planetary powers seen in natural objects. Pseudo-al Majriti: *Ghayatal-hakim [Picatrix]* (mid 15th century)   170
7. Human character in relation to Mars and Venus. Anon.: *Ovid Moralisé* (early 14th century)   175
8. The planetary interaction of Saturn and Jupiter. Marsilio Ficino: *De vita libri tres* (1489)   176
9. Planetary influences on the processes of birth. Michael Scot: *Liber phisionomie* (1209)   177
10. Interpreting Classical myths in the light of astrology. Giovanni Boccaccio: *De genealogia deorum gentilium* (1350–75)   179
11. Medical powers of the planets. Marsilio Ficino: *De vita libri tres* (1489)   180
12. Advice to a King. John Lydgate: *Secrees of Old Philosoffres* (c.1450)   181
13. Astral and planetary magic. Marsilio Ficino: *De vita libri tres* (1489)   182
14. Fraud. Roger Bacon: *Opus maius* (1266–7)   184
15. Imperial acceptance of astrology. Niketas Choniates: *Historia* (early 13th century)   187
16. An Imperial sceptic. Anna Komnena: *Alexiad* (post 1148)   187
17. Doubts about astrology. John Barbour: *The Brus* (1370s)   189

xiv Contents

18 Condemnation of astrology and magic. St Alcimus
    Ecdicius Avitus: *Poemata de Mosaicae historiae
    gestis* (late 5th/early 6th century) 190
19 Condemnation of judicial astrology. Girolamo
    Savonarola: *Trattato contra li astrologi* (1497) 191

Alchemy 193

20 Technical terminology. Pseudo-Geber:
    Summa Perfectionis (early 14th century (?)) 194
21 Metals and minerals. Pseudo-Roger Bacon:
    Speculum alchemiae (pre 16th century) 197
22 Why metals turn to gold. Pietro d'Abano:
    Pretiosa Margarita Novella (1330) 199
23 Alchemical equipment. Pseudo-Geber: *Liber
    Fornacum* (15th century) 201
24 An alchemical operation. Paulus Eck von
    Saltzbach: *Clavis Philosophorum* (1489) 210
25 Alchemical recipes. Arnaldus of Bruxella:
    Alchemical manuscript (transcribed at some
    time between 1473 and 1490) 211
26 The hidden spirit in sulphur. Anonymous
    manuscript: *Alchimiae tractatus* (14th century) 212
27 The need for secrecy. George Ripley:
    The Compound of Alchemy (c.1471) 214
28 Alchemical processes described in symbolic
    language. Alfonso X of Castile: *Tesoro*
    (attributed, 13th century) 215
29 Alchemical processes described more clearly.
    John of Rupescissa: *De consideratione quintae
    essentiae* (mid 14th century) 216
30 Use of the word 'Stone'. Roger Bacon: *Secretum
    secretorum* (13th century) 217
31 The Stone. Avicenna: *De anima* (1021/4) 217
32 Description of the Philosopher's Stone.
    John Lydgate: *Secrees of Old Philosoffres* (c.1450) 218
33 A medicine produced by alchemy. Ortulanus:
    Practica vera alkimica (1386) 219
34 The importance of alchemy to physicians. Roger
    Bacon: *De erroribus medicorum* (13th century) 220

35	Some famous alchemists. Al-Nadim: *Kitab al-Fihrist* (987–8)	221
36	An unfriendly portrait of an alchemist. Geoffrey Chaucer: *The Canon's Yeoman's Prologue*, 64–130, adapted (1380s–90s)	223
37	Impediments to an alchemist's being able to work. Pseudo-Geber: *Summa Perfectionis* (adapted) (early 14th century (?))	225
38	English royal licences granted to practise alchemy. *Calendar of State Papers* (15th century)	226
39	An alchemist terrorised into making silver. *Calendar of Patent Rolls* (3 April 1337)	227
40	Alchemy regarded as fraudulent. Sebastian Brant: *Das Narrenschiff* (1494)	228
41	Fraudulent alchemists. *Calendar of Patent Rolls* (18 August 1452.)	228
42	Papal prohibition against alchemy. John XXII: *Extravagantales decretales: De crimine falsi* (early 14th century)	229

Bibliography	**231**
Index	**242**

List of Illustrations

1	Furnace for calcination	203
2	Furnace for sublimation	204
3	Furnace for descension	205
4	Furnace for smelting	206
5	Furnace for solution	207
6	Furnace for fixation	208
7	Athanor	209

Acknowledgements

All translations are my own with the exception of the passage from David of Ganjak's *Penitential* (page 73), which is that of J. F. Dowsett, and I am grateful to Michael Thompson for his invaluable assistance with Mediaeval Catalan. All images are reproduced courtesy of St Andrews University Library.

Introduction

Of all the epithets popularly attached to the Middle Ages, 'superstitious' is perhaps the most reprehensible. The creation of myths about historical periods has been a feature of general (and indeed scholarly) writing on the subject and may be regarded almost as an intrinsic part of the historian's role as communicator, however much he or she might like to invest the results of his or her researches with the ideal of objective reporting. National myths, as Ronald Hutton has recently pointed out, spring from a combination of individual enthusiasm for a particular point of view and a willingness on the part of the public to be seduced into accepting this as reportage rather than fiction.[1] It is the same, mutatis mutandis, with witchcraft. The view of eighteenth-century *philosophes* that the Middle Ages were representable by the Catholic Church and were therefore backward, superstitious, and 'dark' in contrast to their own times which were forward-looking, rational, and 'scientific', created a myth which successive centuries have found both comfortable and flattering since it supposes that the historical process is, as it were, a vertical progression leading from primitivism to sophistication, with those who make that claim and those who listen to them happily ensconced at the loftier end of the scale. Nineteenth-century romantic historical novels and early twentieth-century anthropology, steeped in both Darwinism, and Imperial and racial assumptions of natural hierarchy, seemed either to reinforce this point of view, or to envisage a quaint but faintly charming peasantry backward and therefore inclined to superstition, liable to be awed by the increasing number of technological inventions the educated were learning to take in their stride; and thus the seductive myth once launched pursued its misleading course. Professional historians battle against such myths with varying degrees of success.

---

[1] *Witches, Druids, and King Arthur*, 2–12. It is instructive to see the effects produced by once-popular histories by John Bury, Arthur Mee, John Trevelyan, and Lytton Strachey.

Like so many myths, however, this one about the Middle Ages contains a grain of truth. Churchmen frequently fulminated against 'superstition', by which they essentially meant beliefs and practices not consistent with strict religious orthodoxy, but not quite wayward or distorted enough to be regarded as outright heresy. The use of Christian names, formulae, or ritual gestures in the course of trying to effect (let us say) a cure was suspicious if it seemed to suggest that these names, formulae, or gestures were sufficient in themselves to bring about that cure; and if they were allied to strange names, formulae in a language unknown, or non-religious gestures – such as passing the sick person through a circle made from the twigs or branches of a particular plant – ecclesiastical opinion turned from suspicion to condemnation, and secular opinion was rarely far behind. Should such a cure work, or appear to work, there arose the question of which power caused the illness to go away. Was it a natural power inherent in the created world, the power of God, the power of some angel or spirit, or the power of Satan or one of his demons?

Here it is important to bear in mind certain distinctions Mediaeval readers or hearers would have made between various kinds of happening, distinctions which were so forcibly made by St Augustine in his *City of God* that they remained thereafter indelible in Christian consciousness. A wonder (*mirum*) was an event regarded as extraordinary in some way or other. If a woman gave birth to a grotesquely deformed child, for example, the child was a *mirum*, and the birth had not happened by accident but by design. That is to say, it meant something. The 'something' could be bewitchment. A person with maleficent intentions had exercised more-than-human power through the agency of, let us say, an evil spirit in order to effect this distortion of nature. The 'something' might be a divine warning to reform the adult's way of life, or a punishment for behaviour long sinful in thought or word or deed. Unusual phenomena such as meteors, comets, dancing lights, particularly sudden and destructive storms, and so on, were also likely to be regarded as *mira* and therefore in some fashion significant. *Mira*, however, were not miracles. They took place within the boundaries of nature, although they probably went beyond the commonly known boundaries of nature and were thus describable as 'preternatural'. *Occultus*, too, it is important to note, simply means 'hidden'. So if anything is described as 'occult', it does not mean 'irrational' or 'the opposite of natural'. On the contrary, it simply implies that human beings do not yet understand the way it works. So 'occult' is natural but so far uncomprehended.

Miracles, on the other hand, were supernatural in origin. They came from 'above nature', which means they originated with God and involved suspension of the ordinary laws governing nature. These laws were either known to human beings or (for the time being, at least) unknown. So if events happened according to the known laws, they were entirely 'natural'. If they happened according to unknown and so 'occult' laws, they were 'preternatural'. Magicians of all kinds, angels, demons, and the whole range of non-human entities, were created beings and in consequence operated within nature. If magicians were able apparently to work wonders, that was because they either understood or, through the assistance of spirits, had access to the hidden laws of nature. Only God could actually interfere with the laws, overt or occult, of His own creation; and therefore miracles were wonders attributable only to God or to saints working through and with the power and consent of God.

The legitimacy of power thus exercised the consideration of both Church and state, and access to illicit power, which was all too easy to obtain, needed very careful watching, if not outright suppression. 'Superstition' with its implications, first of going beyond what orthodox religious practice deemed necessary or appropriate in the worship of God, and secondly straying into unorthodox belief and behaviour which, if not quite heretical in itself, opened the unwary and ignorant to the destructive machinations of evil spirits, was thus a very serious matter, for even at its most harmless, it represented the initial steps along a road which could end in damnation. Mediaeval concern over superstition, however, was frequently reinterpreted by later centuries to conform with their notions of historical 'advance' and scientific 'progress', and thus in large measure misunderstood and, to an extent, trivialised.

The Middle Ages took the view they did because of the concept of creation they held. One might call it 'holistic' in contrast to ours which tends, in practice at least, to treat the various possible realms of being as though they were separate and distinct. A modern western mother is unlikely as a matter of course to take her sick child to a general practitioner, an alternative therapist, *and* a priest in order to seek physical, preternatural, and supernatural help, with more or less equal faith in the efficacy of each. This, however, as Kieckhefer has pointed out, was perfectly possible in Mediaeval society;[2] and it was possible because of the view that Creation was a whole achievement, not a series of discrete

[2] *Magic in the Middle Ages*, 3.

productions. Everything was linked to everything else by 'correspondences', occult likenesses, genuine or perceived, which enabled each separate component of creation to exist in a continuous state of sympathy or antipathy with all the others. Hence one thing could be made to influence another or be subject to its influence in turn, while the supernatural, preternatural, and natural worlds were capable of penetrating each other, and thus existed as a multiformed unit under God. Angels and demons could appear to human beings; God himself took flesh and lived for a while on earth; the Final Judgement would see dead human beings reunited with their bodies which would then exist in Heaven or in Hell, both non-physical states of being. The intrusion of ghosts and spirits upon the physical plane was thus not startling or unusual in theory, whatever reaction it might provoke in practice.

We must therefore learn to look upon magic and its allied branches of knowledge and practice as a continuum ranging from the simple ritual words and gestures, frequently called 'superstitious', intended to fulfil an immediate practical purpose, to the immensely elaborate and time-consuming rituals open only to the learned, and in the later period often involving knowledge of the Jewish Kabbalah – a particular interpretation of the origin and structure of Creation – intended to bring their operators into the very presence of God, or participate, while living, with the hierarchy of angelic beings in their ecstatic vision. Negative magic is to be included with positive on this continuum. Magic is magic. It does not divide itself into 'white' or 'black', as the modern mind trained to list and categorise and subdivide prefers to consider it. Consequently, witchcraft – too often examined on its own, as though it were a distinct species of exercising preternatural power – should be regarded simply as a negative manifestation of the magic which runs the whole length of the continuum; and the very varied Latin and Greek vocabulary of 'witch' and 'witchcraft', which I have retained in the text so that the reader can see how diverse the vocabulary is, illustrates the point that witchcraft was not a unified phenomenon inviting a single, overarching explanation but, rather like French *sorcellerie*, is a rather vague epithet which acts as a misleading *omnium gatherum* for a wide variety of divergent magical practices. So if we are to regain something of the Mediaeval non-discriminatory point of view, we must unlearn the habit of treating magic as though it were botany or zoology, and refrain from imposing upon it genera and species, families and component parts.

The period 500 to 1500 which takes us from the final stages of Classical antiquity to the first stirrings of that intellectual ferment which would produce what are known as 'the Renaissance' and 'the Reformation', and is popularly regarded as something of a stagnant entity, was in fact a millennium of the most intense waves of challenge beating with frequent violence upon the supposedly settled shores of religious, intellectual, and political orthodoxy. People were physically restless. Pilgrimages, warring armies and navies, trading caravans of all kinds, and Christian missionaries opened great stretches of the world to the experience of both the lettered and the unlettered. Islam arose and, after threatening to over-run large parts of the west, was later in its turn threatened by successive crusades seeking to reclaim the Holy Land for Christian governance. People were restless in their religion. Wave after wave of heresy came and went, the Jews in Europe and the Muslims without presented challenges of conversion, not all of which went the Christian way, and new monastic orders were founded to meet the ever-diverse spiritual needs of successive centuries. People were intellectually restless, too. Universities and monastic schools burgeoned, the created universe in its diversity was examined with a constant sense of curiosity and awe, while Latin, one of the great unifying factors in western intellectual life, enabled cross-cultural communication, and therefore largely by its means the vivifying enrichment of Arabic, Hebrew, and Greek learning was transmitted, to leaven the intellects of Europe and produce fresh ideas, fresh theories, and fresh interprctations of everything, theological or temporal: an ebullience which makes the notion of a 'superstitious' Middle Ages misleading at best and nonsensical at worst.

Indeed, it might make a little more sense to call the period 'sceptical', provided we bear in mind that Mediaeval scepticism should not be confused with modern. It was based upon a different view of the universe and therefore had different priorities. Everything was understood, examined, and explained *sub specie aeternitatis*, and history was the unfolding narrative of humankind's relationship with the Creator. Doubt entered into the process because of individuals' mistakes – which the Church had both power and authority to correct – or because the nature of creation was such that interpenetration of one mode of being by another might either lead to misunderstanding or cause illusions and deceits of one kind and another which could be mistaken for reality.

With this possibility of illusion always present, therefore, it is not surprising that the Middle Ages were full of hesitancy, constantly probing 'reality' for its roots and origin. Scepticism was thus almost a necessary condition of Mediaeval intellectual life. Does such-and-such emanate ultimately from God or from the Devil? If the first, it is true: if the latter, it is false. Due recognition of the Devil's superior intellect and experience was always being made – hence the need for deep probing of any phenomenon – and since humankind lived in a porous Creation which allowed various planes of existence to touch and overlap, everything called for interpretation. Signs in the sky, unusual births, marks on the human body, then changing patterns of planets and fixed stars, the interaction between corporeal, mineral, vegetable, and mental worlds known as 'sympathy' which bound everything together in an invisible reticulation of influences – all needed to be understood. For God was always active in His creation, and understanding how the apparently discrete parts of Creation worked, what their inter-relationships revealed about His purposes, and what divagations from His norm were intended to tell humanity, was an important, if not essential aid to the fulfilment of the purpose of both individual and human existence – to transcend the historical process locked in time and to enter into a timeless union with God. Such a view is perfectly rational. Whether we agree or disagree with it is of no consequence for our understanding of the Mediaeval world. It is a view which presents us with a particular, very subtle interpretation of creation, humanity's place within it, and the beginning and end of everything. Given such a view, logical consequences flow. They are unlikely to be ours, but that does not make them either invalid or foolish in relation to the premises which produced them.

For example, the Black Death (1347–51) devastated not only the bodies but also the minds of Europe. Why was God punishing human kind in such an awful fashion? Why did the Church seem to be unable to offer reliable protection against this divine onslaught? Had the multiplicity of heresies tried God's patience too far? Had Satan been unbound and set free to wreak God's vengeance upon a wayward and careless people? Islam, the great challenge to Christian faith, had not been defeated. The Jews were still unconverted. The Church itself was rent by schism, and rival Popes anathematised each other from Rome and Avignon. No wonder, then, if the Council of Basel (1431–47) listened to Johann Nider who summed up, in a manner more succinct and more urgent than others who had gone before him, the case for a Europe-wide conspiracy aimed at Christendom, inspired by Satan and carried out by his deluded henchmen and women, the workers of magic of all kinds, but especially those which did harm and brought illness, starvation, and death to their suffering neighbours. It is Nider's work which, more than perhaps any other of the period, which clarified hostility towards magical operators and stimulated both ecclesiastical and secular authorities to home in on them as particular dangers to the social and spiritual welfare of their communities; and it was upon his work and its aftermath that Heinrich Institoris built his influential, and subsequently famous work on hostile workers of magic, the *Malleus Maleficarum*.

Important to any discussion of the occult sciences during the Middle Ages are the comments and observations of the two great theologians who dominated the thinking of much of the period, St Augustine of Hippo and St Thomas Aquinas. St Augustine condemned as superstitious all forms of pagan religion. Consequently, any practices which were or might be linked with the pagan past were also condemnable, and for this St Augustine tended to use the word 'superstitious', not meaning 'irrational', as in modern usage, or 'going beyond what is appropriate in worship', as the sixteenth century would have it, but 'belonging to an alien, non-Christian cult'. 'Anything is superstitious', he wrote, 'if it has been established by people with a view to making and worshipping idols, or to worshipping anything created, or any part of anything created, as though it were a god; or if it relates to certain kinds of consultation, and pacts made as a sign of good intent agreed and ratified with spirits.[3] Examples of these are the laboured efforts of the arts of magic ... To this category belong all those things people tie round their necks or arms or attach to their clothing as amulets, and remedies which the medical profession condemns as well, whether these consist of incantations or certain marks known as "characters", or in anything people are supposed to hang up or bind or even make dance about in some fashion' (*De Doctrina Christiana* 2.20.30).

The simplest of folk practices comes in for St Augustine's censure: holding your left thumb with your right hand as a cure for hiccupping, going back to bed if you sneeze while putting on your shoes, turning back into the house if you trip while leaving it. His reasons for wholesale disapproval were straightforward. Any manifestation of attachment to non-Christian ways was either futile silliness or an opening through which the Devil might slip into someone's mind and there begin a more insidious and more damaging corruption. It was a practical and well as a theoretical consideration. At the time of his

---

[3] *Daemones*. The *daemon* was a non-human entity acting as an intermediary between the gods and human beings. More or less neutral in implication during antiquity, it gradually took on a negative import under the pressure of Christian condemnation of pagan religions.

writing, for example, St Augustine was sometimes made aware that even his fellow bishops had not understood these simple points. Thus, he had to write to Bishop Boniface that, no, a baptised child could *not* be harmed by his or her parents' sacrificing to spirits in an effort to cure an illness. But all practices smacking of magic were, he thought, parts of the same diabolical whole, and this 'whole' was the apparatus whereby *daemones* sought to control humanity. In 409, he wrote a short book entitled *De divinatione daemonum* ('The Spirits' Art of Foretelling the Future'), the result of conversations he had had with lay-people, in which he makes clear certain key points about *daemones*; (a) they have remarkable perception, they are able to move very quickly indeed, and they have enjoyed very long experience of creation: all these enable them to dazzle human beings with tricks (*praestigia*) which give the appearance of being wonders (*mira*); (b) because they are the authors of their tricks, they can announce them in advance and this looks like accurate prediction: moreover, their long experience enables them to look for things which may escape the attention of human beings, and so, once again, their announcement of these gives the impression they can foretell the future correctly; and (c) they are by no means infallible, but they are very good at hiding their mistakes.

These various observations were repeated, enlarged, and developed by later theologians and thus helped to formulate the standard educated view of magic and the related occult sciences. St Thomas Aquinas expressed this view in full in his *Summa Theologiae* (1266–73), a massive summation of Catholic theology which provided people then and later with a touchstone of orthodoxy. One section (2a.2ae.92–96) is devoted to superstition, idolatry, divination, and popular magical practices and, as may be expected, St Thomas refers again and again to St Augustine as one of his principal authorities. Superstition, he says, consists of either worshipping God in an improper manner, or of worshipping something or someone as though he were God. The latter, of course, is simple idolatry. St Thomas gives an example of the former in relation to the wearing of relics. 'If these are worn out of a reliance upon God and the saints whose relics they are, this will not be illicit; but if this were to be accompanied by some kind of trivial nonsense, such as that their container should be triangular, or anything such as that, which is not relevant to one's reverence for God and the saints, it would be superstitious and illicit.' Divination is sinful because it seeks to usurp a knowledge of the future, a knowledge which belongs to God alone; but there may be degrees of sin involved, in as much as trying to discover the future with the help of demons is self-evidently worse than merely interpreting the flight-patterns of birds, or observing the shapes formed by molten lead when it is poured into water. As for popular practices, St Thomas agrees with St Augustine that these are, in effect, 'signs of intent' (*significationes*) which demons notice and take as indications of weakness in the individual wearing them or doing them. For this reason, if for no other, they should be avoided.

So what the Middle Ages inherited from late antiquity, and re-emphasised in their own time, was a general condemnation of the occult sciences. In practice, of course, they compromised. Converting Europe to Christianity was a long drawn out, piecemeal enterprise which could scarcely be called accomplished until as late as 1200 (some people would argue, not even then), and even after that there were wide tracts in which the full implications of Christian teaching on every subject were either not well known or not rigorously implemented. The frequency with which condemnations of magic by Church and state were issued bears witness to its continuing presence in the culture and subculture, and outbursts of heresy provided indications of the relative failure by both ecclesiastical and secular authorities to impose a single, official view on the diversity of opinion and speculation with which they had constantly to deal. Compromise, therefore, was the general rule rather than the exception when it came to coping with magic and its various manifestations. This is hardly surprising. The mechanical philosophers of the early seventeenth century, who would gradually impose upon everyone else their concept of the universe as a kind of machine to which God or any other non-material being was, at best, irrelevant, had not yet been born: neither had their opponents, the natural philosophers who saturated nature with God and thus tempted human beings to identify themselves with Him and make themselves lords of creation by mastering its secrets. The Mediaeval view was quite different. There was God and there was creation, the latter entirely and always subordinate in every way to the former. Creation consisted of several different kinds of existence – divine, angelic, spiritual, elemental, human, demonic – and they all interacted at different times, in different ways, and in different places according to God's pleasure and permission. Finding means to negotiate the inherent perils of these various existences was therefore a major consideration for human beings, especially since the other types of existence were unpredictable, powerful, and to an extent unknown in their operations. Such a universe contains dangers we have forgotten, or do not heed; but that does not mean the dangers were not perceived as real by those who had to deal with them, and the multifarious ways people sought to ward off harm, keep fear at bay, or seek assistance for problems which, in purely human terms, seemed intractable, may often seem silly to our jaundiced, uncomprehending eye, but were possible life-lines for those afloat in the perilous seas of a spirit-haunted cosmos.

This book is divided into three parts: 'The Created Universe', which describes the various ways in which the material, the preternatural, the angelic, and the demonic worlds were experienced and interpreted; 'The Parallel Universe of Magic', which seeks to give an idea of the various ways in which human beings and non-human entities interacted and sought to use each other; and 'Interpreting and Manipulating the Universe', which concentrates on astrology and alchemy – essentially a mathematical and a chemical technique for exploring the hidden, or occult, laws governing Creation and using the knowledge thus gained for specific utilitarian purposes. Together, these three sections are intended to provide a series of snapshots of an intellectual and emotional attempt, quite different from our own, but perfectly rational in its own terms, to make sense of the universe and humankind's place in it, in the light of God's complete but sometimes apparently capricious dominion of everything and everyone, human or not, and of His plan for human destiny, potentially frustrated by human free will and the machinations of Satan within the created world.

The Created Universe

1 The constituent parts of the world. St Isidore of Seville: De natura rerum (612/13)

[*St Isidore, c.560–636, Archbishop, theologian, encyclopaedist. He wrote extensively on theology, etymology, and the natural world. The* De Natura *was composed at the request of the Visigothic King Sisebut. It is highly derivative. The passages which follow overtly depend on St Ambrose.*]

Chapter 11. The constituent parts of the world are four in number: fire, air, water, earth. Their characteristics are as follows: fire is thin, sharp, and mobile; air is mobile, sharp, and thick; water is thick, blunt, and mobile; earth is thick, blunt, and immobile. When they are mixed together, this is what happens. When thick, blunt, immobile earth is mixed with water, it is bound together with it because of its thickness and bluntness. Water is conjoined with air by its thickness and mobility. Again, air is bound to fire because they are both sharp and mobile. Earth and fire, however, refuse to combine, but water and air are joined by those two characteristics.

Saint Ambrose distinguishes these elements through the qualities whereby each in turn is combined to the rest by a kind of natural kinship. Earth, he says, is dry and cold; water is moist and cold; air is warm and moist; and fire is hot and dry. Each individual element is combined with the others through these 'matrimonial' qualities.[1] For since earth is dry and cold, it is conjoined with water via their kinship expressed in the quality 'cold'. Again, water is joined to air via moistness because air is moist. Indeed, water seems to have embraced earth on the one hand and air on the other as though it had two arms, 'coldness' and 'moistness', with cold embracing the earth and moistness the air. Air itself occupies the middle ground between two things which are mutually antagonistic – water and fire – and reconciles each of those elements with itself; for it is conjoined to water by moistness, and to fire by heat. Since fire is hot and dry, it too is interwoven with air by heat, while it is restored to communion and association with earth because of dryness ...

Chapter 12. The [sky's] parts are the vault, the axis, the pivotal points on the ecliptic, the upper regions, the poles, and the stars. The vault is something which contains the sky. Hence the saying, 'With difficulty they fill the vault with the terrors of the sky.' The axis is a straight line which goes through the central column of the sphere. The cardinal point is the pivot or part of the sky – for example, 'the eastern point' and 'the meridian'. The cardinal points are at the very ends of the axis. The upper regions are the ends of the sky. The poles are the extremities of the celestial circles, and the sphere rests all its weight on them. One looks northwards and is called Boreas; the other looks in the opposite direction and is called Notus. Scholars think that the sky turns once during the day and night from east to west. They described it as spherical and said that it spins and burns. They thought its sphere was above the waters, so that it rolled upon them and thus had its burning tempered. But they maintain that the sphere has neither beginning nor end because its spinning like a circle means one cannot easily understand where it begins or where it stops. It is said that no matter from which direction it is seen, it looks the same: and likewise that the sky itself looks back at everything with equanimity. Each part of it is equidistant from the centre of the earth. Because of its uniformity, it is permanent and regular, and its overall uniformity does not allow it to deviate in any direction anywhere; and pressure from below means that it requires no prop to keep it from falling. Plato, a man of reason, draws upon many arguments to show that the perfection of this sphere or circle implies that it is the work of the Creator of the world. First, because the so-called 'zodiac' is composed of one line from the five angles of the lines of axis. Secondly, because it is without beginning and without end. Thirdly, because from a single point it is constituted of one thing which has motion of itself. Next, because it is exempt from the jurisdiction of the angels, and because it encloses all the constellations, and because it has an undeviating motion. (Six other motions, however, do deviate – behind, right, left, up, and down.) Finally, because it has been constructed to behave that way under compulsion, and so this line cannot be drawn beyond a circle. But, as I said, there are two axes on which the sky is turned: the north, which we call 'Aquilonium' and 'Arctos', i.e. the seven stars of Ursa Major which always appear to us; and opposite, Notus which is called 'the south' ... The pole is said to be borne along with such great speed that unless the stars ran contrary to its headlong course, they would bring about the downfall of the world.

Chapter 13. We read in David, 'Praise God, ye heavens of the heavens'.[2] But there is disagreement about whether there is one heaven or many. Some people maintain there are many, others say there is one and therefore that there are no others. Natural philosophers have proposed seven heavens in the cosmos, that is, planets with a harmonious movement. They say that everything is intimately connected to their revolutions and they are of the opinion that the planets are bound to each other, as though they were physically attached, and are reversed and borne by a movement retrograde to everything else. In *Ecclesiasticus* one reads the phrase 'heaven of heavens', and the Apostle Paul was convinced he had been snatched up to the third heaven.[3] Human impetuosity, however, should not take it upon itself to assume anything about how many there are. God has not made them formless or disordered, but different, each from the other, with its own rank, according to a rational purpose.

Moreover, he has stretched out the sky of the higher circle and separated it from the others by giving it its own boundary, and hemmed it in on all sides by spaces of equal measure, and constituted the powers of the created spirit-beings within it. God, the Maker of this world, maintained the nature of this sky in balance by means of waters, so that the burning of the higher fire may not ignite the lower elements; and thereafter he strengthened the circle of the lower sky with a movement not limited to a single kind, but highly variable, declaring that this [lower sky] was a 'firmament'[4] because it holds up the higher waters.

[1] Isidore frequently uses the verb *commiscere* which means both to mix together and to have sexual intercourse. Hence his introduction of *iugale*s to describe qualities here. The perception of metals and minerals acting as though they were human beings engaged in sexual activity is likewise crucial to understand the language employed in alchemical texts.
[2] *Psalm* 148.1, 'Praise the Lord from the heavens'.
[3] *Ecclesiasticus* 16.18, 'Behold heaven, and the heaven of heavens'. 2 *Corinthians* 12.2, 'I knew a man in Christ ... snatched up to the third heaven'.
[4] Based on the Latin verb *formare* meaning to strengthen, to support.

2 A journey through the cosmos. Bernardus Silvestris: *Cosmographia* (1141)

[*Not much is known about Bernardus Silvestris. A few firm dates place him in the mid twelfth century, and he seems to have died in c.1160. He dedicated his* Cosmographia *to Thierry of Chartres.* Cosmographia *gives an account of the universe and the place of humankind within it. It is written in a combination of prose and poetry, and Silvestris uses philosophical myth to illustrate and expound his several points.*]

[*Natura makes a journey through the cosmos at the suggestion of Providentia.*]

3.8. She followed, as though it were a track, the radiance which a compact mass of stars had poured out and made from its own large numbers, and came upon the Milky Way where the zodiac in its orbit reaches the two Tropics. Consequently, she caught sight of innumerable milling crowds round the boundary of Cancer, a multitude of souls who all looked, I must say, as though they were going to a funeral and were upset by bouts of crying. The reason for this was that those who had been on the point of descending just as they were – free from contamination, free from complications – through the House of Cancer from radiance to darkness, from Heaven to Pluto's empire, from eternity to physical bodies, were starting to be horrified at the drab, dark little dwelling of the body which they saw was being prepared for them.

3.10. The upper regions of the universe and the whole structure of the stars is not composed of [the usual four] elements, but of a fifth element which is first in rank, divine in kind, and unchanging in its nature; for if the sky and the stars to which it gives birth had drawn their material composition from the [four] elements whose nature is subject to change, they would not notify anything reliable or any true prophecy. So this circle which is the outermost boundary does not consist of fire and does not contain fire. In an unvarying circle, always returning exactly to the same spot, it moves round the spheres of the planets, causing them to rotate in company with itself by means of its aggressive rapidity.

5.1. There, [in] a House far removed and withdrawn from grossly physical places, a House of light set free from impurities, with its contamination strained off, is the innermost sanctum of God the Highest and Transcendent, if you are to provide faith with theological arguments.

5.2. On the left and right hand [of God], Heaven is inhabited by ethereal[5] and divine powers whose ranks have been set in place so as to form a series. Each member of the highest, intermediate, and lowest ranks acknowledges the principle of the appointment allotted to him, and the value of his particular activity. A spirit of concordance pervades their dwelling-places which are in contact with each other, each in turn, and are bound fast together by a continuous thread, and suffuses each of them with power. Nevertheless, they do not receive [power] in a uniform fashion from this spirit of uniformity. Those who stand near the seat of God are drawn more closely to His inmost mind when, from time to time, His deliberations are laid bare and revealed. The rest, in accordance with their distance from the

Godhead, keep hold of a contemplation which is reduced and not so unimpaired, and they have a less intense experience of God and the knowledge of future things.

17. Mercury runs down an orbit which touches and is right next to that of the Sun, and is preceded by the very same planet he precedes; and because of the law which governs the orbit which carries him, at one moment he moves in front and above the Sun, at another he vanishes below it. Indifferent and undecided, Mercury does not point out the arrival of wickedness in disposition and behaviour in matters which he directs or alters by his planetary character. But his close association with the other planets either vindicates or perverts him; intimately conjoined with the hot passion of Mars or the kindly indulgence of Jupiter, he decides what to do next from the peculiar attributes of the planets with which he is associated. Adapted to both sexes – and sexually promiscuous in general – it has been his habit to make hermaphrodites which visibly combine both sexes in one body. This god has a slender wand in his hands and a winged foot. He is girded ready for action, in as much as he used to discharge the offices of interpreter and messenger of the gods.

18. Now, Venus touches the line of Mercury and of the Sun in certain places and so encircles the orbits of each with the extensiveness of her own. Having aimed at a climate midway between moist and hot, she draws out the fruits of budding plants by the kindliness of her nature, and assists all seeds by the processes of growth she brings to the marriage-bed. She brings further assistance to the testimonies of favourable stars, and arranges a more indulgent happiness for the nativities[6] she observes. The astrologer believes that any intense arousal of humans' desire for pleasure has crept up on them from the planet Venus. The radiant face of Venus charms the person who looks at it. Her device is a torch, sometimes issuing smoke, sometimes burning with a flame. The little child Cupid used to suckle from her left breast.

20. [At the Moon's orbit] there was a boundary interposed between the lower and upper airs, which was keeping the inherent characteristics of the two regions separate by the mediating Moon's acting as a barrier. Above: endless peace and quiet, perpetual serenity, the unbroken tranquillity of the upper air. Consequently, because the powers above do not move to one state and then to another at the impulse of change, in no way are their inviolability and intrinsic honour subject

to alteration. Because its nature is unchanging, beguiling, and peaceful, the clever Greeks agreed that the Elysian Fields were in this region of the sky, and that its fortunate souls were invested with a nurturing, consecrated, pleasant spot where light would never cease.

21. Below, there is poured forth air of a more turbid, murky character whose changeable aspect is thrown into a turmoil whenever the stress of chance occurrences strikes conditions which have been exposed to the emotions. Consequently, because human beings inhabit this restless place, the equivalent of ancient chaos, they necessarily experience the motions of complete change.

22. So the Moon, running along the midway boundary which acts as a divider, is of a thick and more gross obesity in comparison with the other planets. She feeds on the divine and immortal life-giving forces of the [heavenly] fires, and even supplies to things below the disposition[7] which is a condition of growth. Her luminous body, which reflects the brilliance of the sun's light shining upon it, is constantly being broken down and reconstructed by these same well-organised importations [of life-giving forces of the heavenly fires]. Therefore, because her light is born from the light of another [planet], Ptolemy of Memphis called her 'the planet of the Sun'. In addition to this, just as she stirs up and brings to shore the swellings of the sea, so it is found that she is more powerful the closer she comes to earthy substances. Turning her coming and going in a circle through these same boundaries with an unremitting and tireless speed, she has laid claim to a most extraordinary power over the affairs and destinies of human beings. One and the same divine force, considering the diversity of her power and duty, she used to display herself at one time as Lucina [goddess of childbirth] with her lamp, at another as the Huntress with her quiver, and at another as Queen of the Underworld with a garlanded head.

6. vv.25–30. A witness to its Maker, the very beautiful fabric of creation pleases by its form and the material of which it is made. [But] having disregarded something which is more perfect than the more perfect of the two hemispheres, its position little by little becomes worse and it disregards the stars. Whatever lies beneath the turbulent sky is to be feared because it is deficient and unstable.

[5] I.e. belonging to the *aether*, the upper air beyond the region of the planets.
[6] *Nativitates* may refer to horoscopes or to actual births. The double possibility is exploited in this sentence.

⁷ *Ethin*, which is meaningless. I have provided my suggested translation as though the word were connected with Greek *ethos*.

3 The elements and the humours. Pseudo-Bede: *De mundi celestis terrestrisque constitutione* (second half 12ᵗʰ century)

The world we can feel with our senses is composed from four elements, and from these elements entirely, in such a way that no part of them is left outwith the world. Consequently, nothing is added to the world from elsewhere, and nothing leaves it for another place. But I am saying that the world is composed from these entirely in contradistinction to [the composition] of humans or other bodies made of flesh. Because these are not composed entirely from the elements, something is added to them and also leaves them. Likewise, a certain vital fluid is added to trees and plants from the earth by roots, and when this has been diffused through every part [of them], and hardened by a kind of natural heat, it changes into wood. Furthermore, when something is added to or leaves a human being, if this happens in properly adjusted stages, the person remains complete and unimpaired. But if it happens otherwise, he or she suffers decomposition.

There are, you see, four humours in a person, and these resemble the various elements. They increase at different times [of the year], and are dominant in different period's of one's life. Blood resembles air. It increases in Spring and is dominant during childhood. [Yellow] bile resembles fire. It increases in summer and is dominant during youth. Black bile resembles earth. It increases in autumn and is dominant during one's mature years. Phlegm resembles water. It increases in winter and is dominant during old age. While these flow copiously, neither more nor less than the ideal amount, the person flourishes. Now, in regard to something's being added to or leaving a person, the following natural objects bear witness as apparatus for flowing in and flowing out: namely, the mouth and the lower parts [of the body]. There are, in addition, certain delicate, slender apertures which we call 'pores', and when the wind enters through these it makes the face swell up. They are more noticeable when sweat pours out.

Nothing, as I have said, is added to the world or leaves it, because the composition of the world is fully complete. But according to various authors, a reconstitution of its parts produces a restoration of the whole. When fire has been condensed, for example, it is transformed into air; condensed air is transformed into water, and condensed water into earth. In a reversal of this process, reconstitution dissolves earth into water, water is thinned down into air, and air turns into fire. Now, each of the elements of which the world is constituted chooses a place for itself according to its own character. Fire because of its lightness takes the highest, earth because of its heaviness the lowest, water pours itself round the earth, and air round both the water and the earth. What is more, above the vault of the sky, according to theologians, are supercelestial waters, and above them, spirit-heavens in which the angelic powers are concentrated. Moreover, the earth far below has placed itself in the middle, so that from every direction, except for the prominences of the mountains and the sinking of the valleys, it is an equal distance from the vault of the sky.

Portents and prodigies

4 A travelling star. *Acta et processus canonizacionis beate Birgitte* (c.1391)

[*Swedish saint, 1303–73. Married, mother of eight children, widowed. She then moved into a Cistercian abbey, and finally to Rome where she died. During her Cistercian years, she had revelations about the way the Church and society should be ordered and conducted. These were collected and published after her death. Canonisation began with popular devotion and miracles, both of which were then investigated by Rome which also examined witnesses who were supposed to provide proof not only of the miracles but also of the person's virtuous life. The modern process is essentially the same. The following passage describes an incident which took place while the relics of St Birgitta were being translated to Sweden.*]

While we were in a ship between Germany and Sweden and feeling unsure of ourselves because of the dangers of the wars which were threatening that same kingdom of Sweden from every quarter, we were making for port when suddenly, a little after midday, there appeared in the sky a very brilliant star. The first to see it was an eight-year-old boy who was without guile and not very strong. Then everyone else on board saw it and was astonished and said they had never seen a star at that time of day, when the sun was shining brightly. The star went ahead of the ship as far as a port to which we had not been planning to go, and then it vanished. The following night, one of our men was told: 'The star you saw yesterday, going ahead of the ship and showing you the port, is Bridget, the beloved wife of Christ, whose reputation will gradually advance, like the star, until, like the star, it lights up the whole world.'

5 Two suns. *Chronicum Scotorum* (12th century)

[*Irish chronicle attributed to Abbot Gilla-Christ O'Maeileoin. The following passage refers to the year 909.*]

A wonderful sign appeared this year. People saw two suns journeying together on the same day, 6 May.

6 Eclipses. *Anglo-Saxon Chronicle*

[*This is essentially a collection of chronicles started during the reign of King Alfred (c.848–900) and continuing until the twelfth century. Entries are generally brief.*]

664. In this year, there was an eclipse of the sun on 3 May, and in this year came a great plague to the island of Britain.

734. In this year, the moon looked as though it had been sprinkled with blood, and Archbishop Tatwine and Bede died.

1135. In this year, at Lammas [1 August] King Henry went over the sea and the next day, while he lay asleep on board ship, the light of day darkened over every land. The sun looked like a moon three nights old and the stars were around it at midday. People were astonished and terrified, and said that something of great importance would follow; and indeed it did, for the King died in Normandy the day after the Feast of St Andrew [30 November].

7 Eclipse. William of Malmesbury: *Historia Novella* (1142–7)

[*English Benedictine monk, c.1090–1143. Historian, librarian of his monastery. His most notable works are histories of the English kings and of the English archbishops and bishops. The* Historia Novella, *'Recent History', frequently deals with incidents of which William was an eye-witness.*]

In this year [1140] during Lent, on 20 March, at the ninth hour of the fourth day of the week, I am told there was an eclipse throughout

England. Here – and the experience of all our neighbours was the same – the darkening of the sun was so extraordinary that people sitting at table ... at first were afraid that chaos had come again. But later, once they found out what had caused it, they came out of doors and saw stars round the sun. Many thought and said, quite accurately, that the King would not continue to reign a year longer.

8   Eclipse. Rodulfus Glaber: *Historiae* (late 1020s–1045/6)

[*Glaber (c.985–c1046), Cluniac monk. He was the author of a life of St William, the first abbot of Fécamp, as well as the* Histories.]

4.24. In the same year [1033], the thousandth after the Passion of our Lord, on Friday 29 June ... a really dreadful eclipse or failure of the sun happened from the sixth until the eighth hour of that day. The sun became sapphire in colour, and in its upper part had the look of the moon when her last quarter lights up again. Each person saw everyone else looking pale, as though they were dead, and everything was seen to be under a crocus-coloured mist. Then immense bewilderment and terror took hold of the hearts of the human race, because as they looked at that [phenomenon], they realised it foretold that some grim disaster was about to befall the human race. For on that same day, the birthday of the Apostles [Peter and Paul], certain great men of Rome entered on a conspiracy and rose up against the Roman Pontiff in the Church of St Peter, with the intention of killing him. Their efforts, however, came to nothing although they did drive him out from his see.

9   A rain of blood. André de Fleury: *Vita Gauzlini* (c.1042)

[*French historian, died 1050/60. A monk of the monastery of Fleury under Abbot Gauzlin and his successor. In November, 1004, Gauzlin became abbot in a contested election, but he was supported by the King. In 1012 he became Archbishop of Bourges. Again the election was contested, but this time Gauzlin was supported by Pope Boniface VIII.*]

[*In 1027, Robert II of France wrote to Gauzlin about a prodigy which had caused him alarm.*] Three days before the Feast of St John the Baptist, in certain parts of my realm, namely in parts of Aquitaine, there fell near the seacoast a rain of blood. Its character was such that when it happened to fall on a person's flesh, on clothing, or on a rock, it could not be washed off. But if it fell on wood, it could be washed off perfectly well.

[*This letter had come in a letter to the King, which urged him to make inquiries among the learned to see what it meant. Hence the King's letter to Gauzlin. Gauzlin replied as follows.*]

Since you have been pleased to ask me about the extraordinary event which has taken place, it seems clear to me from history books that blood always stands for a sword, or civil war, or the hostile incursion of one group of people upon another.

In his *Book of Things Worth Recording*, chapter 4, ('Prodigies'), Valerius Maximus tells us: 'During the consulate of Gaius Volumnius and Servilius Sulpicius, the following prodigy happened in Rome not long after the civil war had begun. Pieces of flesh fell down over a wide area, like rain during a cloud burst. Birds flying swiftly overhead grabbed most of these; the rest lay on the ground for several days, but did not begin to stink or become offensive to look at. In Sicily, it was said, two shields sweated blood; blood-stained ears of corn fell into the baskets of the reapers; and in the town of Cerveteri, the waters ran mixed with blood.'[8]

Eusebius's *Chronica* has this to say about prodigies. 'During the reign of Valentinian, after sunset the sky in the north was rendered fire-like or blood-like; the peace was broken, and an incursion of the Huns followed in Gaul.' Likewise: 'In the seventh year of the Emperor Leo, blood burst out from the ground in the middle of the city of Toulouse and ran the whole day, indicating the despotism of the Goths which the people had endured.'

Likewise, *The History of the Lombards*, Book 2, chapter 6: 'At the time of Theodébert, King of the Franks, a bloody sign rather like a bloodstained spear appeared in the sky, and at that moment while Theodébert was waging war on his uncle Lothair, he overwhelmed Lothair's army.' Likewise, in the same History: 'In the days of Justinian, there occurred a very serious outbreak of plague, especially in the province of Liguria. In no time at all, certain marks began to appear on houses, doors, utensils, and clothing, and if anybody wanted to wash them off they simply persisted in appearing. A full twelve months later, small swellings like nuts or dates started to form on people's groins or in other more tender places. These were soon followed by an unbearable feverish heat, and under such circumstances the person died within three days. But if anyone survived beyond three days, he or she had a hope of living. But everywhere there was panic, everywhere there was grief, everywhere there were tears, because popular rumour had it that everyone was going to die.

So houses were abandoned, deserted by their inhabitants, and only the young of their pets[9] to look after their homes. Sheep remained all alone in the fields, untended by any shepherd. You might see farms or hamlets bursting with a press of people one day, and the next everyone had fled, leaving their parents' corpses unburied; parents forgetting their natural duty abandoned their feverish children; and if by any chance anyone was gripped by an old-fashioned duty and wanted to bury his relative, he himself lingered without burial and was overcome while carrying out his task, for while he was performing the funeral rites for another, he himself was left without any such office. You might see the world reduced to its ancient silence: no voice in the countryside, no hissing or whistling, no attacks by wild animals on livestock, no losses among farm-birds. Crops went past the time of harvest and awaited the reaper, ungarnered. The vine lost its leaves, its grapes shone, and it remained untouched as winter approached. During the hours of darkness and of daylight, many heard the roaring of an army; yet there were no tracks to show that people had passed by, there was no sight of a killer, and yet the bodies of the dead overwhelmed the eyes [of the living]. Sheep-runs had been turned into burial places for humans, and human dwellings into refuges for wild animals.'

These are a few of the instances I have noted in history books. Now, the fact that the blood fell upon a rock seems to mean that Holy Church, which was founded upon a rock (that is, Christ), is going to suffer tribulation. The fact that it fell on someone's flesh and clothing and could not be washed off, one may, without stretching things too far, interpret thus: the flesh indicates the people, and the clothing property which is granted to us as a support in this life. By the wood, we are given to understand the vivifying wood of the holy cross and baptism whereby we have been reborn to life: for wood begins to bear fresh growth in the humour of water. When the Jews were thirsty in the desert and could not drink the water there because it was bitter, at the Lord's instruction Moses threw a piece of wood into the water and the bitterness was changed to sweetness, and the people were restored to life once more;[10] and as for Noah's ark which was made of wood, you are not unacquainted with what that signifies. In all these instances, the Lord performed his mercy particularly through wood. So because the blood was washed off the wood, I assume that, through penance, alms-giving, and the other things produced by mercy which are practised in the bosom of our mother the Church, the rigorous anger of God, the just judge, which is the deserved result of sinners, can be turned again to mercy. For the Lord is so merciful, as the Psalmist says, that he saves not only people but also beasts of burden.[11]

[8] *Factorum et dictorum memorabilium libri novem* Book 1, chapter 6, section 5. The book was composed over a period of time, probably before the end of 31 AD.
[9] *Catuli*. This refers to the young of any animal, but in Classical Latin it frequently means 'puppies', while Mediaeval Latin may also use the word specifically for 'kittens'.
[10] A reference to *Exodus* 15.23-25
[11] *Psalm* 35.7 (Vulgate) = 36.6 (Authorised Version).

10 A storm. *Annales Fuldenses*, referring to the year 857

[*Various manuscripts written in the Abbey of Fulda, containing annals between 714 and mid 882. Those referring to 714–838 were composed by Einhard, Abbot of Seligenstadt; those referring to 838–863 by Rudolf of Fulda, who also wrote hagiography; and those referring to 865–882 by Meginhard of Fulda. This anecdote was thus probably written by Rudolf.*]

[*A synod held at Mainz heard a letter from the Bishop of Cologne, relating the following incident.*]

At Cologne on 15 September there was a dreadful storm. The whole population, terrified out of its wits, sought refuge in the church of St Peter and, while the church bells were being rung,[12] as one body implored the mercy of God. Suddenly an enormous bolt of lightning, like a snake made of fire, entered the church and rent it. Three people in different places in that large gathering were killed by a single blow: a priest near the altar of St Peter, a deacon near the altar of St Dionysius, and a layman near the altar of the Virgin. Six others were knocked over by the same blow with such force that when they were picked up, half-alive, they only just managed to recover.

[12] In order to drive away any evil influences which might be causing the storm – a common practice all over Europe.

11 A globe of fire. *The Myracles of Oure Lady* (1496)

[*Published by Wynkyn de Worde, apprentice to William Caxton. Alsatian printer, died c.1534.*]

Also a certain layman that was of holy living dwelled with the Friars Preacher in a certain house in England, which oftentimes saw a great globe of fire going from one side of the choir to the other side, and descending down of every brother's head while they sang devoutly after Compline, *Salve Regina*.

12 Various portents. Sigebert of Gembloux: *Chronica*, on the year 1000

[*Polemicist, historian, and hagiographer, c.1030–1112.*]

Many prodigies were seen in the thousandth year of Jesus Christ, according to the reckoning of Dionysius. There was an immense earthquake; a comet appeared; on 14 December, around the ninth hour, the sky was split apart and there fell to earth something like a burning torch with a long trail like a lightning flash. Its light was so great that not only those who were in the fields, but also those indoors were struck by the light which had burst out. This split in the sky gradually began to vanish, but in the mean time there was seen a shape like a snake. Its head was getting bigger and its feet were light blue.

13 Various signs. *Annales Fuldenses*, referring to the year 870

[*Probably recorded by Meginhard of Fulda.*]

At Mainz for several nights the whole air was bathed in a redness, as though with blood, and glistened brightly; and other extraordinary things were seen in the sky. A cloud came down from the north one night; another, by contrast, came from the east at midday. Both continuously emitted fiery arrows by turns, and then at last they mingled in the highest point of the sky, jumbling together as if they were armies engaged in battle, and bringing at once no little fear and astonishment to those who saw them. Everyone was asking [God] to change these signs into something good. The city itself was twice struck by an earthquake. Several people who were bringing in the harvest in the district of Worms were brought back dead because of the sun's heat which was stronger than usual, and a very large number also drowned in the river Rhine, and died. But, on the Feast of St Lawrence, while everyone else was hurrying to church, a woman baked some loaves of bread which she intended to sell. Her neighbours reminded her that she should honour this important day and go to church, but she was unwilling to leave off completing the work she had started with a view to earning some money; and since she preferred earthly lucre to honouring the saints and made bread from the same flour she had used before to make healthy, gleaming loaves, and then sent them to the oven, suddenly she found that they were blacker than ink. So, thoroughly ashamed, she ran out of doors and without trying to cover anything up told everyone who was present about the sin she had committed in offending such an important feast-day, and the loss she had suffered by the ruin of her loaves.

14   Further portents. *Chronicum Scotorum* **(12th century)**

811. This was a year of portents. It was during this year that the Célé Dé came over the sea from the south, dry foot, without a boat. He would be given a scroll from Heaven, and from this he would teach the Irish. It used to be taken up into Heaven again after he had finished teaching … In this year, too, cakes were changed into blood, and blood used to flow from them when they were cut. In this year, birds would speak with human voices.

885. A boy spoke at Craibh Lairre scarcely two months after he had been born.

900. A big woman was thrown up on to the shore by the sea in Scotland. She was 192 feet tall; she measured 6 feet between her breasts; her hair was 15 feet long; her fingers were 6 feet long, and her nose was 7 feet long. Every part of her body was whiter than a swan or the foam of the sea.

15   A mysterious voice. Georgios Kedrenos: *Compendium historiarum* **(late 12th century)**

[*Biography unknown. His work covers world history from the Creation to 1057 and, as its title suggests, is essentially a compilation based on the works of various other historians.*]

At this time [the reign of Romanos III] in the province of Thrace something happened at the foot of Mount Kuzena where there is a spring of very clear water. A voice full of unhappiness was heard there, giving vent to cries and lamentations. This did not happen once or twice, but continuously day and night from March until June; and when a number of people came to reconnoitre the place whence the voice was issuing, the wailing migrated elsewhere. In my opinion, this portent was a sign that the Byzantines had suffered a disastrous defeat in Coelesyria.

16   Further portents. *Annales Fuldenses*, referring to the year 878

[*Probably recorded by Meginhard of Fulda.*]

There was a village called Walahesheim in Worms, not far from the manor of Ingalenheim, where an extraordinary thing happened. While dead animals were being hauled every day from their byres into the fields, the dogs of the village would eat their corpses, as dogs do. But on one particular day, nearly all the dogs gathered in one spot and then went away, and not one of them could be found later, either living or dead.

Referring to the year 823

[*Probably recorded by Einhard of Seligenstadt.*]

In this year, certain extraordinary events are said to have taken place. The most notable of these were an earthquake in the manor of Aix-les-Bains; and in the region of Toul, near the village of Commercy, a girl aged about twelve ate nothing for ten months. In Saxony, in a small village called Firihsazi, twenty-three houses were burned to the ground by fire from heaven, and lightning fell in daylight from a clear sky. In the region of Como, in the village of Gravedona, in the church of St John the Baptist, the statue of the Virgin Mary holding the child Jesus in her lap, and a painting in the choir of the church depicting the gifts offered by the Magi, which was darkened and almost obliterated by the long passage of time, shone for two days with such a very bright light that it seemed to those who saw it that the beauty of this old picture almost outshone the beauty of the one which was new. That brilliance, however, scarcely illumined the figures of the Magi at all – only the gifts they were offering. In many areas the crops were destroyed by a devastating hailstorm, and in certain places real stones which were very heavy, were seen to fall along with the hail. Houses are said to have been struck from the sky, and in several places human beings and all other living creatures were frequently killed by thunderbolts, beyond what one might expect. There followed an immense plague and great mortality among people.

17 Expectations of the end of the world. Abbo of Fleury: *Apologeticus ad Hugonem et Rodbertum, reges Francorum* (c.994/6)

[*French scholar and hagiographer. Abbot of the Benedictine Abbey of Fleury sur Loire, c.945–1004. He founded several monastic schools in England and reformed a number of abbeys in France. After he died, miracles happened at his tomb.*]

Anent the end of the world, when I was a young man I heard a sermon preached to the people in the church of Paris, which said that as soon as a thousand years had been completed, the Antichrist would arrive and would be followed not long afterwards by the Last Judgement. I objected to that sermon as strenuously as I could, quoting the *Apocalypse* and *Daniel*; and then my abbot of blessed memory, who had a sharp intellect, rejected another error about the end of the world, which was beginning to grow. He received letters about it from the Lotharingians and instructed me to answer. For a rumour had filled almost the entire world that when the Feast of the Annunciation fell on Good Friday, the end of the world would be at hand – no question about it.

18 Doubts about how to compute the arrival of the end of the world. Anon.: *Blickling Homily on Holy Thursday* (971)

We learn that the time [of the end of the world] is so secret that no one in this world, no matter how holy he may be, and no one in Heaven, either, except the Lord alone, has ever known when our Lord might decree an end to this world on the Day of Judgement. Nevertheless, we know it is not far off; for all the signs and portents our Lord said would come before the Last Judgement have happened – with one exception. The accursed stranger, the Antichrist, has not yet come into the world. The time is not far off, however, when that too is bound to happen. For this world must necessarily come to an end with this present age, because five [ages] have come and gone. So this world must end in this age, most of which – 971 years this year – has taken place already. These [ages] were not all the same length, but in this one there have been three thousand years.[13] Others have had fewer, others more. Now, since no one knows how long our Lord will take to end this [age], whether this millennium will be shorter or longer than another, is quite unknown to anyone except our Lord.

[13] This does not make sense, of course, but the text is likely to be corrupt at this point.

19 Evil portents at Emperor Alexios's coronation. Niketas Choniates: *Historia* (early 13th century)

[*Byzantine government officer, historian, theologian, 1155/7–1217. His* History *takes a particular interest in the quirks and peculiarities of human behaviour.*]

VI.1. [When the new Emperor Alexios Angelos was about to mount his horse during his coronation ceremonies], an unexpected and noteworthy marvel happened. The horse did not come forward for him to mount it, but snorted and leaped about, its eye suffused with blood, its ears pricked up. It struck the ground many times, threw up its front hooves, made a great noise as it moved, and shied away from him, disdaining to have him ride upon its back, and driven into a savage frenzy against him. Many times it beat off Alexios as he was trying to mount it, shaking its front hooves and rolling its eyes back into their sockets. After a good many whistles and calls of encouragement and soothing pats on its neck, however, it seemed to settle down, stop its insolent convulsions, and kicking its hooves in the air. The Emperor sprang up on to it and seized the reins; but the horse, as though it had been tricked into receiving its rider when it did not want to do so, became wild as before, lifted its hooves, and whinnied loudly. It did not stop behaving like a drunk and maddened follower of the god Dionysos until it had knocked the jewelled crown off the Emperor's head on to the ground, where parts of it broke in pieces, and flung the Emperor off like a ball, as well. A second horse was brought up and Alexios led his procession, wearing the broken crown, which seemed to be an unlucky sign of things to come – that people would blame him for not preserving the Empire, that he would fall from his lofty position, and that he would suffer much at the hands of his enemies.

20 A monster. Georgios Kedrenos: *Compendium historiarum* (late 12th century)

[*In the ninth year of the reign of the Emperor Maurice = 590*], a woman from Daon gave birth to a child which had no eyes, eyelids, hands, or feet, but at its hips had sprouted a fish's tail with a shell to it like a potsherd. On the same day, too, was born a dog with six feet and a lion's head, which grew to an enormous size. On the same day, the Emperor's horse which was wearing a golden harness suddenly fell down in convulsions.

21 The meaning of monsters. Sebastian Brant: *De monstroso ansere atque porcellis in villa Gugenheim* (1496). Adapted

[*German lawyer, civil servant, and satirical poet, c.1458–1521. His best-known work*, The Narrenschiff (1494) *was immensely popular, partly because of the woodcuts with which it was illustrated. It consists of 112 sections, each devoted to a particular type of foolish person. Together these constitute the passengers in the ship which is taking them from Basel to Fools' Paradise. "The Monstrous goose and the Pigs in the Villa Gugenheim" is a typical blend of factual information and social-cum-moral comment.*]

Even if I were a magician [*magus*], a soothsayer [*ariolus*], or a diviner [*vates*] from Tuscany, an interpreter of dreams, and an oracle, I should still be unable adequately to explain what so many monsters portend at the present time ... Births which produce monsters, animals joined together, things of a kind never seen before are openly visible in defiance of civilised behaviour – as I may easily establish, since our dear creatrix, Nature, brings them to our notice by means of marvels and prodigies ... For example, in one place recently she joined twins together at the forehead; in another, two children were born, each with two heads, and many more extraordinary things in other places. You often see this kind of duplication in people born under Gemini. No matter how Nature is accustomed to produce these things, however, they are still monsters, and both show and mean new wonders ... [Bad faith and potential disaster] are indicated in a monstrous specimen, an extraordinary goose whose picture was sent to me recently. It had two heads, one throat, crooked wings and feet, and an unkempt body ... [Let me explain what it means. In ancient Rome the sacred goose saved the city from attack by screeching and so alerting the citizens.] Let us hope this modern goose drives away the frenzied enemy and averts his threats from us – as indeed it can. Because it has two mouths, it has two tongues, and its outcry will thus be the greater. If it sleeps, it will move its heads separately hither and thither, and in flight it will move them all over the place without constraint. Alas for the Rhinelanders and for our own people whence dreadful things, harmful to the Empire, will come ... We see all the kingdoms joined together, beginning to coalesce; soon the Empire which is divided against itself comes to grief. I speak the truth in verse; but to many people what I say is idle and ridiculous. If only I were a false prophet in all circumstances! But those things which are going to come will certainly come (so the gods decree): those things which frequent, repeated monsters portend.

22 Why the original inhabitants of Britain were giants. Anon.: *De origine gigantum* (mid 1330s)

[*After a plentiful meal of meat, Albina and her sisters became inflamed by sexual desire.*] Demon incubi weighed up the situation, took on human shape and, after overpowering the women, mingled their seed with that of the women: after which, they vanished immediately. The women did not see the 'men', but simply felt their male activity. Each woman conceived from her own demon and gave birth to a gigantic child; and when the giants reached puberty, the mothers gave birth to children from their sons, and sisters from their brothers. Naturally, the monstrous offspring were of excessive height, immense bulk, and astounding strength. Indeed, the appearance of the giants was absolutely terrifying. Dreadful demons procreated dreadful giants, and the giants' mothers were notable because they were dreadfully obese; and it was appropriate that dreadful creatures should give birth to dreadful creatures, and beasts reproduce beasts. Therefore the giants multiplied themselves exceedingly and filled this land. They made for themselves subterranean caves and surrounded them with large walls and ditches. Some of these walls are still standing: one can see them. The rest have been knocked down and ruined by the weather.

Occult properties of the natural world

23 The meaning of stones. Marbodus: *Liber lapidum* (c.1090)

[*French Benedictine, c.1035–1123. Chancellor of Angers in 1069, then later Bishop of Rennes. Prolific writer of both prose and verse. He tells us he based his poem on an Arab author who dealt with the medical qualities of precious stones. Actually it is derived largely from St Isidore of Seville and the late antique writers, Solinus and Damigeron.*]

(4) Jasper. There are said to be seventeen types of jasper. This one is known to be of many colours and is reputed to grow[14] in many parts of the world. The best has a green, translucent colour and is the type proved to have more than ordinary power. While the person who is wearing it remains sexually pure, it drives away both fevers and dropsy, and when it is applied to a woman in labour, it helps her. It is believed to be a protective talisman for the person who carries it; for once it has been consecrated, it makes him or her well-liked and powerful. According to popular belief, it repels harmful ghosts or fancies of the mind. This type is thought to have greater power when set in silver.

(5) Sapphire. The sapphire is particularly suitable for the fingers of kings. It shines with a most splendid light, just like that of a cloudless sky. The cheaper kind has neither power nor distinction. Many people also call it the 'syrlites stone' because it is mixed up with Libyan sand round the Syrtes Islands; the waves cast it up and it is found in the seething strait. But the best is the one brought forth by Doctor Earth. It is claimed that it never allows you to see through it. Powerful nature has endowed it with such great honour that it is rightly called the sacred gem of gems; or it invigorates the body and keeps the members unimpaired. The person who wears it cannot be harmed by any mischief. He or she conquers envy and is not disturbed by any terror. This stone, they claim, sets free those who are in prison, opens barred doors, loosens chains at a touch, and when accompanied by prayer restores God's forgiveness and favour. It is also said to be effective in restoring peace; and the art of hydromancy esteems this gem above all others for the purpose of being able to elicit divine responses with its help. Because it chills internal heat, it draws out sweat, causing it to flow in abundant torrents; if it is rubbed and smeared over someone's

side, it cures ulcers; it removes impurities from the eyes and pain from the forehead, and likewise heals defects of the eye.

(9) Onyx. When the onyx is worn suspended round the neck or tied round the finger, it gives form to malevolent ghosts and all other grim things [which appear] during sleep. It multiplies quarrels and stirs up disputes all over the place. It is said vastly to increase the flow of saliva in children. This stone comes to us from Arabia and India, and there are said to be five types. The name is derived from the Greek word for finger-nail.

(19) Loadstone. The loadstone was discovered in the land of the Troglodytes, but does not come from India, the mother of gemstones, at all. Its colour is known to be dark purple, almost black; by a power of nature it picks up iron anywhere near it. It is said above all to have the great use that its wearer knows there is nothing more powerful in the art of magic. Circe, the notorious worker of poisonous magic [*venefica*], is said to have made particular use of it in her magic tricks.[15] When people had started using it here and in the land of the Medes, further experience revealed the power of the stone. For if anyone wants to know whether his wife is an adulteress or not, he should carefully put the stone on her head while she is snoring and, if she is chaste, she will soon try to embrace her husband, (and not just while she is waking up). Every adulteress falls out of bed as if struck by a hand or driven out by a foetid stench; the stone, acting as the revealing sign of a hidden crime, expels her. If a thief comes through closed doors and windows into a house bursting with loot and treasure, scatters burning coals round the place, and sprinkles bits of loadstone over them: soon afterwards, whoever has stayed in the house is driven out as a thick cloud of smoke fills the courtyard. All those who were still inside will scatter in different directions, their minds overturned as though by impending disaster, and the thief, now secure, will do whatever he wants. The stone can reconcile husbands with their wives and wives with their husbands. At the same time, it furnishes good will, charm of conversation, and the ability to argue. When administered in sweet wine, it cures dropsy by purging the body, and when scattered over burns or scalds, it cures them.

(32) Haematite. Haematite takes its name from the Greek word for 'blood'. The stone was created to be at the service of human beings,

and it is proved that it contains a great deal of symbolic power. For if it is held over rough eyelashes, it cures dulled vision by driving away the cloudiness. If you take shavings from it, and ground-up egg-shell, and dilute it in pomegranate juice, or dissolve it in water in a medical pestle, just as you would while making an eye-salve, it helps those who discharge bloody froth from their mouths. It cures ulcers; when drunk, it acts as an astringent for a woman suffering from menstrual flow; the power in its dust suppresses fleshly excrescences growing in a wound; it immediately retains fluid from the abdomen when diluted in old wine and drunk frequently. When dissolved in water and rubbed on, it provides a wonderful cure for snake-bite or the wound which comes from an asp. When mixed with honey, it can cure painful eyes, and when drunk it is said to dissolve stone in the bladder. Its colour is recorded as being dark purple or reddish, and it comes from Africa, Ethiopia, and Arabia.

(50) Pearls. The type of stone I am going to discuss now is taken from sea-shells. It is called *unio* ['a single pearl'] because one pearl is taken from one shell. You never find two or more together in the same shell. Its shining white appearance is much praised as an ornament, and when it adorns clothing, gold fades to nothing by comparison. It is recorded that at certain times the shells gape open to the sky and imbibe heavenly drops of dew from which are conceived little shining white orbs. Morning dew makes the pearl brighter; evening dew usually eats away its dusky offspring; but younger shells produce whiter, more shining pearls. Greater age darkens the offspring of the shells. The more dew there is in the air, the more a fall of dew gives birth to a larger pearl. No pearl, however, is thought to grow larger than half the size of a walnut. But if the high vaults of heaven are filled with flashing thunder, the shells close up and run away in sudden dread; and, by its intervention, [the thunder] aborts what the dew had started to create, and thus the pregnancy is drowned and perishes. The Indian ocean gives birth to the finest pearls. In olden times, Britain also gave birth to very fine pearls.

[14] *Nasci*, which also means 'to be born'. The notion that metals and minerals grow in the earth, like plants, goes back to Aristotle. See his *Meteorologia* Book 3, and *De generatione et corruptione*, Book 2.
[15] Circe turned Odysseus's men into pigs by giving them a herbal concoction to drink, *Odyssey* 10.233–43. Hence Marbodus calls her a *venefica* which is a more specific term than the catch-all English 'witch'.

Signs on the human body

24 Physiognomy. James Yonge: *The Governance of Princes* (1422)

[*Little is known for certain about James Yonge. He belonged to an English family living in the Pale in Ireland at the beginning of the fifteenth century. His translation of the* Secreta, *a work traditionally attributed to Aristotle, was probably made from a French version by Gofroi of Waterford.*]

Chapter 58. Physiognomy is a science to deem the conditions or virtues and manners of people, after the tokens or signs that appeareth in fashion or making of body, and namely of visage and of the voice and of the colour. One light manner and general of physiognomy is to deem virtues and manners of man after the complexion. Complexions been iiii for a man is [ie. namely] sanguine, or phlegmatic, or choleric, or melancholy. And these four complexions answer to the four humours of the body, which answereth to the four elements, and to the four times of the year. The blood is hot and moist to the likeness of the air; phlegm is cold and moist after the kind of the water; choler hot and dry after kind of fire; melancholy cold and dry after kind of earth. The sanguine by kind should love joy and laughing and company of women, and much sleep and singing: he shall be hardy enough, of good will and without malice: he shall be fleshy, his complexion shall be light to hurt and to impair for his tenderness, he shall have a good stomach, good digestion, and good evacuation: and if he be wounded he shall soon be healed, he shall be free and liberal, of fair semblance, and active enough of body.

The phlegmatic by kind he should be slow, sad, full still, and slow of answer: feeble of body, lightly fall in palsy; he shall be great and fat, he shall have a feeble stomach, feeble digestion, and good evacuation. And as touching manners he shall be piteous, chaste, and little desire company of women.

The choleric by kind he should be lean of body, his body is hot and dry, and he shall be somewhat rough; and light to wrath and light to peace; of sharp wit, wise, and of good memory, a greater busybody, full large and foolhardy, active of body, hasty of word and of answer; he loveth hasty vengeance; desirous of company of women more than him needeth. He should have a stomach good enough, namely in cold time.

The melancholy man should be lean of body and dry, he should have good appetite of meat, and commonly he is a glutton and good evacuation hath of his belly. And as touching manners, he should been pensive and slow, and of still will, still and dreadful, and a small busybody. More later is he wrath than a choleric man, but he holdeth longer wrath; he is of subtle imagination and of handworks, and well are wont the melancholic men to be subtle workmen.

The sanguine men should been ruddy of colour, the phlegmatic white and pale, the choleric should have yellow colour somewhat streaked with red, the melancholic should be somewhat black and pale ...

Those that have red eyelids loveth commonly well wine, and been greater drinkers; heavy eyelids tokeneth good sleeper; little eyes tokeneth a little heart and a slow; great eyes tokeneth a rude wit; mean eyes, neither great nor small, tokeneth good complexion without vice. Deep eyes, malice; over-open eyes, like as they were thrust out, commonly tokeneth a fool; somewhat deep eyes tokeneth hardiness, but eyes neither too deep nor too far out but meanly been best.

Those that have fully black eyes tokeneth that they been cowardly, for black colour approacheth nigh to darkness, and in darkness a man lightly is a-dread more than in light. And those that have eyes not well black, but declining to yellow, been of good courage. Speckled eyes and white eyes tokeneth dreadfulness, for white colour tokeneth dread. Those that have eyes of the colour of a camel's hair been courageous likened to the lion and the eagle. And those that have eyes coloured like red wine been disposed to madness, likened to beasts which may not be daunted. And those that have eyes like flame of fire burning and sparkling been angry and shameless, likened to hounds. Those that have eyes discoloured and troubled tokeneth dread, for he that is a-dread waxes pale; and they that have eyes shining been lechers likened to rooks and cocks.

Whoso hath full great eyes, he is envious and not shamefast. Slow and disobedient, and namely if he have pale eyes. He that has the eyes of mean greatness, black or grey, he is of perceiving, understanding, courteous, and true. Whoso hath long eyes and straight, and the visage much strait, such is malicious and felonious. Whoso hath eyes like an ass's eyes, he is a sot and of hard understanding. Whoso hath eyes moving and flying and sharp looking, he is a deceiver, a thief, and a beguiler. He that hath red sparkling eyes, he is fierce and courageous. Eyes that been white freckled or spotted or black or red scattered through the eyes been most to blame among all others and most reprovable; and such a man is worst among all others.

25 The evil eye. Robert Grosseteste: *Expositio in epistolam Sancti Pauli ad Galatas* (c.1225)

[*English Franciscan, 1168/9–1253. Scholar and translator. Bishop of Lincoln in 1235. He produced a large number of works on natural philosophy and two very influential commentaries on Aristotle. He had a particularly high regard for mathematics which he though provided a sound basis for reasoning about the other sciences.*]

3.2 [*Grosseteste is commenting on Galatians 3.1:* 'O Galatians, mad to the point of frenzy, who has infected you with the evil eye (fascinavit) so that you do not believe the truth?'] Note that he does not say, 'who has deceived you', but 'who has cast the evil eye upon you', showing by this that it had happened to them because of envy; that is, that those who persuaded them of something other than they heard from [Paul] did not do this because they cared about them or were solicitous for them, or because they wanted to restore what had been taken from them, but because they wanted to get rid of what was already fulfilled in them. For this is the essential characteristic of envy, that it wants to diminish someone else's good. 'Casting the evil eye' is when someone who is filled with envy infects by a glance or by words of praise someone of tender age, someone born recently, and changes what is perfect into something which is worse: like the Devil who first envied Man and by his jealousy opened the door for death to enter the world. Now he was envious of the new period in which Galatians were believers and, just as previously he used the mouth of a serpent, so now falsely he poured the poison of his envy upon them through [others'] mouths, infecting these people first by means of the corruption of jealousy, after which they infected the Galatians with the error of faithlessness.

3.3 But whether the Evil Eye (*fascinatio*) as the common people understand it is something else or not, I cannot easily say. For who knows whether an envious person's sight is poisonous and infects those of tender years, as the sight of a basilisk infects the air and anything it looks at, and as the sight of a menstruating woman infects a new mirror, freshly clean and polished? Or whether because of people's lack of belief, the Devil has been allowed to make something happen at the exchange of glances between an envious person and a tender, recently born child? Or whether there is a frequent concurrence between two events – an envious person looks at a newly born child, and a disease comes from some other source and makes the child ill after he or she has received the envious person's glance – and, by a false suggestion of the Devil, some people are persuaded that the disease comes from the glance which coincided with the arrival of the disease? The philosopher Avicenna says in his *De anima*, 'On many occasions, the soul acts in someone else's body just as it does in its own, which is what happens in the case of the evil eye and the judgement of the person causing it.' But the soul does not act upon its own body simply by possessing it and having a powerful effect on it, as when a very sick person gets better through the process of healing, and vice versa. Perhaps, according to this way [of thinking], the evil eye exists only in a rational soul. The philosopher Algazel says, 'For this reason, the emotion of love makes its body imprint love upon it. But sometimes the imprint of some soul crosses over to another body in such a way as intentionally to destroy the spirit and intentionally to infect the person. This is called "the evil eye", and hence comes the proverb that the eye sends a person into a ditch and a camel into a cauldron, and it is said it is true that human beings are bewitched by the evil eye ...' Whatever may be the truth about this, the Apostle certainly intends us to understand this word [*fascinatio*] in its popular sense, and is using it metaphorically to designate a body infected with corrupting envy.

26 The evil eye. Alfonso de Tostado: *Las catorze questiones* (mid 15th century)

[*Alfonso de Madrigal Tostado de Rivera, was Bishop of Avila. He died in 1455.*]

Question 14. It must be said that very many of those who strongly adhere to Catholic truth say there is no such thing as the evil eye, and that no creature casts the evil eye (that is, strikes dead with the eye), and that neither good nor evil is caused by the eyes. What these people believe undoubtedly has the ring of truth. For the common people, who are not wise as their name suggests, think and maintain that certain people do have evil eyes: and they add that if these people want to look at something with a maddened or envious eye (or however) in order to do evil, they will harm it and kill it; and if they look at it with a kindly eye, they will do it no harm. This is completely false and contrary to nature.

Non-human entities

27 Orders of angels. Nicholas of Cusa: *Dialogi de ludo globi*, Book 2 (1463)

[*German philosopher, theologian, and mathematician, 1401–64. A prolific author, he was also a major participant in the Council of Basel (1431–49). The game of the globe he describes in these dialogues involved nine globes + one, which seem to relate to the ten Sephiroth of the Kabbalah.*]

Angels are Intelligences and because they are of various kinds, one must distinguish intellectually the ways they appear to our intellects, and the distinctions one should make between them, by ranks and grades from the lowest to the highest (who is called 'Christ' and 'the angel of great counsel'). This distinction produces three ranks and, in each rank, three choirs ... The first rank is that of the intellectual spirits who, by simple intuition, join everything simultaneously to the centre (or the Omnipotent Archetype) without either temporal or natural succession. They stand near the divine majesty, and this enables them to see everything. For, just as God derives from himself this power of discernment so that, in His singleness of nature, he sees everything at once because he is the Realising Cause: so he grants to those spirits who are placed next to him that they may know everything in divine singleness of nature. What is more, although they are created beings, they are called 'eternal' because they understand everything simultaneously.

Another ranks consists of Intelligences who understand everything simultaneously, but not unless it is accompanied by natural succession (i.e. one thing issues naturally from another). So, although they understand things which do not flow from a *temporal* succession, if they don't have their place in nature, these Intelligences don't understand because a certain weakness of perception sneaks up on them. Consequently, they are not called 'eternal', as are those apprehended by mind alone, but (appropriately) 'perpetual' because they understand in natural ranks and succession.

The third rank is called 'rational' because, although their understanding is indisputable, they have a less perfect comprehension than the others. The first rank has three choirs which contemplate the divine will in God, (although they do so in different ways), and imitate the distinctions He makes; the three intellective choirs comprehend the divine will in intellectual things, the three rational choirs in intellective. Therefore there are nine orders, and God includes and contains everything in himself ... Each of the nine orders has its own 'theophany', or divine manifestation, and God is the tenth [order] from which all of them emanate.

28 Angels and demons. St John of Damascus: *De fide orthodoxa* (early 8th century)

[*Syrian theologian, controversialist, and hymn-writer, c.675–c.750. He became a monk in 726 and was noted for his defence of the veneration of images against Emperor Leo the Isaurian, and of the Catholic faith against Greek Orthodoxy.*]

Chapter 3. [Angels] are held within limits; for when they are in Heaven, they are not on earth, and when God sends them to earth, they do not remain in Heaven. They are not confined by walls, doors, bars, and seals: for they are indeterminate. I say 'indeterminate', although they are actually not, in so far as they appear to worthy people to whom God wishes them to appear, but they do so in altered form, so that those who do see them are enabled to bear the sight. Only that which has not been created is properly indeterminate by nature. Everything which has been created has bounds put upon it by God the Creator ...

[Angels] are strong, and ready to fulfil the will of God, being discovered everywhere at once by the speed which is theirs by nature, wherever God indicates [they should go]. They keep watch over the regions of the earth, and are set over their peoples and places, just as they have been appointed by the Creator. They regulate our affairs and come to our aid. But in every way, according to God's will and command, they are above us and always have their real existence around God ...

They see God in accordance with their nearness to Him, and this sight is their nourishment. They are above and beyond us, in that they do not have physical bodies and are released from all physical suffering, although they are not devoid of feeling, because only God is devoid of feeling.

They transform themselves into whatever the Lord God orders them, and in this form show themselves to human beings and unveil to them the mysteries of God.

Chapter 4. [Demons] do not have authority or power over anyone unless they have been granted a meagre amount of it by God, as in the case of Job, and the pigs described in the Gospel.[16] But with God's agreement, they are powerful. They change their shapes and transform themselves into whatever appearance they want, according to the image they have in mind.

Neither the angels of God nor evil spirits know the future. Yet, all the same, they predict it. In the case of the angels, God lifts the veil for them and tells them to predict, and so whatever they say actually happens. The demons, too, predict – sometimes they see things happening a long way off, sometimes they guess. In consequence, for the most part they lie and one should not put any trust in them. On a number of occasions, however, they tell the truth.

[16] *Mark* 5.2–13. Jesus exorcises evil spirits from a man. They then occupy pigs which run off a cliff into the sea and drown.

29 The use of demons. John Barbour: *The Brus* (1370s)

[*Scottish poet, c.1370–1395. Archdeacon of Aberdeen. He is sometimes called the father of Scottish vernacular poetry.* The Brus *is centred upon the exploits of King Robert I during the Wars of Independence.*]

[*King Edward I of England invaded Scotland, and fell sick at a place called Burgh.*]

But people said he had a spirit enclosed[17] which gave him replies to things about which he used to ask questions. There is no doubt he was a fool to believe that creature, because demons are by nature jealous of humankind. For they know for certain that those who lead good lives here will gain the mansion from which they [the demons] were pulled down through their great pride. Consequently, it will often happen that when demons by the power of an invocation are compelled to appear and give a response, they are so deceitful and wicked that they give an ambiguous answer in order to deceive those who are willing to believe them. I shall now give an example of a war which, so I heard, took place between France and the Flemings. The mother of Count Ferrand was a necromancer, and she raised up Satan and asked him at that time what would happen as a result of the fighting between the King of France and her son. Satan, as he has always done, turned his answer into a piece of deceit.

[17] Probably in a ring or a bottle. This was how spirits were usually imprisoned. It made them easier to carry around and have at one's disposal.

30 Fairies. *The Trial of St Joan of Arc* (1431)

24 February 1431. She was asked about a certain tree which grew near her village. She answered that quite near the village of Domrémy there was a tree called 'The Ladies' Tree'. Some people called it 'The Fairies' Tree'.[18] Not far away is a spring of water.[19] She has heard it said that people who are ill with fever drink from this spring, and come to seek its water to restore their health. She has seen this herself, but she does not know whether they are cured thereby or not.

She says she has heard that when the sick can get up, they go to the tree in order to walk round it. It is a big tree, called a 'beech', from which comes may [blossom]. It used to belong to Pierre de Bourlemont, a knight.

She said that sometimes she used to walk round it with other young girls; and close by that tree she used to make garlands of flowers for the statue of the Blessed Virgin of Domrémy. On many occasions, she has heard from the very old – not those of her own family – that the fairy-ladies used to visit it frequently. She has heard it said by one woman called Jeanne, the wife of Mayor Aubery of Domrémy, who was her godmother, that she had seen the said fairy-ladies; but [the defendant] does not know whether this is true or not.

She said that she has never seen the said fairies at the tree, as far as she knows. Has she seen them elsewhere? She does not know whether she has or not.

She said she has seen young girls putting garlands on the branches of the tree, and she herself has sometimes put them there, in company with other girls. Sometimes they would take the garlands away with them, sometimes they would leave them there …

[18] *Arbor fatalium*. The fatales, according to the root of the word, are those who are concerned with destiny, or who act as the instruments of Fate. By the early twelfth century, however, the fatales had become associated with 'fairies', and this, as a phrase in the record of St Joan's trial makes clear, is how the word should be understood here.

[19] *Fons*, which may also refer to a well.

---

31 A werewolf. Giraldus Cambrensis: *Topographia Hiberniae* (c.1187)

[*Welsh historian, theologian, hagiographer, and belle lettrist, 1146–1223. The* Topographia *was written out of his experience in Ireland as a member of the English army's expedition thither in 1185–6.*]

2.9. Now, I am going to tell you about things which have happened in my own time, and which are worthy of your astonishment. About three years before Earl John arrived in Ireland, a certain priest happened to be travelling from Ulster towards Meath, and was obliged to spend the night in a wood adjoining Meath. He had kindled a little fire for himself under a tree in full leaf, and was working by the firelight, with only a young boy for company, when lo and behold! a wolf came up to them and immediately burst into speech as follows.

'Be at ease, don't be afraid! There's no need for you to be alarmed when there is no fear,' and since they were stupefied and their minds were thrown into complete confusion, he added some sensible words about God. The priest implored him and called upon him, through almighty God and their allegiance to the Trinity, not to harm them but [to tell them] what kind of a creature he was who, beneath the shape of an animal, was uttering human words. The wolf gave a reply conformable in every way with Catholic doctrine, and finally added, 'Because of the curse of St Natalis – that is, Natalis the Abbot – two of us, a man and a woman, are compelled every seven years to live in exile from our [natural] shapes as well as from our native territory. We doff our human form entirely and put on that of a wolf. At the end of the seven-year period, if by chance these people have survived, two others are substituted for them and take their places under similar conditions, while they return to their former country and former nature. My companion in this wandering is seriously ill not far from here and since she is on the point of death, please do her the favour of granting her your priestly consolation, in consideration of the duty laid upon you by God.'

After he had said this, the wolf led the way to a tree which was not far away, and the priest followed, quaking with fear. In a hollow of the tree, he caught sight of a she-wolf who, in her shape of a wild creature, was uttering human groans and cries of distress. As soon as she saw the priest, she spoke a quite human greeting and gave thanks to God because He had deigned to provide her with such great comfort at such a critical moment; and thus she received from the priest every [rite of the Church] performed with due formality, as far as [but not including] final communion. But this too she demanded insistently, begging him earnestly to complete his good deed by granting her the viaticum. The priest told her firmly he did not have it with him. The male wolf, who had withdrawn a little out of the way, came forward again and brought to the priest's attention a small Missal which, according to the custom of his country, the priest was carrying hung round his neck under his clothing. This had some consecrated Hosts inside it. The wolf asked him not to refuse, at this juncture, the gift of God and an assistance destined for them by divine providence; and in order to wipe away all hesitation, using his paw as though it were a hand, he dragged back all the skin from the she-wolf's head and unrolled it as far as the navel, and thus at once the clearly defined shape of an elderly woman appeared. When he saw this, the priest compelled more by terror than by rationality, finally gave her communion, since she was resolute in her demand for it, and she received it with devotion.

When this had all been done, more in ritual than in justifiable fashion, the he-wolf exhibited to them a human rather than an animal sociability during the whole night at their little fire. When morning came, he led them out of the wood and spent a long time pointing out to the priest, who was continuing his journey, the most reliable road. While the priest was leaving, the wolf also gave him many thanks for the act of kindness he had done, and promised that he would give him much more practical thanks if the Lord called him back from this exile, two parts of which he had already completed ...

Now, two years later I happened to be travelling through Meath when the Bishop of Meath, as luck would have it, summoned a synod. He had also brought in the neighbouring bishops and abbots so that he could consult them about this business (which by this time he had learned from the priest's confession), and have a clearer idea of what to do about it. Hearing that I was coming through the area, he sent two of his clerics to me, asking if I could be present in person, if at all possible, when a matter of such great importance was being discussed; and if I could not attend (he said), could I at least assure them, in writing, that I agreed with their assessment? So I listened to what each of the clerics had to say about the business, even though I had actually heard it before from other people, and as certain pressing matters meant I was unable to attend the synod, I did them the courtesy of writing them a letter. The Bishop, together with the synod, complied with its instructions and dispatched the priest to the Pope along with a letter from the Bishop, containing an account of what had happened and the priest's confession, to which the bishops and abbots present at the synod attached their seals.

So, you see, it cannot be disputed, but rather must be embraced with a completely confident faith, that the divine nature took on human nature in order to save the world; and in this case, simply by God's assent in order to testify to his power and exaction of punishment, by no less a miracle human nature took on that of a wolf. But should an animal of this kind be called a beast or a human being? An animal endowed with reason seems to be far removed from a brute beast. Moreover, who will assign to the human species a four-footed animal which leans forward towards the earth and has not the ability to laugh? Likewise, supposing someone kills this animal. Surely he has not killed a human being? Surely he cannot be called a murderer? But divine miracles must not be drawn into the process of reasoning in a [purely] human discussion. Rather, they should be objects of astonishment. In Book 16, chapter 8 of his *De Civitate Dei*, Augustine raises a question about monstrous races of people who are born in the East, some of whom have dogs' heads, while others have no heads at all, and are said to have eyes on their shoulders and to be deformed in various ways: can these actually be said to be people, generated from the first parent [Adam]? At the end, he concludes we should think the same about these as we do about monsters born from human beings, something we hear happens very frequently, and that whatever is defined as a human being, (i.e. a mortal creature endowed with reason), is attested by true reasoning to be a human, regardless of what shape it has[20] ...

When he had finished what he had to say about various transmutations of people into wolves, he finally added, 'When I was in Italy, I used to hear such things about a particular district in that region. Women who kept stables and lodging-houses there were steeped in these wicked acts and, according to popular gossip, used to give something to travellers in their cheese. This would turn them into pack-animals and they would carry all kinds of commodities; and after they had completed their tasks, they would turn back into themselves again. Yet they did not develop the mind of a beast, but preserved their human rationality.'[21]

In our day, too, we have seen[22] certain people who, steeped in the arts of magic, would produce what appeared to be fat pigs – they were always red – from any material they had in front of them, and then sold them on market-days. But they vanished as soon as they began to cross any water, and would return to their own true nature; and no matter how carefully you looked after them, their assumed shape did not last beyond three days. Likewise, it is a frequent modern complaint, which also goes back a long way, that certain elderly women in Wales, as well as in Ireland and Scotland, change themselves into the shape of a hare so that, under their counterfeit form, they may secretly steal other people's milk by sucking [their farm animals'] teats. So I agree with Augustine that while neither evil spirits nor wicked people can create or really change their natures in this way, those things which have been created by the true God with his permission do change in appearance, meaning that they seem to be what they are not; and when people's senses have been taken prisoner and put to sleep by an extraordinary hallucination,[23] things are not seen as they actually are but, by the power of an apparition or of a magical incantation, they are distracted in an extraordinary fashion so that they see certain false and unnatural shapes.

[20] This does not appear at the end of Augustine's chapter. It is a paraphrase of something he says earlier therein. The monsters to which he refers were described by Pliny the Elder in his *Naturalis Historia* 7.9-30 which was probably Augustine's source. Pliny himself owed something to Herodotus 4.191.

[21] Augustine's further remarks about werewolves come in *De Civitate Dei* 8.17. His personal reminiscence appears in the next chapter which, significantly, is headed, 'What we should believe about transformations which seem to happen to people through the craft of evil spirits'.

[22] This may be an inclusive 'we', i.e. Caesarius and his reader, or an editorial 'we', meaning Caesarius who is relating a personal experience.

[23] *Illusio* also means 'mocking play, ridicule', a comment on the game which evil spirits play on human beings.

---

32 Unearthly visitants. *De gestis Herwardi Saxonis* (late 11th/early 12th century)

The following night, Hereward saw in his dreams a man of incalculable shape standing near him. He was old, with a frightening expression and, judging by the way he was dressed from head to foot, more unusual than anything Hereward had seen or conceived of. He was threatening Hereward with a great sword he was carrying in his hand, and gave him the dreadful instruction that, if Hereward wanted to provide for his salvation/safety and avoid a wretched death the following day, he should restore at once everything belonging to his church, which he had taken the previous night. Hereward woke up, seized by fear sent from God, took back everything he had removed, and so passed on with all his men and left the place. While they were on their way, they suddenly lost the straight track and wandered off; but something wonderful and miraculous happened to them while they strayed (if it is reasonable for one to say that such things can happen to men of blood). For it was the dead of night, there was a thick fog, and they did not know where to turn through the trackless woods. An enormous wolf appeared in front of them, fawning on them like a house-dog. Then it drew to one side of the path and began to go in front of them, keeping quite close. In the foggy darkness, however, they thought it was a white dog because of its grey coat, and kept urging one another to follow the dog, maintaining that it was from a village nearby. So they followed it and, in the dead silence of night, realised they had successfully come off the track and now recognised their way. Suddenly lighted candles appeared, attached to all the soldier's spears. These, however, were not very bright, but rather like those popularly known as 'fairy candles'.[24] Nobody, you see, could have torn them off or extinguished them at all, or thrown them away. Each man was astounded at this and yet, although they were taken aback, they saw the way to go and followed it, always under the guidance of the wolf. As daylight grew, (if one can believe it), everyone found out at last that their guide was a wolf – something they found amazing – and while they stood there, full of uncertainty over what had happened to them, the wolf could not be found and the candles vanished. They arrived on the further side of Stanford, where they had arranged to go; and when they realised their journey had been successful, they gave thanks to God, and were full of astonishment at what had happened to them.

[24] *Candelae nympharum*. 'Nymphs' has too many Classical associations to be appropriate in this passage, so I have adapted its meaning to fit the context.

33   The dead. Peter Damian: *Letter to Pope Nicholas II*, (written between December 1059 and July 1061)

[*Italian Benedictine, 1001–72. Abbot of Fonte Avellana in c.1043. He was used in Papal diplomatic missions to France and Germany, and was named Cardinal-Bishop of Ostia but eventually resigned therefrom. He was never formally canonised, but Pope Leo XII declared him a Doctor of the Church in 1828.*]

[No. 72] In the German states, a rich and very powerful Count who was also – and this is an extraordinary thing to be found in people of his rank – of sound faith and blameless life (a general judgement entirely consistent with his worth), died just before completing his tenth year. After the Mass held on the anniversary of his death, a monk descended in spirit to the realms of the dead, and saw the Count set on the highest rung of a ladder. He said that the ladder seemed to have been set up among the hissing, crackling flames of an avenging fire, arranged so as to receive all the members of this same Count's family. There was a foul chaos and a dreadful chasm gaping endlessly and sunk into depths from which the extended ladder was rising. A succession of people, following each other in order, was thus being woven into a continuous sequence in such a way that when any new person joined them and occupied the first rung of the ladder, the person who had been occupying it and all the others stepped down on to the nearest rung below. So when more and more of the same family gathered at intervals on the foresaid ladder after their physical death, some of them submitted to the demands of the judgement which cannot be avoided, and made their way to Hell. Obviously the man who was looking at this asked what was the cause of this dreadful punishment, and especially why his contemporary, the Count, who had lived such a decent, honourable life, was being punished; and he heard, 'A certain piece of property belonging to the Church of Metz was alienated by his great-great grandfather from [its patron] St Stephen. This Count, as you can see, is tenth in line of succession from him, and all these people have been assigned to the same punishment. For, just as the sin of greed has affected them all equally and conjoined them in the commission of the sin, so also a common punishment has linked them to make them endure the penalties of the atrocious fire.'

34 Dead monks. Trithemius: *Beati Rabani Mauri Vita* (refers to 837)

[Hrabanus *or Rabanus Maurus, c.776–856, was Abbot of Fulda and Archbishop of Mainz. An extensive writer, his major encyclopaedic work,* De rerum naturis, *later called* De Universo, *was published in 842. He also composed* Carmina figurata *which were poems written in symbolic shapes. One of his most popular poems was in praise of the cross,* De laudibus sanctae crucis.]

It happened in the twelfth year Rabanus was abbot, the year of Our Lord 837, that a number of monks in the monastery of Fulda were called by the Lord and passed from this misery to a future life. Consequently, the saint, full of compassion for the dead and for the living poor, earnestly gave instructions to Adelhard, the monastery's steward, saying to him in front of everyone, 'Take especially careful pains, Brother, to distribute faithfully to each of the poor the full and undiminished allowances of food which were allotted my dead brethren for their sustenance [in life]. If you fail to do this, understand that your guilty soul will be liable to the uncompromising justice of God and will be punished.' Adelhard answered that he would willingly carry out Father Abbot's commands.

[*But Adelhard, overcome by greed, held back for himself those charitable offerings which were meant to assist the souls of the dead.*]

Divine justice, however, did not endure his rash insolence without revenge. For one day, when he had been very much preoccupied with worldly affairs, it became rather late and the rest of the brethren were already asleep. Adelhard was making his way alone to the dormitory through the chapter-house carrying a small oil-lamp, as usual, when he saw a large number of monks seated there in rows, clad in their accustomed black. Seized by an immense fear, he did not know what to do; for it was too late at night for him to believe that a chapter had been assembled. When he looked more closely, he realised that each was the ghost of one of the recently deceased brethren whose allowances he had held back. Terrified out of his wits, he began to try to withdraw. But his blood drained away and panic made his legs and feet grow stiff, as with freezing cold, so that he could not move from the spot. In an instant, the dreadful ghosts of the dead, seeing him struck down by great fear, rose up with sudden violence and, with hidden power, stripped him of his clothes and beat the wretched man with sticks – not just on his naked back, as is the custom in monastic punishments, but over his whole body – in such a way that he could actually feel it. While they struck him, they uttered [the following words] in the awful semblance of a voice. 'Wretched man, take the punishment you deserve for your greed. You will receive worse in three days' time, and then you will be numbered with us among the dead.'

At about midnight, when the brethren got up to sing Matins and Lauds, they found the wretched man who had been beaten, lying in the chapter-house more dead than alive. They took him to the infirmary and, after a while, when the brothers' efforts had restored him to himself, he told them what awful things he had suffered and that, according to the spirits who had appeared to him, he was going to die in three days' time. Lest they imagine he had dreamed it, or that it was merely a sick fantasy of his mind, he said, 'Look at the blows; observe the livid marks. No one could get the signs of a violent assault and remain asleep.'

35 A disturbing vision. Thomas of Cantimpré: *Bonum universale de apibus* (1256–61)

[*Belgian encyclopaedist and hagiographer, c.1201–c.1270/2. First an Augustinian, then a Dominican. His* Bonum universale *is a guide to monastic life, based on an analogy between the monastery and the bee-hive. It proved very popular and was translated into Dutch, German, and French.*]

Book 2, chapter 57. Gunerchena is a prominent and well-known township in Brabant. Here a young man once fell in love with a virgin, but when he asked her parents to let him marry her, they refused. Meanwhile, the girl contracted an acute fever which became worse and everyone thought she had died. Consequently they mourned her, and bells were tolled as if for a dead woman. The girl's young lover did not wait around, but left Gunerchena. At some thickets he heard a voice like that of a woman wailing. Full of concern, therefore, he ran about looking for its source and found the girl he thought was dead. 'Your family is mourning your death', he said to her, 'so where have you come from?' 'Look', she replied, 'the man who led me astray is coming into my presence!' The young man was taken aback at this, since he saw no one else except the girl; but boldly he seized hold of her, carried her off, and hid her at once in a house outwith the township. From here he came back into Gunerchena, spoke to his friends, and then went to the girl's father who was sitting with his friends near the dead body. He asked him if he would give him the daughter for whom he was wailing as though she were dead. The father replied in astonishment, 'Surely you are not proposing to play God for me by raising a dead woman and taking her for your wife?' The young man said, 'Just give me your favourable answer, that I may have your daughter for my wife if I restore her to life and health.' The father agreed and ratified his consent in front of everyone. Then the young man pulled back the linen cloth which they thought was covering her, and they found an extraordinary image, the likeness of which no human being could have made. It is said by those who have inspected diabolical images of this kind that the inside is like decayed wood, and the outside is covered with a thin layer of skin. After this, the girl was brought back and restored to her father. In full health, she married the young man several days later, and has survived safe and sound right up to the present day.

---

36 An evil spirit. *Vita Sancti Roberti Abbatis* (11th century)

[*St. Robert of Molesmes. French Benedictine, founder of the Cistercian order dedicated to the strict observance of St Benedict's Rule. He died in 1098.*]

One night, the holy man saw something malign lingering at the entrance to the choir. It made frequent attempts to enter, but was unable to do so. It looked like someone wearing peasant dress. Its shanks were long and bare. It was carrying a little basket on its back and a piece of wood bound with rope at its chest. Well now, it began to circle the choir, its neck thrust forward, intently casting its eyes upon the brethren to see whether it could discern any mark of favour to itself in anyone. But the man of God [St Robert] prayed vehemently, rousing the brethren from their torpor, and the insolent spy lingered expectantly for a long time in vain. Since it saw it was making no headway, it took itself off, full of indignation, to the lay-brothers' choir. There it stared attentively at everyone, and if any of them was nodding off, it cackled loudly and made a scornful gesture as if to repudiate him. If anyone was engrossed in wicked thoughts, it applauded, spurning him in a remarkable manner. At last, it found a young man among the novices, whose mind was wandering off to forbidden subjects, present only in body and actually thinking about running away in secret. Noting, therefore, that it and the young man were two of a kind, the malignant creature picked him up with a little trident, thrust him into its little basket, and quickly rushed away. Seeing this, the holy man, very anxious and solicitous for the youth's safety [or 'salvation'], ordered that diligent search be made for him in the morning. But the youth had wandered off before dawn and had run away, shaking off the pleasant yoke of Christ, and had followed the Enemy. He attached himself to criminals and spent his time in banditry. But not long afterwards, he was arrested and beheaded and so died a wretched death.

---

37 A mysterious transvection. Peter Damian: *Letter to Abbot Desiderius and the Abbey of Monte Cassino* (c.1065)

[*Italian Benedictine, 1001–72. Abbot of Fonte Avellana in c.1043.*]

No. 119. The five-year-old son of the most noble Ubald who has spent time with me in a hermitage, had become a monk in my monastery. Every so often in the silent dead of night, he would go out (or be taken out, I don't know which), while the brethren were asleep. On one occasion, there was a miller lying in his mill who could not get back to sleep. To ward off the cold, he wanted to put on his clothes which were lying close by, stretched out his arm, and discovered the boy asleep next to him. Immediately he was bewildered and very frightened. He got up in haste, lit a lamp, and going round the whole house in a state of mingled unease and curiosity, he found all the doors and windows closed and barred. When morning came, the brethren were not a little astonished. How could the boy have gone into the mill when all the doors were closed and when everyone knew perfectly well he had gone to sleep in his own bed the previous evening? They had all seen it for themselves.

Of the Apostles we read that when they were to be removed from the common prison, 'the angel of the Lord [came and] by night opened the prison doors, and brought them forth, and said: Go, stand and speak in the Temple to the people all the words of this life' [*Acts* 5.19–20]. Again, we read of Peter that when the angel went before him from the prison 'to the iron gate, it was opened to them of its own accord' [*Acts* 12.10]; and of Paul, that 'suddenly there was a great earthquake, so that the foundations of the prison were shaken: and immediately all the doors were opened, and everyone's bonds were loosed' [*Acts* 16.26].

Now, since even the angels did not bring the blessed Apostles out of prison without first opening the doors, it is quite extraordinary how the boy could have entered a house completely shut up if its entrances had not been opened either by the magic arts of human beings or the tricks of unclean spirits. For when the boy himself was painstakingly questioned, he added that certain people had lifted him up in their hands and brought him to a great banquet where there seemed to be every type of rich dish, and made him eat. He also told them they carried him right up to the castle which looms over the monastery, and put over him the bell which hangs in a high place next to the church.

I have been led to describe this incident so that each one of us may consider that even children who do not yet know how to sin are subject to the snares of a malignant Enemy, and so that each one of us may bear whatever he suffers with equanimity.

---

38 A political use of demoniacs. Niketas Choniates: *Historia* (early 13th century)

[*Byzantine government officer, historian, and theologian, 1155/7–1217.*]

V. Book 1. [In order to urge the Bulgars and Vlachs to rebel against the Emperor Isaac, two brothers, Peter and Asam] constructed a prayer-house in the name of the Excellent-Martyr Demetrios, and here were assembled many from both races, who had been seized by evil spirits. Their pupils were stained with blood and wrenched out of place; their hair was loose; and they embodied in accurate detail everything else relevant to those held in the grip of demons. Peter and Asam obliged them to shout aloud in their ecstatic states such things as, 'the God of the race of the Bulgars and the Vlachs consented to their freedom and agreed that they shake off the yoke they had worn so long. In support of this, Demetrios, Christ's martyr, would abandon the metropolis of Thessalonika, his shrine there, and the places where the Byzantines took their leisure, and join them as their helper and partner in the coming enterprise.'

These frenzied people reined themselves in for a short time, but then all of a sudden they would take a deep breath and behave like epileptics, creating a frightening disturbance and shouting in the manner of those inspired by a god a piercing cry that it was no time to sit still, but to take hold of weapons and close with the Byzantines. Prisoners of war (they said) should not be taken alive or granted life, but have their throats cut and be torn in pieces without mercy; nor should they be let go upon payment of ransom, nor turn people from their purpose by their prayers and entreaties, and make them womanish by going down on their knees. No, their captors, like diamonds, should be unyielding to every appeal, and slaughter every person they had taken prisoner.

By means of diviners such as these, Peter and Asam won over the whole race, and everyone took up arms.

39 Torments inflicted by demons. Blessed Angela of Foligno: *Vita* (late 13th century)

[*Married, with several children, she had a vision in 1285, which changed her life. She became a Franciscan tertiary. She experienced vivid visions, and dictated accounts of them to her confessor.*]

Chapter 19. I suffer more or less continually at the hands of these demons torments and martyrdoms of the soul which, in my opinion, are incomparably more bitter and worse than those of the body. I don't know to what my situation may be compared other than to that of a hanged man on a scaffold, his hands tied behind his back, his eyes blindfolded, suspended at the end of a rope, who has been left on the gibbet and is still alive, without any chance of help or remedy or support. I say I am still being tortured by demons in a way more hopeless and more cruel than that; for I perceive that the demons suspend my soul in such a way that, just as the hanged man has no support, so my soul seems to have no support left and all its powers are being overthrown, with my soul knowing that this is so, and watching it happen. When my soul sees all its powers being overthrown and departing, and because it cannot put up a fight, its pain is so great that I can hardly utter a cry of grief because of my hopeless pain and anger. Sometimes I cry out and cannot stop or be stopped. Sometimes so great an anger comes upon me that I can barely stop myself from tearing myself to pieces. Sometimes I can hardly stop myself from hitting myself in a quite dreadful way, and this hitting has sometimes caused swelling in my head and other parts of my body. When my soul sees its powers collapse and go away, it protests and I cry out to my God.

Likewise, I suffer another torment because all my sins have revived in me and sometimes come to life again. They don't suborn my reason by lasting a long time, but they do bring and expose me to great punishment. Even sins which have never been in my body come into me, are made more intense, and bring me great punishment. But they do not have a continuous life, and when they die once more they give me great relief; for I perceive I have been handed over to many demons who bring to life again the sins I abhor and which were dead, while adding sins which have never existed [in me]. When I call to mind that God was afflicted and despised in this way, and poor, I should like all my woes to be doubled; as also whenever I am in the most dreadful darkness of demons, where all hope seems to be lacking entirely, and there is that dreadful darkness, and the sins I know deep within my soul are dead are being stirred to action, while outwith the soul demons are stirring them up – yes, and also stirring up those sins which have not existed in me.

I suffer bodily in at least three places. In my shameful parts there is such a great fire that it was my practice to burn them with real fire in order to extinguish the fire of lust, until my confessor forbade me to do so. When I am in that darkness, I believe I should sooner choose to be roasted than suffer what I have been describing. Then I cry out and summon death, asking God to grant it to happen to me in some fashion or another; and then I say to God, 'Lord, if you must send me to Hell, please do it quickly and don't hold back; and in as much as you have abandoned me, end my life and drown me in the deep.' Then I realise it's the work of demons and that those sins are not alive in my soul because my soul never agrees to them. But my body suffers violence and there is such great pain and disgust that, were it to last, my body could not bear it. But the soul also sees that all power has been taken away from it, even though it does not consent to the sins: and yet it does not have the ability to resist the sins at all. It perceives that it is in opposition to God, and so falls, and is tortured in these sins.

There is a particular sin which God allows to come into me. This sin is so great that it surpasses all the other sins; and there is a particular power, clearly given to me by God, against that sin, whereby I am set free by God by virtue of possessing this special power; and even if I did not have a firm faith in God, for this reason alone and for no other it would stay with me. Therefore I retain a firm and secure hope and should not be able to fall into sin. It is a power of such great strength of virtue that, really, I recognise God in it, and I am enlightened. I am strengthened so much that none of the people in the world, none of the demons of Hell, and nothing else, either, can move me to the slightest sin, and with this power I keep my faith in God. But the sin is so great that I am ashamed to speak it. Whenever the power I have been describing is hidden from me and I think it has left me, there is nothing I could keep hold of, either for shame or for any other punishment, to prevent me from rushing into sin at once. But then the power comes back and sets me free in its powerful, virtuous fashion, in such a way that I would not be able to sin for anything good or evil in this world. These struggles I have endured for two years and more.

40 Exorcism. Hieronymus Radiolensis: *Miracula Sancti Joannis Gualberti* (late 11th century)

[*St Giovanni Gualbert, c.995–1073, Benedictine monk originally from Florence, was the founder of the Abbey of Vallumbrosa in 1039. His aim was to restore traditional Benedictine monasticism. Hieronymus was a monk of the same abbey.*]

(51) A girl by the name of Francesca, from the city of Civita Castellana, afflicted by acts of magic and incantations, was brought to the monastery of Santa Maria, and we took her in. For a while she was untroubled in mind and body and her life was tranquil, to the extent that no one would have said she was being tortured by an evil spirit or suffering in any part of her body. At length, however, she tried to kill herself with a sword, began to attack others and tear them with her teeth. But the priests and monks who were exorcising her put up with this (albeit in great distress), because the demon upon whom they inflicted immense torments would give no response. We could come to little or no agreement about the reason for this: he may have been behaving like this because of [our] diligent activity, or because a

certain type of evil spirit is dumb by nature. But after the priest had tormented him for a long time and commanded him on several occasions in the power of God at least to make some reply, on the chance he was devising some evil, at last he made the following response.

'I have been confined and held prisoner here a long time by the incantations of a wicked priest who stank of a shameless love for this girl. He did not admit the truth of this to himself, and although all the other evil arts which lovers use were not available to him, he preferred to try anything and everything rather than be exposed to the heat of a fire he could not endure. [52] I come into it because he roused me by incantation so that I might force her to his will. But – and here let me speak the truth – I was not in the least successful; for she had been very well brought up by her parents, been given first rate warnings and good advice, and devoted herself to prayer from her earliest years, perpetually calling upon the Virgin Mary with prayers and tears. Therefore these and other good works of hers stopped me, and when I was unable to carry out the priest's wicked will, I lost my temper and took possession of her. Contrary to our usual custom, I proved to be considerate and kind, and she became entirely used to me. For among other things, however frequently a greater zeal set her on fire in heart and mind to follow the religion of God, either by silent prayer or by visiting churches or going to sermons, I never refused without first doing works of piety.'

The [exorcising] priest said, 'O you who lead everyone astray, bringing a thousand misfortunes, disputes, rages, quarrels, and murders! You do works of piety? Ha! Most villainous of all demons who have fallen from the regions above, I know you inside out. Whatever was done in a holy, honourable fashion was done by the merits of the Virgin Mary, not by yours, and you dare not at all say otherwise.'

[53] Then the demon cackled and laughed aloud and said, 'It's true, Father, as you say.'

The priest wanted to know why the demon had dared to take possession of a girl who had been so very well brought up.

'It's not something which was done by God', replied the demon, 'and for that reason it is not for mortal beings to investigate these things. Rather, in these and indeed anything else which does not pertain thereto, one must lapse into an everlasting silence.'

So St Giovanni spent a fruitless two days in prayers and orisons until finally the devil, unwilling to endure the saint's power any further, thundered forth these words with a cry of pain.

'Why are you persecuting me? Why are you inflicting so many and such varied torments [upon me] to make me go away? Didn't I say I was being kept here by someone else's command? Let the man who bound me come here – the wicked priest – and let him set me free, and I shall go willingly.'

Then, when the laymen who were present wanted to ask him the name of the priest, the [exorcising] priest said, 'Be off with you! It's the Devil's trade to sow discord and to bring upon mortals whatever evil he can. So please don't put any trust in him.'

The demon took offence at this and, in a loud voice, said, 'It will all become clear shortly, whether I have lied or told the truth. O wicked priest at whose hands I endure so many tortures and torments! What great punishments you will suffer!'

[54] As for the rest, by the grace of Jesus and the prayers of holy Mary and St Giovanni, the girl was freed from the demon. But – and I don't know why this happened – in an instant such an intolerable and wearisome disease attacked her that her whole body was covered in sores, she discharged black bile from every orifice, and finally, driven by suffering and her illness, she pulled out all her hair, making a spectacle of herself to everyone, especially her relatives and neighbours. Several years went by and, by the grace of the Virgin Mary and St Giovanni, to whom she had very often commended herself, she was restored to her former health. Her face remained extremely pale and certain blotches did not go away; otherwise she was well. It was then told to those who were looking after her at home that the [identity of] the priest I mentioned earlier had been revealed to her kinsfolk by the agency of the Devil or (and this is more likely to be true), he had been recognised because people guessed who he was: that he had taken himself off elsewhere, fearing judgement for his misdeeds and, by the judgement of God, had spent his life in wretchedness, plotting revenge upon the girl. There have been those who have maintained that he was murdered by the girl's brothers beyond the limits of their own district; but this is merely gossip. The truth of the matter is in the hands of those who witnessed the events. As far as I am concerned, it is an established fact that for many years the young girl devoutly came to this church of the Virgin Mary barefoot, carrying a wax candle, on the Feast of St Giovanni. So, anent these and other miracles I have related and will go on to relate, it is quite clear that incantations are done by people who are perverted.

Miracles

41 Curing the sick. Andrew of Strumi: Vita *Sancti Joannis Gualbert* (referring to end of 12th/beginning of 13th century)

45. At the time when the Simoniac heresy had sprouted all over Tuscany, while Saint Giovanni was staying at a monastery in Florence, a religious man from a noble Florentine family, whose son had been confined to bed with a serious wasting illness and was now out of bed, awaiting death which was not far off, approached the saint to ask him to cure his son and give him back to him. The man said that these were not his own words but those of the Apostles and, full of groans, prostrated himself at the saint's feet and persisted with his prayers until the holy Father, moved by pity, sent him back home and promised he would petition God on his behalf. Then he went downstairs, summoned the brethren, and devoted himself to prayer and supplication. While they were humbly prostrate on the round in prayer, He in whose hands rests everyone's salvation, restored the sick man to complete health through the intercession of his beloved; and the person on whom this favour of health was bestowed as a miracle through Giovanni, as I have described, is a living witness to it at the present time.

---

42 Blood in the chalice. Giovanni Villani: *Croniche Fiorentine* (early 14th century)

[6.7] On 30 December 1229, the Feast of St Firenze, a priest of the Church of St Ambrogio di Firenze, whose name was Father Uguccione, had said Mass and celebrated the sacrifice but, because he was an old man, he did not wipe the chalice properly. So when he came to pick it up, he found inside it living blood, freshly shed and bright red. This was shown to all the women of the convent, all those who lived nearby and were present in the church, the Bishop, all the clergy, and later on, all the inhabitants of Florence. They then came with great devotion, took the blood from the chalice, and put it in a crystal flask which they then displayed with great reverence.

43 An anointed King's ability to cure the sick. Robert Fitzhugh: *Memorandum*, 31 May 1435

[*Fitzhugh was Bishop of London and was attending the Council of Basel when he wrote this memorandum.*]

6. The Kings of France and England are anointed on their heads; others on their shoulders or other parts of the body. According to Archdeacon Hostiensis, and to scholars, this way of anointing and the place on which it is done implies a greater dignity and excellence, because it is just like that of David and Saul whom Samuel anointed in this manner, as the Canons attest. Experience proves that by virtue of this anointing, as is firmly believed and held in England, those infected by transitory disease and suffering from various other wasting illnesses are cured by a touch of the royal hand, along with certain rings consecrated on Good Friday. The anointing of the King of France gives him a similar power to cure the sick.

44 A false miracle. Giovanni di m. Pedrino Depintore: *Cronica del suo tempo* (mid 15th century)

[*Giovanni Merlini, Italian historian, died 1465.*]

No. 2008. In 1383 people were saying throughout Romagna that a miracle had happened in Faenza, in the Church of San Piero, at about the end of May. A painting or crucifix in the said church, near the piazza of the same name, worked miracles and cured the sick. Several men were said to have seen them, and once the news had spread, many of the region's sick went all together to the said church. They wanted to go to the altar, and once they were there the men and women began to quiver and dance like lunatics. They flung themselves all over the place in the church, and went into raptures three or four times before they could go to the altar. Whenever they got as far as the altar, they would turn back and fall down, and did not get up without assistance. No one was free from this. At last it was noticed that this was happening because of some wicked person's incantation, because of diabolical conjurations; so the crowd of people stopped.

Methods of divination and discovering truth

45 How to cast lots. *Sortes XII Patriarcharum* (second half of 11th century)

[*A set of verses containing instructions on how to cast lots to find out about the future. The questioner undergoes a rigorous preparation, then throws the lots in a space in church next to the altar, having chosen his or her questions beforehand from a prescribed list.*]

If you want the lots to be fortunate and not a curse, take care to know in advance what it is you need to know. Do it this way and you will receive an answer to all your questions. When you want to find out the future by casting lots, pray and fast for two days, keep vigil and make humble entreaty for the whole of the previous night, and have a candle of double weight. Then, after Mass has been said and you have been sprinkled with holy water, don't forget [to say] 'Our Father' and the Creed, and don't fail to make the sign of the cross over the place nearest the altar. Then genuflect three times and, in that place, cast two lots; and while this is happening, make sure that twice six indigent people are being fed. In this way, the trustworthy lot, once thrown, tells you whatever you want to know. Put the following questions to the lots and hope that the lots do not deceive you.

1. Will you be deceived or not?
2. If you are thinking about doing something, should you dismiss it from your mind? At what time should it be done?
3. Is your journey safe or difficult?
4. Is a person weakened by illness going to recover or die?
5. Is peace going to ensue or disappear from sight?
6. Is someone who is absent safe and sound, or is there a hope of his safe return?
7. If you happen to be looking or asking for something, is it a mistake to do so?
8. If you want to make someone your friend, is he trustworthy?
9. If you are proposing to do something, will it turn out well?
10. Will you survive the war or die during it?
11. Is a body of men defeated in battle going to spread itself through the region, or will it be put to flight?

12. Does a piece of good fortune apply equally to everyone or just one person?

46 Imperial patronage of divination. Niketas Choniates: *Historia* (early 13th century). Adapted

[*Byzantine government officer, historian, theologian, 1155/7–1217.*]

[The Emperor Andronikos Komnenos] saw that the ancient skill of the *haruspex*[25] had disappeared, and that its use to reveal the future was dead and already completely forgotten; and that likewise, revealing the future through the juggling art of reading the movements of birds in flight had flown away beyond the borders of the Byzantine empire along with interpreters of dreams and observers of signs and portents; and that the only survivors were liars who made their divinations from the troughs in which dirty clothes are washed by being trodden, and little pots or dishes: and those who carefully observe the positions of the stars and deceive others no less than they deceive themselves. He disdained astronomy [i.e. astrology] as an art which had been far too common hitherto, and which indicated things to come in an obscure fashion, and gave himself up entirely to those who, so to speak, interpret the signs of secret things in waters and certain shapes of future events which co-exist therein as though faintly illuminated by certain rays of the sun.

Andronikos therefore refused to be present at initiations into secret religious rites, and while he turned aside, it seems, from the prattling voice which sees through things done in secret and betrays them to everybody when it came to this abominable night-work, he used Stephanos Hagiochristophorites as his substitute ... and Stephanos invited Seth to be his assistant. Seth had taken part in operations such as these ever since he was a grown boy, and the Emperor Manuel had had his eyes gouged out because of it ... Stephanos posed a question – and how he did so is something it gives me no pleasure to inquire about or to tell, so anyone who wants to know must find out from elsewhere – who is the next ruler after the Emperor Andronikos, or who will depose him? The evil spirit[26] gave an answer: or rather gave an indistinct representation, as in troubled waters, not of the whole name, but of the first letters: a sigma in the shape of a half-crescent moon, with a perfectly formed iota behind it, suggesting the interpretation 'Isaac'. The oracle therefore was an obscure piece of abomination, rather like a pattern of what was to come, pricked out beforehand,[27] or (to express it more truthfully) something which that many-shaped demon who feeds on wickedness by night did not understand with any accuracy and wrapped round in obscurity so that he could not be convicted of telling a lie.

[25] A diviner who foretold the future by interpreting signs on the internal organs of specially slaughtered animals, other extraordinary phenomena, and lightning.
[26] *Pneuma,* literally 'breath'. Hence the following reference to the ruffled surface of the water.
[27] Painted pictures could be lightly drawn, or in the case of frescoes pricked out in the wet plaster before the artist began on the final version.

47 How to uncover a murderer. *Lex Frisionum* (late 8th/early 9th century)

If someone has been killed in an uprising or a popular riot, and the person who killed him cannot be found because of the large number of people who were there, it is permissible for the person who wants to seek blood-money for the killing to accuse up to seven people and to blame each of them for the killing. Each of them must purge himself of the crime laid to his charge by taking a solemn oath.

Then they must be taken to a church and lots thrown on the altar or (if this cannot be done because there is no church nearby) on to relics of the saints. These lots must be of the following kind: two nodes (which they call *teni*) cut from a shoot, one of which is marked with the sign of the cross, the other left blank. They are wrapped in clean wool and thrown on to the altar or the relics. A priest, if there is one available, or if not, a virgin boy, should pick up one of the lots from the altar. Meanwhile God must be entreated to send a clear sign to indicate if those seven who have taken an oath about the killing have sworn the truth. If [the priest or boy] picks up the lot which is marked with the cross, those who have taken the oath will be innocent. But if he picks up the other one, then each of the seven must make his own lot (i.e. *tenus*) from a shoot, and sign it with his own mark so that both he and the rest of the bystanders can recognise it. These lots should be wrapped in clean wool and placed on the altar or relics. A priest, if there is one available, if not, a virgin boy as before, should pick up each of the lots from the altar, one by one, and ask each man to identify his own lot. The one whose lot is last to be picked up is the person who is forced to pay the blood-money, and the rest whose lots were picked up before his are acquitted.

48 Organising an ordeal. Eberhard of Bamberg: *Breviarium* (12th century)

[*The second Bishop of Bamberg by the name of Eberhard. Dates = 1100–1172.*]

When anyone is accused of theft, adultery, fornication, poisonous magic (*veneficium*), or any act of harmful magic (*maleficium*), and after interrogation denies the charge, he should be investigated as follows:

Ordeal by boiling water.

(a) The priest should go to church with the accusers in the case and the person who is to be investigated. While everyone waits in the churchyard, the priest should go and vest himself (except for a chasuble); take the Gospel, a reliquary and the relics of the saints, and the chalice; make his way to the church door, and say as follows to all the people standing by,

(b) 'See, brethren ...'

(c) Then let him address the person who is to be investigated thus: 'I enjoin you, N, in the presence of all these bystanders, by the Father and the Son and the veneration of all the saints, that if you are guilty of this forenamed matter, or have done it, or have consented to it, or have knowingly seen those who have committed this particular sin, you do not enter the church, you do not mix with Christian society unless you are willing to admit and confess your guilt before you are examined in public ordeal.'

(d) Then he should point out a place in the churchyard where fire is lit to heat the water or [a piece of] iron. First, let him asperge the place with holy water, and the cauldron (if it is to be hung up), along with the water. He should asperge the water because of the illusions of the Devil.[28]

(e) Then he should enter the church with everyone else and celebrate Mass as follows ... After he has celebrated Mass, the priest should go to the place of ordeal with the people, carrying the Gospel under his left arm, while the cross, the thurible, and the relics of the saints are carried in front of him. During this procession, he should chant the seven penitential psalms and the litany ...

(f) Over the boiling water: 'God, just judge, strong and patient'.
(g) 'Almighty and everlasting God, the searcher out of hidden things, we your suppliants pray that if this person is guilty of the aforesaid matter imputed to him, and the Devil is making him stubborn ... you may see fit to get rid of[29] the herbs which have been prepared by the Devil's art.'
(h) The blessing of the boiling water.
(i) Prayers. 'Almighty and everlasting God, we your suppliants pray you ...'
(j) 'Almighty and everlasting God, who by your unchangeable providence ...'
(k) After this, cense with myrrh the person who is to be investigated, and the cauldron or pot containing the boiling water, and then say this prayer:
(l) 'God, who [has established] the very great sacraments ...'
(m) Then the person to be investigated should wash with soap the hand which is to be put into the water, and examine it carefully to see that it is clean; and before it is put in, let the priest say: 'I exorcise you, pot or cauldron, by the Father ...' etc.
(n) After this, the person to be investigated should put his hand into the water and it should be marked immediately. After the ordeal, he should drink some holy water. Right up to the test by ordeal, it is a good idea that salt and holy water be mixed in all his food and drink.

[28] I.e. to make sure the Devil does not interfere with the water in such a way as to render it painless to the person undergoing the ordeal, which would frustrate the whole process and turn it into a blasphemous mockery.

[29] *Evacuare*, which means 'to purge' or 'to empty the bowels'. Since the person undergoing the ordeal might well be terrified, the latter could certainly happen and, if it did, might be taken as a sign that God was indeed removing protective magical herbs from his system.

49 Championing a witch. Adémar of Chabannes: *Chronicon* (late 1020s)

[*French Benedictine, c.988–c.1035. Historian, illustrator, and musician.*]

Book 3, chapter 66.
[*Throughout the 1020s, apocalyptic fears fed by signs and wonders multiplied. Count William of Aquitaine, through the King of France, sought advice from the bishops on what these marvels meant, and was told they presaged war and calamities.*]

In that same year (1028), the Count was seized by a debilitating physical weakness which brought him to the point of death, while at the same time the city of Saintes (and it pains me to speak of this), together with the Cathedral of St Peter, the Episcopal seat, was burned to the ground by heathenish Christians. No divine worship took place in the cathedral for a long time thereafter. The foresaid Count wanted to avenge this insult to God. Little by little he was beginning to lose his physical strength, so he gave instructions for a house to be prepared for him in the city of Angoulême, near the Church of St Andrew, where he could hear the divine office; and there in his sickness he began to die. He received constant visits from all his magnates and nobles and because several of them attributed his illness to acts of harmful magic, for he was usually physically robust and healthy, and because he was fading away in a manner unlike that of old or young men, it was revealed that some female worker of harmful magic [*malefica mulier*] had used the maleficent arts against him by burying images made from mud and wax in his name in streams, dry places, and next to the roots of trees, and enclosing some of them in the throats of dead bodies. Since she did not confess to having done these things, it was decided that, as the truth lay hidden, it would be left to the judgement of God and tested by the outcome of victory between two champions.

On Tuesday, 8 April 1028, after Mass, Stephan, champion of Count William, and William, champion of the witch (*malefica*), fought each other hard with cudgels and shields for a long time beyond the city on an island in the River Charente. The witch's champion had been bewitched that very day by certain enchanters, and 'consecrated'[30] by certain herbal potions. Stephan, on the other hand, trusted in the true judgement of the one Lord and was victorious without suffering any physical injury. William, his head battered and himself covered in blood, stood on his feet from the third hour to the ninth; but then, unable to move any more and having changed neither shield nor cudgel, shouted out in front of everyone that he was defeated, and a moment or two later fell to the ground and vomited up the instruments of harmful magic (*maleficia*) he had drunk. Defeated and half-dead, he was picked up and carried away, and for a long time confined to his bed. His enchanters, who had been standing at a distance, reciting certain magical chants, fled terrified soon afterwards. Stephan stayed where he was then, jumping up and down for joy without a scratch on his body, he came running along that same shore-line to the tomb of St Eparchius where he had kept vigil the previous night, to render thanks to God. Then he rode back to the city to recover his strength.

Not long afterwards, the witch was subjected to a good many tortures (although Count William knew nothing about this), but refused to confess to anything and, her heart hardened by the Devil, uttered not so much as a word or syllable. She was convicted, however, by the testimonies of three women who took part with her in these acts of harmful magic; and in the presence of everyone, these same women pulled out from beneath the earth a number of quite extraordinary images fashioned from mud. But they had already disintegrated because of the passage of time. Accordingly, Count William was merciful to the witch-woman (*malefica mulier*), did not allow her to be tortured further, and granted her her life.

[30] *Initiatus*, literally 'had been introduced to a certain skill or practice', or 'had been initiated into a religious or pseudo-religious association'.

The Parallel Universe
of Magic

Popular practices

1 The various kinds of magic. Hugh of St Victor: *Didascalion* (late 1120s)

[*German Augustinian, c.1096–1140/1. Master of the school of the Abbey of St Victor in Paris. His book aims to describe all those branches of knowledge which are important for human beings so that they may achieve what God intends for them.*]

Book 6, chapter 15. The person who first discovered magic is believed to have been Zoroaster, King of the Bactrians. Some people maintain he was Cham, the son of Noah, under a change of name. Later on, Ninus, King of the Assyrians, defeated him in battle, killed him, and made a bonfire of his books which were filled with the techniques of working harm by magic (*maleficia*). But Aristotle writes of him that his books handed down for posterity to remember contained up to two million, two hundred thousand verses on the art of magic, which he himself had dictated. Subsequently, Democritus extended this art at the time Hippocrates was considered to be foremost in the art of medicine. Magic is not counted as a philosophical system; its false creed puts it beyond the pale. A teacher of every kind of wickedness and evil-doing, who lies about the truth and in actual fact does harm to people's minds, it leads them astray from God's religion, persuades them to worship evil spirits, lets loose a degeneration of virtuous behaviour, and drives the minds of those who pursue it towards every type of crime and forbidden wickedness.

It is generally accepted that there are five ways in which one can do harm by magic: *mantike*, which denotes 'divination', futile mathematica,[1] casting lots (*sortilegia*), acts of harmful magic (*maleficia*), conjuring-tricks and illusions (*praestigia*). *Mantike*, however, contains five sub-divisions. The first is necromancy, by which is meant divination by means of the dead. *Nekros* is the Greek word for a dead person – *mortuus* in Latin – and this gives us the word 'necromancy', divination which takes place through the sacrifice of human blood, [because] demons have a thirst for it and take pleasure in it when it is poured out [for them.] The second is geomancy, that is, divination by means of earth. The third is hydromancy, that is, divination by water. The fourth is aeromancy, that is, divination by air. The fifth is divination by fire, which is called 'pyromancy'. Varro, you see, said that there are four things which can be used for divination – earth, water, fire, and air. So the first, necromancy, seems to be directed towards the region underground,[2] the second to earth, the third to water, the fourth to air, and the fifth to fire.

Astrology (*mathematica*) has three sub-divisions: interpretation of internal organs, portents, and lightning (*aruspicina*); interpretation of the movements and flight of birds (*auguria*); and the art of casting horoscopes (*horoscopia*). *Aruspices* are so called as though they were *horuspices*, that is, 'inspectors of the hours',[3] people who note the times during which things should be done, or as 'people who examine the altars' and judge the future in the entrails and bowels of sacrificial animals. Augury or auspicy sometimes relates to the eye and is called *auspicy* as though it were derived from 'looking at birds', because it pays close attention to the movement and flight of birds. Sometimes it relates to the ears, and then it is called *augury* as though it were derived from 'the chattering of birds', because this is perceived by the ear. Horoscopy, which is also called 'constellation', is when people's destinies are sought in the stars. This is what those who cast birth-horoscopes (*genethliaci*) do. They examine birth-horoscopes and once had the particular name *magi*. We read about them in the Gospel. Casters of lots (*sortilegi*) are people who use guesswork or intuition while they try to discover [the future]. Workers of harmful magic (*malefici*) are those who achieve dreadful things by means of demonic incantations, or magical ligatures,[4] or any other accursed type of treatment,[5] with the assistance and at the prompting of evil spirits. Conjuring-tricks and illusions (*praestigia*) are when a skill inspired by or dependent upon a demon plays games with human senses via fantasies and hallucinations in connection with the change of one thing into another.

[1] I.e. astrology. The Latin word is a singular noun. It may thus refer to the *art* of mathematics or to astrology, and the latter makes better sense in this context.
[2] *Infernus*. Here it is unlikely to refer to Hell because the dead cannot visit the earth from either Hell or Heaven. They can, however, come from Purgatory, as is clear from a large number of Mediaeval ghost stories.
[3] A false etymology. The word *aruspices* sometimes appears with an initial 'h', but the alteration of the 'a' to an 'o' in order to suggest *hora* = hour is unwarranted. The other attempted etymologies in this paragraph are equally mistaken.
[4] These may have been amulets worn round the neck, tied round the arm, or attached to the clothing; or they may have ben knotted strings intended to produce impotence in men.
[5] *Remedia*. The word *remedium* refers to a mean of treating illness, or a mean whereby one can avoid or prevent some non-physical harm. It may

therefore cover the magical cure of sickness and the use of counter-magic to ward off a magical attack.

2 Magic as part of everyday life. David of Ganjak: *Penitential* (c.1130s)

[*Armenian priest and canonist, c.1070–c.1140/1. His penitential is meant to be a guide for priests who are obliged to impose penances or temporary excommunication.*]

And they devise many other soul-destroying texts which estrange them from God, and write them on parchment together with those names and passages from the gospel of Christ. And they write them jumbled together so that with the Word of Life one might more readily receive the death-bearing words. And writing these things on parchment, they roll them up and seal them with the Lord's Cross, so that one should think them to be of God, and they put them in a box. And they bind them on the arms and around the necks of their children and animals, horses, oxen and sheep, and call them 'phylacteries'.

Also they make passes with the hand over their young children, and say, 'Let there be no pain in their bodies.' And they rub the spittle of their mouths on them with their hand, and say, 'The evil eye is upon him, he has become sick, may he not attract the evil eye.' And wicked old crones yawn and stretch round the sick child; and they cast sparks into water and give it to the children and other sick persons to drink, in order [to see] whether they have been the victim of the evil eye or not. Also they melt lead and cast it into water in a vessel and place it upon people's chests, saying that it is a cure for palpitations and toothache. In remote places they cut roots of plants and stuff them in pear trees and other bushes around the room, and say that it is a cure for fever.

At births they perform many auguries; also when they remove a corpse from the house and at weddings, [they draw] auguries concerning the route. And [they do the same] when one goes before the elders and when the wine is pressed and bottled, and at business transactions, and when clothes are being cut, and at slaughterings, and funerals, and when things are taken from vessels, and for hunting expeditions, and also for dyeing and weaving [operations] and all manner of crafts.

And when anyone asks for water in the night, they pass a knife with three rivets through it and then give it him to drink. Also they forbid [anyone] to give a sieve to a person who asks for it towards evening, or fire likewise. And on the fifth of the intercalary days they forbid one to give anything to anyone who asks. And when the New Year comes, they cast iron into a pitcher and draw a circle round the dwelling, and on the morrow send the girls to turn over the rocks and to open them and look inside; if a white hair be found, they say that she has met her fate and shall marry a greybeard; if a black hair be found, they say she has met her fate and shall be given to a young man.

Also, if a cock crow towards evening, they draw auguries, and if the call of the crowing come from the woods, they cut off its head. And at the beginning of the year all the craftsmen seek auguries in their crafts. The blacksmith beats the anvil with his hammer, the weaver/spinner draws a thread from the bobbin and strikes it three times with his comb, draws the thread on to the distaff and winds it round the spindle. They even introduce many acts of divination into the annual feasts and church offerings. Also when the rattle sounds [to call people to church], they draw auguries from the time, and on their own and strangers' entering and leaving through the door of the house. And when clothes are washed, or the heads of men and women, they draw auguries ...

3 Advice to beware of using divination and magic.
Aelfric: *Homily on the Octaves and Circumcision of Our Lord* (1020s–40s)

[*Archbishop of York 1023–51.*]

Now foolish men practise manifold divinations on this day, with great error, after heathen custom, against their Christianity, as if they could prolong their life or their health, while they provoke the almighty Creator. Many are also possessed with such great error that they regulate their journeying by the moon, and their acts according to days, and will not undertake anything on Monday because of the beginning of the week; though Monday is not the first day in the week, but the second. Sunday is the first in creation, in order, and in dignity. Some foolish men also say that there are some kinds of animals which one should not bless; and say that the decline by blessing, and by cursing thrive, and so enjoy God's grace to their injury, without blessing, with the Devil's malediction. Every blessing is of God, and curse of the Devil. God created all creatures, and the Devil can create no creatures, for he is an inciter to evil and worker of falsehood, author of sins, and deceiver of souls ...

Woe to the man who uses God's creatures without his blessing, with diabolical charms, when the Apostle of the gentiles, Paul, has said, 'Whatsoever you do in word or in work, do always in the name of the Lord, thanking the almighty Father through his Son.' That man's Christianity is naught who passes his life in diabolical charms. He is in appearance a Christian man, and is a miserable heathen; as the same Apostle said of such, 'I believe that I laboured in vain when I inclined you to God, now you observe days and months with vain auguries.'

Every bodily creature in the creation, which the earth produces, is, however, according to nature fuller and stronger in full moon than in decrease. Thus trees also, if they are felled in full moon, are harder and more lasting for building, and especially if they are made sapless. This is no charm, but is a natural thing from their creation.

---

4 Mixing religion and magic. Etienne de Bourbon: *Anecdotes historiques* (early 13th century)

[*French Dominican, 1190/5–c.1261. He preached a crusade against the Albigensians in c.1235 and was named an inquisitor soon after.*]

Nos. 370–1. Insulting to God are superstitions which pay divine honours to evil spirits, or to any other created being – as idolatry does, and as wretched women, female witches [*sortilegae*], do when they seek health by worshipping elder-trees or making offerings to them, despising churches or the relics of the saints, carrying their children thither or to ant-hills or to other things in pursuit of health. People were doing this kind of thing recently in the diocese of Leiden. I was preaching there against acts of sorcery [*sortilegia*], and hearing confessions, and many women confessed they had taken their children to Saint Guinefort. Since I believed this was a saint, I asked about him and was told, after much reluctance on their part, that he was a greyhound.

[*There follows a brief account of the legend of Saint Guinefort.*]

Equally insulting to God are such things as using the sacraments, or sacramentals, or sacred things, or things pertaining to the worship of God as instruments of sorcery [*sortilegia*] – as may be seen in the example of a peasant keeping the body of Christ in his beehive. I have also been told that a woman from the diocese of Leiden, while taking communion on Easter Sunday, kept the body of Christ in order to do sorcery with it, wrapped it in a piece of cloth, and put it in her bag. While she was asleep, she saw a most beautiful choir coming down from Heaven, worshipping a very handsome young man, and taking him back with them into the heavens. At this sight, she became frightened and woke up, and full of despair decided she would never admit [to having seen] it. But soon she was struck by an extraordinary sensation and, not finding the body of Christ where she had put it, began to suffer excruciating pains sometimes in her feet, sometimes in her hands. Because of these, she decided to confess, summoned a priest, and after confessing her sin with much weeping and bitterness, she was restored to health.

5   Heretics and magic. Heribert: *Epistola de haereticis Petragoricis* (c.1147)

[*French Cistercian, later Archbishop of Torres in Sardinia.*]

I, Heribert, a monk, have a strong desire that it should be generally known by all Christians that they should act in a circumspect manner with false prophets who are striving to cause the downfall of Christianity .... A large number of people has already been led astray – not only nobles who have thereby abandoned their property, but also clerics, priests, monks, and nuns .... They cannot be held in prison by any means because, if they are arrested they cannot be restrained by being tied up or put in chains, since the Devil sets them free; and the consequence is that all of them, without exception, hope and want to find people who will torture them and put them to death. They also do many remarkable things. For example, if they have been put into a tun of wine (it doesn't matter where), bound in chains or fetters, and the tun is turned upside down, and guards full of courage are posted: the guards do not find them the next day until they have revealed themselves once again of their own accord; and the wine cask which had had its contents hurriedly removed, is [found to be] turned the proper way up next day and full [of wine].

6   Magic by means of a pact. Heinrich von Gorkum: *De superstitionibus quibusdam casibus* (early 15th century)

[*German theologian, c.1358–1431. Professor of Theology at the University of Cologne.*]

People make a pact. They do what they do with the help or advice of evil spirits through some pact, tacit or explicit, they have entered into with them; and this happens every time people do something and insist on doing it because of a false, worthless opinion. Now, any opinion which claims there is any way whereby one may strive to obtain any outcome which does not arise naturally therefrom is both false and worthless. For example: someone about to go and fight stands in a place where two roads meet and carefully scrutinises the motion, the flight, and the twittering of birds, and from their movements is able to speculate on the future disposition of the air – whether it will tend to fine weather or rain, calm or storm. For the bodies of brute beasts are under the influence of the heavenly bodies, and so there is nothing to prevent their activities' being signs of certain things to come, in as much as the creatures are conformable to celestial prompting. Thus, when a little crow or rook caws frequently, one concludes that rain is on its way. So, according to what I have said, the man may calculate from the signs of birds whether it is more advantageous to him to follow one road rather than another, and whether he will be victorious in his fight. Such a false and worthless opinion extends the movements and voices of birds to things which have nothing to do with birds, and he is asking for information via a medium which cannot supply it. By these means, evil spirits secretly fall over themselves to do as the person asks, and it is understood that this constitutes a secret pact between the person and the evil spirit.

If someone writes a document, using the normal alphabet, and sends it to someone who knows how to read what he has written, the writer can thereby produce the following outcome: he makes his intention clear to the other person. But if he writes a highly distinctive document, using unknown words, and believes that by means of these unusual characters he can make another person fall in love with him, this opinion is false and frivolous, and gives an evil spirit permission to meddle therein; and this makes the action illicit and superstitious.

---

7 The dangers of divination. Nicholas of Cusa: *Sermon, 'Ibant Magi'* (6 January 1431)

[*German philosopher, theologian, and mathematician, 1401–64. A prolific author, he was a major participant in the Council of Basel (1431–49).*]

(13) There is an infinite number of superstitious acts of all kinds which lure every soul beyond the true foundation of the Christian faith by their

deceptive, devilish light. The person who falls away from the foundation of faith is 'a son of perdition'. Hence, such superstitious people should be driven out and not tolerated. *Deuteronomy* 13[1–3]. 'If a prophet rises in your midst, or someone who says he has seen a vision in a dream, and gives warning of a sign or a portent which actually happens, don't listen to the words of this prophet or interpreter of dreams, because the Lord your God is testing you to make it clear whether you love him or not. Follow the Lord your God in your whole heart and fear him and keep his commandments.' [v.5] 'That prophet, the deviser of dreams, shall be killed because he has spoken in order to turn you away from the Lord your God;' and because, if you wish to be made blessed, 'You must not pay heed to false nonsense' [*Psalm* 39.5] because God 'hates all those who pay attention to silly illusions' [*Psalm* 30.7] …

(17) Good and evil spirits are able to send out thoughts; the bad, by throwing light upon fantasies one has had already, or by supplying fantasies one has not yet had: the good, by imprinting them directly. Sending out [thoughts] in these circumstances brings about a certain virtue, and so although the evil spirit cannot have a direct effect upon one's natural desire or emotional state, he can nevertheless arouse them in a proficient and persuasive manner. The first thing the Devil does in sending out this type of thought against the faith is to send out divinations whenever he wants to turn someone into a prophet and a diviner. Now, it would take too long to talk about this matter now – how an effect stems from a cause, how the spirits know what the causes of future events are at any time, and how people know how eclipses happen and showers of rain, and how physicians know about health, etc. But in all these cases, evil spirits are as prone to error as human beings, because the truth of the future is in no way determined and consequently it is ridiculous to foretell it. Because it is said in *Isaiah* 41[23], 'Announce the things which are going to come in the future, and we shall know that you are gods,' the person who takes upon himself the office of predicting the future blasphemes God who alone knows, of himself and in himself, those things which are going to happen. Understand this faithfully, thoughtless individual! To tell the future is to make divinations, and that is suitable only for God. Astrologers [*astronomi*] go beyond their boundaries and fall into heresy and are led astray in their opinions by the Devil.

'The wise person is governed by the stars. All judgements', according to Ptolemy, 'exist between what is inevitable and what is possible'. Many things obtrude on one's attention, such as imaginings, presentiments, etc. The Devil who frequently urges us to do a great penance, (so that he may kill us), or to make a prediction so that we can, in some way, save the people is recognisable in this, because he is a liar. Often the prediction does not come true or, if it does, it should not be believed ...

(18) There are many classes of divination sent out (with hostile intent) by the Devil: aeromancy, pyromancy, hydromancy, geomancy, etc. Geomancy includes seeking answers to questions in the mirror of Apollo, in an incense-burner,[6] in polished stones, in a boy's finger-nail. Haruspicy is done using the innards of sacrificed animals and [their] shoulder-blades. Augury includes horoscopes, astrology, and prophecy, the twittering of birds, repeated sneezing, and the omen when someone says something unexpectedly which is then interpreted as referring to the future. It also includes chiromancy, the art of interpreting marks on shoulder-blades [*spatulamancy*], and the casting of lots to discover things which are hidden or secret. There are many types – books [of prophecies], dice, melted lead, touching a wheel to discover treasure or thieves, ordeals by red-hot iron or boiling water, duels, corshed,[7] etc. All these are prohibited ...

(19) I should also mention that there are some perfectly natural things done by herbs, stones, human ingenuity, physiognomy, chiromancy, dreams, and astrology, which appear worthy of astonishment; There are also natural magic, seeds, the extraordinary appearances in things which nature can produce as, for example, on Monte Pincio;[8] and treasure and deceivers who make their way through the world ... There is no power on earth which can equal that of the Devil (*Job* 41). For God alone, and the angels, and human beings through divine grace, have power over evil spirits; but a human being does not have this of himself except in as much as God gives it to him. Therefore those peasants who strive to drive out an evil spirit by means of characters, and certain words and incantations because those characters and so forth have power, are in error; and although sometimes the Devil yields by not doing harm, as one may read in the legend of St Bartholomew, nevertheless he does so merely in order to lead us astray. Enchanters who want to shut up a spirit [*spiritus*] in a finger-nail or a piece of glass are stupid, because a spirit cannot be shut up in a physical body. Astrologers with their imaginings are stupid ...

(20) Why do you supplicate the sun with blessings and incantations to protect you, fool; and the new moon to do likewise, by fasting on the day she first makes her appearance? The Lord is your spouse; he created them; and you are an idolater! What are you asking for in amulets,

characters, and unknown devilish names? 'Your God is one' [*Mark* 12.29]. The Devil leads you astray in all of these ... How is it that superstitious people seek God by [the Devil's] light and acknowledge His kindness by praying in a manner other than that established by the Church? It is not lawful for anyone of his own authority to add to, or subtract from those things established by the Church for the worship of God. Likewise, it is a superstition when worship is paid to another cult rather than to God; it is, in fact, idolatry. Therefore it is idolatry to make a pact with evil spirits, to sacrifice to them, and to accept advice from them. It is superstition to ask for health by using characters, ligatures, words, and those things which doctors condemn. When evil spirits are openly invoked, it is called 'nigromancy'; if portents are invoked, it is called 'trickery by tying up people's ears'; when it involves a dream, it is called 'divination through dreams'. Nigromancy is ostensible divination by means of the dead because 'the dead are brought back to life and are made visible through incantation and the provision of blood'.[9] If [evil spirits] foretell the future by means of living human beings, such as those who are possessed or obsessed, it is called 'Pythonian divination' [a name derived] from Python-Apollo, the originator of divination.

(22) When it comes to herbs and stones, it is obvious that when they are used for their natural effect, there is no sin involved. If they are used in any other way, however, this is not so, because they are being used as a mark of esteem to the Devil. The Devil pretends to run away after a peony or a jasper has been applied to the neck, so that he may be given respect by this action. If [herbs] are collected to the accompaniment of incantations, the Lord's Prayer or the Creed add nothing to their efficacy. Notice, at point, that if consecrated objects are applied to other than their proper use, it constitutes superstition: for example, drinking holy water to guard against illness, or sprinkling it to ensure fertility, or (sometimes) giving it to animals; having a light made from the wax of the Paschal candle; using water which has been used in baptism. Other things likewise constitute superstition: complete fasting in honour of St Apollonia or using the consecrated light of St Blaise;[10] making a cross from palm-wood; having a bath on Christmas Eve and at the beginning of Lent to ward off fevers, or to pay honour to St Nicholas so that one may acquire riches; seeking the benefit of going to St Valentine to ward off a transitory illness; weighing a child together with wheat or wax; carrying a cross round a field during Spring to ward off storms. Likewise, offering certain things on the altar, such as stones on the Feast of St Stephen and arrows on the Feast

of St Sebastian. Likewise, words combined with objects give rise to various superstitions. It is the same when it comes to [magic dealing] with hate and love; the maleficent, devilish operation with a needle which has touched a dead person's clothing; the wooden pieces making up a *furca*;[11] pieces of wood joined together to ward off fevers; unconsecrated Hosts, for the same purpose, and to ward off jaundice; the use of urine, chickens, etc.[12] ... enchanting mares to ward off worms or other evils; using four fingers to lift up a heavy individual; using superstitious observances on the feast-days of the year in order, beginning with Christmas Day; using things engraved, things written, etc.

(23) According to St Thomas Aquinas, *Summa Theologiae* 2.2, question 96, article 4, *responsio*: 'When it comes to any kind of incantation, there are two things which seem to call for caution, whether the incantations consist of spoken words or things written down or spells worn round the neck or suspended from the clothing. If there is anything in them which belongs to the invocation of evil spirits, it is obviously superstitious and unlawful; the same may be said if it contains unknown names, in case something unlawful lies hidden beneath them. Chrysostom on *Matthew* says, 'Many now follow the example of the Pharisees who enlarged their phylacteries, and invent some kind of Hebrew names of angels, write them down, and tie them to themselves. Such things appear to be alarming to those who do not understand them. One should also be cautious in case [the words] contain some error,' for then they really do not come from God. Likewise, one need not believe that these words have any power which God has not given them. Take, for example, those who believe that if they carry St John's Gospel with them, they cannot be drowned or taken prisoner. Likewise, take care not to mix any foolishness with sacred words (such as characters, apart from the sign of the cross), or put any faith in the way words are written or spoken or read ... One may carry or wear things other than the Gospel or the Lord's Prayer or relics, provided there is no foolishness mixed up in it, such as doing something in a particular way or carrying it in a particular container or doing it for a particular purpose.

[6] *Manubrius*. Everything Nicholas mentions here has a shiny surface in which visions can, under the right conditions, be seen. A thurible, however, is still a somewhat unusual object to be used for such a purpose.
[7] Trial by morsel. A piece of bread weighing about an ounce was exorcised and then the suspect had to swallow it without choking or any other ill effect. Touching the wheel is similar to turning the sieve. Shears were stuck in the rim of a sieve. One then held it by one finger placed in one handle of the shears,

and the sieve would move when (let us say) the name of the suspect thief was mentioned.

[8] There used to be a tree overhanging the Flaminian Gate, in which the demon-guardians of Nero's body used to hide.

[9] See St Isidore of Seville: *Etymologiae* 8.9 ('On magicians').

[10] St Blaise was the patron saint of sore throats and throats were blessed with candles dedicated in his name.

[11] A forked frame put on someone's neck as a punishment. The arms were fastened to the projecting ends.

[12] Sacred chickens were used in ancient Rome for purposes of divination. When they were fed corn, did they eat or not? Thus they indicated the gods' favour or displeasure anent a particular enterprise.

8 Days regarded as unlucky. Jean Gerson: *De superstitiosa dierum observantia* (1421)

[*French theologian, 1363–1429. Prominent in Church Councils, in fighting heresy, and advocate of intensifying spiritual life in all ranks of society. Eager to eradicate superstition in the practice of religion.*]

The Apostle [Paul] finds fault with those who observe days and years, such as the large number who think that 'Egyptian days' are unlucky, and believe that the Day of the Holy Innocents brings danger to health throughout the whole course of a year. Some people say that the Feast of St Paul has been affected one way or another with regard to its weather; and certain people have maintained that 'Clear skies on St Paul's signify good crops that year. If there's snow or rain, the times will be dear. If it's clouds, all the animals die,' and other such superstitious nonsense.

Against these and similar [beliefs], one may argue as follows. If the Day of the Holy Innocents is said to be unlucky or inauspicious for starting anything and as a result other days are set up in similar fashion throughout the whole year, one must give the root cause of this lack of good fortune, because no effect is without an efficient cause.

Let us select the cause, then, from one of the following, in order of their likelihood: (1) the disposition of the stars, according to astrology; (2) the disposition of inferior bodies, according to medicine; (3) the conditioning pattern or the complete type, according to natural philosophy; (4) the disorder of behaviour and morals, according to moral teaching; (5) the divine order of things, according to theology; (6) the action of evil spirits, according to the art of magic; (7) the merit or action of the Holy Innocents, according to the

Christian religion; (8) the fantasy or imagination of the observers which adduces experience [as an explanation].

But none of these causes [by itself] is sufficient or reasonable enough to make this observation; nor are they, taken all together, sufficient or reasonable. Such an observation is, therefore, frivolous and should be condemned.

9 Finding a thief by divination. Etienne de Bourbon: *Anecdotes historiques* (early 13th century)

[*French Dominican, 1190/5–c.1261.*]

No. 360. There are various kinds of divination, as Augustine points out, in chapter 26 of his book *On the Nature of Demons*. One is called 'pyromancy' because it involves fire; another 'aeromancy' because it involves air; 'hydromancy' involves water, 'geomancy' earth, and 'nigromancy' [i.e. necromancy] the dead ... Another type involves sneezing, another dreams, another the so-called 'Apostles' lots'. There is one involving finger-nails, one mirrors, and one swords in which the Devil makes you see various images which lead people into error and give the good a bad name, as does indeed happen sometimes. While I was a student in Paris, my fellow-students were at Vespers on Christmas Eve, and a very well-known thief entered our lodgings, broke into the room of one of our friends, and made off with a number of law books. After the holidays, our friend wanted to study his books and when he did not find them, he ran to consult male workers of harmful magic [*malefici*]. Many disappointed him,[13] but one magician did as follows: binding demons by oath, and holding a sword, he made a boy look at [the blade]. The child saw a great deal therein but at last, in a show of many images, he saw that one of our fellow-students was stealing the young man's books – someone related to him, and a person we believed to be one of the more decent members of our society. This man blackened the name of the owner of the books, not only in the eyes of the students but also of his friends, by suggesting that he had stolen the books from *him*. But this thief stole some other things and was caught and fled to a church where he hid in the bell-tower. Then, in answer to questions, he revealed everything he had stolen, where it was, and what he had done with it afterwards.

[13] The Latin verb may also mean 'deceived' or 'tricked'.

10 Geomancy. Rolandino da Padova: *Cronica in factis et circa facta Marchie Trivixane* (1262)

[*Italian historian, 1200–76. He taught grammar and rhetoric at the University of Padua, and was an eye-witness of some of the later events he describes in his chronicle.*]

Book 10, chapter 11. For behold in those days, while your Highness[14] was besieging Padua during your campaign, some of the prisoners anxiously used divination (*sortes*) to find out what would happen to your army. One of them, by means of special dots used in one technique which they call 'geomancy' (a word I haven't come across before), seemed to say that Padua would not be captured at this time, claiming – and I don't understand this – that the first house, relating to the army, seemed to be Lesser Fortune, while the figure of the seventh house, which represents 'enemies', was Greater Fortune.

[14] Ezzelino da Romano.

11 Magic at the Papal Court. Pope John XXII: *Letter* (27 February 1318)

[*Pope between 1316 and 1334. He settled the Papacy at Avignon, suppressed those Franciscans known as 'Spirituals' who wanted to separate from the rest of the Order, and was himself condemned as a heretic by the University of Paris in 1332. This letter is addressed to Bishop Bartholomaeus of Fréjus, Prior Peter Textoris, and Provost Peter de Pratis*].

The Roman Pontiff, the principal requirement of whose office is to look after the salvation of souls, must therefore, in the case of sons straying from the faith and standing in need of correction, nullify whatever is perceived to be quite incapable of tending towards salvation if it is not founded and rooted in the faith. Now, We have recently been brought a statement, worthy of belief and containing a clamorous report of public opinion, that Giovanni de Lemovici, Jacques alias 'the Brabantine', Giovanni de Amanto, a physician, Randolf Penchaclau, Walter Loflamene, Guilielmo Marini, Konrad 'the German' and the late Thomas called 'the German', both clerics, and Innocenzo, the barber of Our venerable brother the Archbishop of Leiden, and several others residing at Our court, unwilling to have a sensible understanding of the teaching of the Apostle, and striving by base endeavours to lose their reason in the drunkenness of overweening vanity, have involved and continue to involve themselves in the exercise of necromancy, geomancy, and other magic arts. They are in possession of manuscripts and books dealing with these subjects which, since they are the arts of evil spirits and arise from a noxious association between humans and angels, should be avoided by any Christian and condemned from the bottom of his heart by every kind of curse. These people have frequently used mirrors and images consecrated in accordance with their accursed ritual. They have often stood within circles and invoked harmful spirits so that, by their aid, they may labour against people's salvation/health,[15] either by destroying them with the violence of their incantation or by shortening their life by sending a violent sickness upon them. They have, on a number of occasions, enclosed evil spirits in mirrors, circles, or finger-rings so that they may ask them not only about past but also future events in order to predict the future – foreknowledge of which belongs to God alone – from their consultations with them. They have involved themselves in acts of divination and casting of lots/sorcery,[16] and on occasion mistakenly make use of demons popularly known as *diani*; and at some point they also invoked evil spirits and carried out a very large number of experiments concerning these and other matters. They are not afraid to claim that they can shorten or prolong people's lives, or even destroy them, or cure them of any illness by getting them to drink or eat, or simply by uttering a single word: and they steadfastly maintain that they have employed such means. Moreover, they have abandoned their Creator and, putting their trust in evil spirits of this kind and thinking them worthy of it, they serve them and pay them divine honours and presume to worship them after the fashion of idolaters, with a display of veneration and reverence. To these and other detestable superstitious practices which are opposed to the Catholic faith, the foresaid clerics, the beard-trimmer, and any one of them, are said to have applied themselves not once but many times, not only to the danger of their own souls, but to those of many others.

Therefore, because We neither wish nor have the power to ignore and turn a blind eye to a plague of superstitious acts of this kind, whose reprobate followers social opinion considers to be hostile to the common welfare, and to be enemies of the human race, especially as they smell of the disaster which is the wickedness of heresy: with respect to each and every one of the aforesaid, and in the zeal of the faith whose interests should be prosecuted everywhere in such a way as to gain people's good opinion, We have decided to proceed to an inquisition against the aforementioned clerics, barber, and others. The fact that the foresaid late Thomas has died makes no difference since, when dealing with crimes of this nature, one is permitted to accuse the reputation of a dead person whose proven perfidy must necessarily be punished after his or her death.

Therefore, by the authority of these presents, We ordain and command you and any of your people conjointly in whose judgement We have complete faith in the Lord, to inquire into all the general circumstances, specific details, and consequences flowing therefrom, and into anything else at all you may find publicly said to the detriment of the foresaid clerics, barber, and any others living at Court. You are to investigate them and other persons you think pertinent and useful anent this matter summarily, without unnecessary formality and judicial form, and without any appeal to a higher court, having only the Lord before your eyes; and you are to determine, with scrupulous care, the truth and the scrutiny thereof as may be in accordance with what is just, and draw the appropriate conclusion.

[15] *Salutem*. The Latin word is capable of both meanings, and may also refer to personal safety or freedom from damage.
[16] *Sortilegia*. The former is the word's literal meaning, the latter its possible broader usage. Translating fourteenth-century use of *sortilegium* as 'witchcraft' is likely to be misleading in view of the English word's associations derived largely from the early modern period.

12 Magic at the Imperial Court. Theodore Balsamon: *In epistolam Sancti Basilii canonicam III* (1170s)

[*Byzantine canonist, c.1130/40-post 1195. Patriarch of Antioch between c.1185 and 1190.*]

Often the rather simple-minded and stupid fall rather ill and, when they are not cured quickly, have the idea of getting themselves treated by magical conjuring-tricks or herbal magic [*pharmakeiai*];[17] and so they go to certain heathens who boldly claim that they will bring into the open secret magical compounds [*pharmakeiai*] which rob the patient of his or her physical health and so purge what is defiling him. Therefore St Basil says that those who make such predictions and do not believe that any illness and any sickness is cured by calling upon the name of the Lord and God and Saviour, Jesus Christ, and the Mother of God, and all the saints: and that any act of poisonous magic [*pharmakeia*] and devilish conjuring-trick is banished by the faithful through the power and protection of the honourable cross: but rather follow to the letter the tellers of tall stories, those who do conjuring-tricks, and the customs of the heathen, and introduce such people into their homes to see if they can produce a quick cure for the illness which has been caused by acts of poisonous magic – these, says the Saint, are to be subject to penitential discipline for a period of six years ...

But those [sick people] who have strayed on only one occasion and have abandoned [their use of magicians] will, within limits, be cured. I actually saw this happen. The Lady Zoe, wife of the most blessed Lord Alexios Komnenos, son of the famous Emperor, fell gravely ill, and the doctors gave up any hope of curing her because of the large number of conflicting diseases from which she was suffering. Certain heathens claimed they could cure her, because her illness actually sprang from magical conjuring-tricks, and assembled many of her women (who were of admirable character) and, what is more, many of her men, too, in order to examine them – an unjust and improper proceeding. They would secretly throw in corners images fashioned from wax and, in a Satanic manner, give advance information relating to every detail of these and the fact that they would be discovered. They also did thousands of other dreadful things in contempt of God and the vengeance of many, and when these godless men had proved ineffectual, they vanished. The most noble lady not only failed to derive any good from this: having been nailed fast to her illness, and having been loaded down with an evil burden, she departed this life. But the Lord God, in recognition of other good works she had done, relieved her of the physical pain inflicted on her by divine principle.

[17] This is the equivalent of the Latin *veneficium*. Both words refer to a compound made of herbs, minerals, or other materials, which is meant to be taken internally and which may result in poisoning rather than curing the patient. The preparatory administration of such compounds might be accompanied by magical words or gestures or both. Hence, both the Greek and the Latin may imply an act of poisonous magic, even though the supplier's intention could have been to cure.

13 How to investigate workers of magic. Bernardo Gui: *Practica inquisitionis heretice pravitatis* (1323/4)

[*French Dominican, c.1261–1324. Theologian, historian, Inquisitor at Toulouse, Bishop of Túy in Galicia. He wrote a large number of historical and theological works, the best-known of which is this handbook for inquisitors.*]

Casters of lots/sorcerers (*sortilegi*), diviners (*divini*), and invokers of evil spirits.

1. The diverse plague and error of casting lots/sorcery, making divinations, and invoking evil spirits, which takes many forms, is found in various lands and regions in keeping with the various inventions and false notions belonging to the vanity of superstitious people who pay attention to the spirits of error and the teachings of evil spirits.
2. The lot-caster/sorcerer or diviner or invoker of evil spirits under examination should be asked what kind of divinatory/magical techniques (*sortilegia*) or methods of prognostication (*divinationes*) or invocations he knows, how many he knows, and from whom he learned them.

Item: when you get down to details, take note of the person's rank and circumstances. You should not interrogate everyone without discrimination or after a single fashion. Men and women are questioned differently. Questions can be posed about the following points: what do they know or what did they know or do about children or infants who had been ill-wished or were to have the ill-wishing lifted?
Item: question them about lost or injured animals.
Item: thieves who should be locked up.
Item: agreement or disagreement between married couples.
Item: the impregnation of those who are barren.
Item: the things they give people to eat – hairs, finger- or toe-nails, and certain other things.
Item: the state of the souls of the dead.
Item: foretelling future events.
Item: the fairies whom they call 'good deeds' who, according to what they say, move about in the night.
Item: enchanting fruits and plants, thongs, and other things, or casting a spell on them by means of chanted words.
Item: whom has he taught how to enchant or how to conjure by means of chanted spells? Who taught him such enchantments and conjurations, or from whom did he hear them?
Item: the cure of the sick through incantations or chanted words.
Item: collecting plants on bended knee with the face turned to the east while reciting the Lord's prayer.

Item: telling people to go on pilgrimage, to go to Mass, to offer candles, and to give to charity.
Item: discovering who has committed a theft, or uncovering things which are secret and hidden.
Item: very diligent inquiry should be made about those things which smack of any kind of superstition, irreverence shown or harm done to the sacraments of the Church, especially to the sacrament of the body of Christ, and also to divine worship and holy places.
Item: retaining the Host [in one's mouth instead of swallowing it], or stealing baptismal oil, or holy oil from the church.
Item: the baptism of images made of wax, or the baptism of other things; how they are baptised, and to what uses or effects these things are put.
Item: making images from lead, how they are made, and for what purposes.
Item: from whom did he or she learn or hear such things?
Item: how long is it since he or she began to use such things?
Item: how many people have come to him,[18] asking for a consultation, especially during the present year? Who were they?
Item: has he ever been prohibited on an earlier occasion from doing such things? Who prohibited him? Did he abjure such things, and did he promise never to do or use such things again?
Item: has he lapsed after making an abjuration or giving a promise?
Item: did he believe that what he was telling others was true?
Item: what benefits or gifts or recompense has he had and received for such things?

[18] *Ad ipsum*, specifically masculine.

---

14   Image magic. Athelwold: *Record of an exchange of lands* (late 10th century)

[*Bishop of Winchester.*]

The land at Ailsworth formerly belonged to a widow and her son. For this reason, she then drove a thick iron pin into [an image of] Aelsi, Wulfstan's father. This was discovered and they removed the death-image from her room. Then they seized the woman and drowned her at London Bridge. Her son escaped and became an outlaw.

15 Maleficent images. Niketas Choniates: *Historia* (late 12th/early 13th century)

[*Byzantine government officer, historian, and theologian, 1155/7–1217. His* Historia *is an important source of information for 1118–1206, and highlights the active role played in history by human beings, with God acting more as a moral overseer of the historical process.*]

II. Book 4. [*An incident dating to the 1160s*] Not long afterwards, [the interpreter Aaron] was arrested while carrying out magical practices, and there came to light an image in the form of a pregnant tortoise. Inside the tortoise shell was a human figure with both feet bound and a nail struck clean through its chest. Aaron was taken in the act of unrolling a book of Solomon.[19] When this is unrolled and read aloud, it brings together evil spirits by the legion and makes them visible. They keep on asking for what purpose they have been invoked, and when urged to carry out what they are enjoined to do, they willingly fulfil the command.

[19] Famous in legend as a powerful magician. Aaron was thus using a book containing magic formulae.

Ritual magic

16 Conjuration of Spirits. Pietro d'Abano: *Heptameron seu elementa magica* (late 13th century)

[*Italian physician and philosopher, 1250–1316. He was twice brought before the Inquisition which acquitted him the first time. He died during his second trial which proceeded to find him guilty.*]

The circle and how it is to be made. The structure of circles is not always one and the same, but is usually changed according to the kind of spirits which are to be invoked, places, seasons, days, and hours. For when it comes to constructing a circle, you must consider at what season of the year, on what day, and at which hour you are making it: which spirits you want to summon, over which planet and region they preside, and what tasks they carry out. Consequently, make three circles nine feet wide and a palm's breadth away from each other. In the central circle, first write the name of the hour in which you are doing the work: secondly, the name of the angel of the hour: thirdly, the sigil of the angel of the hour: fourthly, the name of the angel who presides over the day on which you are doing the work, and the names of his attendants: fifthly, the name of the present time: sixthly, the name of the ruling spirits during that segment of time, along with those standing guard over it: seventhly, the name of the commander of the sign ruling over that segment of time in which you are doing the work: eighthly, the name of the earth according to that segment of time in which you are doing the work: ninthly, and in order to complete the central circle, write the names of the sun and moon according to the foresaid guiding principle of time. Once the time is changed, the names are changed too. In the outermost circle, assign to the four corners the names of the angels of air who are presiding over the day on which you are doing the work, namely, the King and his three ministers. Outwith the circle there should be pentagrams in the four corners. In the innermost circle, write four names of God with crosses in between them. In the central circle, write Alpha facing east and Omega facing west, and divide the middle of the circle by means of a cross. Once the circle is complete, you will proceed according to the regulation which follows.

The names of the hours and of the angels which preside over them. You must know that angels preside over the hours in successive rank, according to the guiding principle of the heavens and planets they govern. So, the spirit which governs the day also rules over the first hour of the day; the second from this planet presides over the second hour, the third over the third, and so forth in sequence. When the seven planets and hours have gone the rounds, the sequence comes back to the first spirit who governs the day. So I shall first tell you the names of the hours.

Hours of the day		*Hours of the night*	
1	Yayn	1	Beron
2	Idnor	2	Barol
3	Nasnia	3	Thamis
4	Salla	4	Athir
5	Sadedali	5	Mathon
6	Thamur	6	Rana
7	Ourer	7	Netos
8	Tamic	8	Tafrac
9	Neron	9	Saffur
10	Iayou	10	Aglo
11	Abai	11	Calerva
12	Natalon	12	Salam

I shall tell you about the names of the angels and their sigils later on. Now let us see what the names of the seasons are. A year is divided into four, and its four parts are Spring, Summer, Autumn, and Winter. Here are their names.

Spring = Talvi
Summer = Casmaran
Autumn = Ardarael
Winter = Farlas

The angels of Spring = Caracasa, Core, Amatiel, Commissoros
The commander of the sign of Spring = Spugliguel
The name of the earth in Spring = Amadai
The names of the sun and moon in Spring = Abraym (sun) and Agusita (moon)

The angels of Summer = Gargatel, Tariel, Gaviel
The commander of the sign of Summer = Tubiel
The name of the earth in Summer = Festativi
The names of the sun and moon in Summer = Athemay (sun) and Armatus (moon)

The angels of Autumn = Tarquam, Guaberel
The commander of the sign of Autumn = Torquaret
The name of the earth in Autumn = Rabianara
The names of the sun and moon in Autumn = Abragini (sun) and Matasignais (moon)

The angels of Winter = Amabael, Ctarari
The commander of the sign of Winter = Altarib
The name of the earth in Winter = Gerenia
The names of the sun and moon in Winter = Commutaf (sun) and Affaterim (moon)

The consecrations and blessings: first, the blessing of the circle. After the circle has been completed in due form, sprinkle it with holy or lustral water, and say: 'Thou shalt purge me with hyssop, o Lord, and I shall be clean. Thou shalt wash me, and I shall be whiter than snow.'[20]

The blessing of fumigants.[21] 'God of Abraham, God of Isaac, God of Jacob, bless for this purpose the creatures of these kinds [of things], so that they may increase the power and potency of their odours, and so that neither enemy nor phantasm may be able to enter them, through our Lord Jesus Christ, etc'. Then sprinkle them with holy water.

The exorcism of the fire on which the fumigants are put. The fire to be used for the fumigations should be in a new earthenware vessel. You should exorcise it as follows. 'I exorcise you, creature of fire, by Him through whom all things have been made, so that you immediately expel from yourself every phantasm so that it cannot harm anyone.' Then say, 'Bless, o Lord, this creature of fire. Sanctify it so that it becomes blessed, to the praise of thy holy name, and so that no harm may come to those who are working [this rite] or to those who are watching it, through our Lord Jesus Christ, etc.'

The clothing and the pentagram. You should wear a priest's garment if possible. If you cannot get one, wear clean linen clothing. Then take this pentagram [illustrated in Abano's text], which has been drawn on a kid's skin parchment on the day and in the hour of Mercury, while the moon is waxing. First, let a Mass of the Holy Spirit be said over it; then let it be sprinkled with water used during baptism.

A prayer to be said when the garment is put on. 'Ancor, Amacor, Theodonias, Anitor: through the merits of thy holy angels, o Lord, I shall put on the garment of salvation so that I may bring to completion this thing which I desire. Through thee, Most Holy Adonai, whose kingdom lasts for ever and ever, Amen.'

The manner of working. The moon should be half way through her period of waxing, if possible, and not burned up [by the rays of the sun]. The operator should be clean and free from defilement for a period of nine days before he begins the work, and he should have been to confession and received communion. He should have the fumigant appropriate to the day on which he is doing the work, water blessed by a priest, a new earthenware vessel full of fire, his garment and the pentagram, all of which should have been properly and duly consecrated and prepared. One of his pupils should carry the earthenware vessel full of fire, another his book, and another the garment and pentagram. The master should carry a sword over which has been said the Mass of the Holy Spirit, and which has inscribed in the middle the name AGLA+, and on the other side ON+. While he is going to the place which is to be consecrated, he must continually recite the Litanies, with his pupils giving the responses; and when he arrives at the place where he wishes to make the circle, he should draw the lines of the circle as I have already instructed, after which he should sprinkle the circle with holy water, saying, 'Thou shalt purge me, o Lord' etc.

Well now, once the Master has been purified by fasting, chastity, and abstinence from all indulgence in good living for a total of three days before the day of the working, on the day itself he should put on clean garments, and will then enter the circle along with the pentagrams, fumigants, and things necessary for the work. From the four corners of the world, he will invoke the angels who govern the seven planets, the seven days of the week, the seven colours, and the seven metals, whose names you will see later. On his knees, he will invoke the said angels by name, saying, 'O angels N.N. assist me in my request and come to my aid in what I do and in what I ask.' Then from the four corners of the world he will invoke the angels which rule the air on the day on which he is doing the work or giving the demonstration;[22] and, having called in particular upon all the names and spirits written around the circle, he should say, 'By the throne of Adonai, by God who is holy, strong, immortal, the intercessor, Alpha and Omega: and by these three secret names, Agla, On, Tetragrammaton, I entreat and command you all that today you fulfil what I desire.'

When he has done this, he must read the conjuration assigned to the day on which he is giving the demonstration, as I shall indicate later. If [the angels] are obstinate and refractory and refuse to be obedient either to the conjuration assigned to the day or to the preceding prayers, use the following invocations and conjurations.

A conjuration of the spirits of the air. 'We who have been made in the image of God, endowed with the power of God, and made by his will: by the most powerful and supportive name of God, El, we strongly and wonderfully conjure you' (here he will name the spirits he wants to appear, of whatever rank they may be), 'and we command you by him who spoke and it was done, and by all the names of God, and by the name Adonai, El, Elohim, Elohe, Zebaoth, Elion, Escerchie, Jah, Tetragrammaton, Sadai, Dominus Deus, the Most High: we conjure you and powerfully command you to appear at once to us here next to the circle in pleasing (that is, human) form, without any kind of misshapenness or deformity. Come, all of you of this kind, because we command you by the name Y and V which Adam heard and spoke: and by the name of God, Agla, which Lot heard and was saved along with his household: and by the name Joth which Jacob heard from the angel as they were wrestling together, and was freed from the hand of his brother Esau: and by the name Anephexeton which Aaron heard and was made wise in speaking it: and by the name Zebaoth which Moses pronounced,[23] and the rivers and marshes in the land of Egypt were turned to blood: and by the name Ecerchie Oriston which Moses pronounced, and all the rivers spouted frogs which came up into the houses of the Egyptians and destroyed everything: and by the name Elion which Moses pronounced, and there were locusts appearing over the land of the Egyptians, which ate what had been left behind after the hailstorm: and by the name 'Alpha and Omega' which Daniel pronounced and destroyed Beel and killed the serpent: and in the name of Emanuel which the three boys Sidrach, Misach, and Abednago chanted in the furnace of burning fire and were set free: and by the Holy One and the throne of Adonai: and by God, the strong, the immortal, the intercessor: and by these three secret names, AGLA, ON, TETRAGRAMMATON, I invoke, I appeal, and by these names and by the other names of our Lord, the living, true Almighty God who for your sin has expelled you from the heavens to the place beneath: we conjure and manfully command you through Him who spoke and it was done, whom all created things obey, and through that awe-inspiring judgement of God: and by the sea of glass, unknown to everyone, which is in front of the sight of the divine majesty, a thing moving and full of power:[24] and by the four divine animals [NN] moving in front of the throne of the divine majesty, with eyes in the front and the back [of their heads]: and by the fire gathered before his throne: and by the holy angels of the heavens [NN]: and by that which is called the Church of God: and by the highest wisdom of Almighty God, we manfully conjure you to appear to us here in front of the circle in order to carry out our will in everything, as it may please us. By the throne of Baldachia, and by the name Primeumaton which Moses pronounced and Daton, Corah, and Abiron were plunged into or engulfed in caverns of the abyss:[25] and in the power of that name Primeumaton which drives together the whole fighting-force of Heaven, we curse you, we deprive you of all your office, place, and joy, all the way to the depth of the abyss, and we put you there right up to the final Day of Judgement; we relegate you to eternal fire, to the swamp of fire and sulphur, unless you appear before us at once in this place in front of the circle, to carry out our will.

In every case, come, by these names, Adonai, Zebaoth, Adonai, Amioram. Come, come! Adonai, Sadai, the most powerful and most awe-inspiring King of kings commands you. No created thing can evade his power. Unless you will be most obstinate, obey and appear here in front of this circle immediately and be easy to talk to, a lamentable, wretched destruction and a fire which never goes out awaits you. Come, therefore, in the name of Adonai, Zebaoth, Adonai, Amoram. Come, come! Why are you holding back? Hurry! Adonai, Sadai commands you, King of kings, El, Aty, Titeip, Azia, Hyn, Jen, Minosel, Achadan, Vai, Vaa, Ey, Haa, Eie, Exe, a El, El, El, a Hy, Hau, Hau, Hau, Va, Va, Va, Va.

A prayer to God, which should be said in the four parts of the world in the circle. 'Amomle, Alpha and Omega, Leiste, Oriston, Adonai. My most merciful heavenly Father, take pity on me even though I am a sinner; glorify in me today, although I am thy unworthy son, the arm of thy power against these most obstinate spirits so that I, by thy consent, having become an observer of thy divine works, may be enabled to achieve illumination with all the wisdom there is, and always glorify and worship thy name. I humbly implore and beseech thee that in accordance with thy judgement these spirits I invoke may be bound and constrained, come when summoned, and give true answers to the questions I put to them; and that they may give and bring to us those things either I or we may enjoin upon them, doing no harm to any created being, doing no damage, uttering no angry, incomprehensible noises, not hurting me and my companions or any created being, and not terrifying anyone. Rather let them be obedient to my requests in everything I shall enjoin upon them.'

Then, standing in the middle of the circle, he should stretch out his hand towards the pentagram and say, 'By the pentagram of Solomon our patron, let them give me a true answer.'

Then he should say, '[By the] thrones of Beralans, Baldachis, Paumachia, and Apologia: by their kings and proud powers and powerful princes: by the attendant spirits of Liachis, the servant of the throne of Hell: Primac, the Prince of the throne of Apologia, along with the ninth cohort: I invoke you, and by my invocation I conjure you and, powerfully guarded by the power of the heavenly Majesty, I powerfully command by Him who spoke and it was done, and to whom all created things are obedient: and by the name which should not be pronounced, Tetragrammaton, Yod He Vau He, Jehovah, in which the whole world has been given form, at the sound of which the elements collapse, the air is shaken, the sea retreats, fire is extinguished, the earth trembles, and all the armies of celestial, earthly, and infernal beings tremble, are thrown into confusion, and collapse: [I command you] to come quickly without delay, from every part of the world, since every opportunity for not doing so has been removed: to reply coherently to any and every one of my questions: and to come in peace, in visible form, and in friendly manner. Now, without delay, we wish you to show yourselves, having been conjured by the name Helioren of the eternal, living, and true God, carrying out our instructions, continuing always in existence right to the end and in accordance with my purpose, visible to us and easy to talk to, with a loud voice which we can understand, and without any double-meaning.'

Next the magical operator should hold out his hand in the direction of the pentagram and say, 'Behold the pentagram of Solomon, which I have brought into your presence. Behold the person of the magician in the midst of the conjuration. He is very well protected by God. He is without fear. He has exercised his foresight and now, filled with power, invokes and summons you by conjuration. Come, therefore, in haste by the power of these names: Aie, Saraie, Aie, Saraie, Aie, Saraie. Do not postpone your arrival, through the eternal names of the living, true God – Eloi, Archima, Rabur. By this pentagram here present, which has power to command you, and by the power of the heavenly spirits, your lords: and by the person of the magician, once you have been conjured, hurry up and come and be obedient to your master who is called Octinomos.'

Once this is done, you should whisper in the four corners of the world, and immediately you will see great movements. When you have seen these, say, 'Why are you holding back? Why are you delaying? What are you doing? Prepare yourselves and obey your master in the name of the Lord Bathat or Vachat who arrives at Abrac at full speed, and of Abeor who arrives at Aberer likewise.'

Then immediately they will come in the form appropriate to each. When you see them next to the circle, show them the pentagram covered in a sacred cloth. Uncover it and say, 'Behold your prison. Do not be disobedient;' and all of a sudden you will see them in peaceable form. They will say to you, 'Ask what you want because we are prepared to fulfil all your commands, for the Lord has made us subject to them.' When the spirits have appeared, you should say, 'You have duly come, spirits (or, most noble Kings), because I have summoned you through Him to whom is bent the knee of every celestial, earthly, and infernal being: in whose hand are the realms of kings, and there is no one who can oppose His majesty. Therefore I bind you that you remain here before this circle, visible and easy to talk to, as long as I wish and just as you are at present, without any permission to leave until you fulfil my wish without any deception and in full reality, by virtue of that power which has placed its boundary upon the sea which cannot go beyond it and does not cross its bounds by the ordinance of that power, namely, God Most High, King and Lord, who has created everything, Amen.'

Then command what you wish and it will be done. Afterwards, give them permission [to depart] as follows: 'In the name of the Father, the Son, and the Holy Spirit, go in peace to your various places, and may there be peace between us and you. Be prepared to come when summoned.'

²⁰ *Psalm* 50.9 (Vulgate). It is recited by the priest at the beginning of a High Mass when he sprinkles the congregation with holy water.
²¹ Not necessarily 'incense', because all kinds of materials might be used, something smelling pleasant, some unpleasant according to the nature of the spirits to be invoked. *Fumigia* simply means 'various kinds of material which will give off smoke when placed on fire'. Later in the text, for example, we are told that that the fumigant for use on a Sunday is red wheat: on Monday, aloes: on Tuesday, pepper: on Wednesday, mastic: on Thursday, saffron: on Friday, pepperwort: on Saturday, sulphur.
²² *Facit experimentum*. This could mean 'carrying out an experiment', but the passage is couched in terms of instruction, which does not seem quite to fit the concept of experiment, and we are told that the master-operator is accompanied by pupils or apprentices (*discipuli*), which makes the notion of 'demonstration' somewhat more likely than 'experiment'.
²³ Moses is constantly mentioned largely because he and the plagues of Egypt became types of the magician, and a magic legitimate because it was authorized and supported by God.
²⁴ A reference to *Apocalypse* 4.6. The animals in vv. 6–9.
²⁵ See *Psalm* 105.17 (Vulgate); 106.17 (AV).

17 Types of magical procedure. Moses Maimonides: *Dalalat al'Ha'rin* [A Guide of the Perplexed] (1190)

[*Spanish Jew, 1135–1204. One of the greatest European scholars of his time. Dalalat is a work addressed primarily to an intellectual audience. It aims to explain the spiritual meaning of Biblical terms which may caused puzzlement if taken too literally. It was written in Arabic, using Hebrew characters.*]

[Part 3, chapter 37] Magical procedures are very varied, and I shall divide them into three classes: (1) those connected with some living creature such as plants, animals, or minerals; (2) those dependent on a particular time for their performance; and (3) certain actions performed by people, such as dancing, clapping, laughing, jumping on one leg, lying supine on the ground, burning something, making a particular kind of fumigation, speaking certain words which may be intelligible or unintelligible. These are the different kinds of magical procedure.

Certain magical operations need all these simultaneously in order to be effective. They say, for example, that you must take a certain number of leaves of such-and-such a plant just when the moon is under a particular sign [of the zodiac] in the east, or at one of the other cardinal points. You must also take a certain animal's horns, or a certain amount of its droppings, or hair, or blood when the sun is, for example, at its zenith, or in some other specified place; and you must take such-and-such a metal or metals which you will melt while such-and-such a sign [of the zodiac] is rising, when the stars are in a particular alignment. Then you must speak aloud and say certain words, make a fumigation with the leaves, and offer [the smoke] to a figure made from the metal; and such-and-such a thing will happen as a result. There are other magical operations which they believe will work, using only one of these three types of procedure.

Most of these magical operations need to be done by women. Thus, they say that in order to cause rain, ten virgins wearing jewels and red garments must dance, push each other, go backwards and forwards, and make signs to the sun. By these means, they believe that water will fall. They also say that if four women lie on their backs, lift their legs and spread them and, in this indecent posture, pronounce certain words and do a particular act, hail will stop falling in that area. There are many more of these stupidities and madnesses, all of which have to be done by women.

In all these magical operations one must observe the position of the stars; for they claim that each plant is linked with a particular star, as is each animal and each mineral. According to their belief, what is done by those who work magic is a kind of worship offered to such-and-such a star which takes pleasure in this particular operation, these words, or that fumigation, and does for us what we want it to do.

18 Making amulets. Alexander of Tralles: *De arte medicina* (late 6th century)

[*Byzantine physician, 525–605. He was especially famous for his encyclopaedia on medicine in twelve books, and for his essay, 'A Letter on Intestinal Worms'.*]

Book 12. *A precaution against gout.* Take a small, thin sheet of gold and, while the moon is waning, write on it the following [inscription]. Tie it with a crane's sinews; then make a small cylinder the same size as the gold sheet and enclose the sheet in it. Wear this round the ankle-joints. [The inscription] 'Mei, threu mor, phor, teux, za, zon, the, lou, chri, ge, ze, on. As the sun is strengthened in these names and is renewed each day, so strengthen this figure as it was before: at once, at once, quickly, quickly, quickly. For look, I speak the great name wherein the things which are resting from labour are strengthened: iaz, azuph, zuon, threngx, bain, choök. Strengthen this figure as it was at first: at once, at once, quickly, quickly.'

A wonderful thing, proven by experiments, against gout which has not yet got hold of the joints. Take a chameleon. Cut off its feet and the tips of its toes or its knee-caps. Keep the ends of the right feet separate. Again, cut off the ends of the left feet likewise, and keep them separate, too. Use one of the chameleon's nails to cut notches in two fingers of its right hand, the thumb, and the ring-finger; likewise, cut notches in the second finger of its left hand with the animal's nail. Stain the extremities of the right-hand limbs of the chameleon with blood from the fingers of the right hand, and the animal's left extremities with blood from its left hand. Make cylinders. Enclose the pieces of the chameleon you have cut off, and wear the cylinder containing the right-hand extremities of the animal on your right foot, and that containing its left- hand extremities on your left foot until the disease has been cured. Take the chameleon whose extremities you have cut off and, while it is still alive, wrap it tightly in a piece of clean linen and bury it where it will face the rising sun. If it turns out that the patient we have been discussing has pain in his or her hands, take pieces of the chameleon's hands, put them into cylinders, and you will cure the patient's hands, too. Do this while the moon is waning.

19 Making magical seals. Arnald of Villanova: *De sigillis* (c.1301)

[*Catalan physician and religious reformer, c.1240–1311.*]

In the name of our Lord, Jesus Christ. [The seal of Libra] Take very pure gold and melt it. Then make a round seal and, while it is forming, say: 'Arise, o Lord, upon this gold disk and hear my voice because I have called to thee. Have pity upon me and hear me.' Then say the psalm, 'The Lord is my light' [26.1, *Vulgate*], and when you have done that, put it down again. Do this while the Sun is entering Libra (17 September), and after the Moon is in Capricorn or Aquarius. On one side engrave a human figure holding scales in his hands, with his arms stretched out in the form of a cross. Do this while the Sun is in Libra. Round the edge, engrave 'Eli, Eli, Lama Sabachthani', and 'It is finished'; and round the edge of the other side, 'Jesus of Nazareth, King of the Jews'; and in the centre, 'Michael, Yod, Matthew, Vau'. This very holy seal has power against being ambushed by demons on land or sea. When you wear it, it frees you from sudden death. Whoever wears it will be gentle and compassionate, wise and decent, and full of good advice. He also has the power to acquire money in any business-affairs, and the affection of both men and women; and whoever wears it along with the seal of Aries will not be able to be accused unjustly before a prince. It has power against illnesses arising from the blood, against violent winds and swelling seas, and against pain in the kidneys. Acts of harmful magic (*maleficia*) and bewitchments (*sortilegia*) will not harm his household; and it has power anent much else. Whoever wears it will sail safely upon the sea, provided he always prays earnestly for God's mercy; and if he is begging forgiveness for his sins, he should wear it with reverence and fear of God.

[The seal of Taurus] Take gold or silver and melt it while the Sun is in Taurus. Make a seal therefrom, and while you are hammering it out say, 'Arise, o Lord, my God, my helper', and the psalm, 'The heavens declare the glory etc.,[26] Then on one side engrave the figure of a bull, and round the edge the sign of Taurus, 'Theonel', and St Paul. On the other side, round the edge, 'May the name of the Lord Jesus Christ be blessed', and in the centre, 'On, Joseph, Oytheon'. The seal of Taurus has power over all types of diseases and morbid swellings of the eye, any malformations thereof, quinsies, and any pains in the neck and throat.

The sixth seal is that of Leo, 22 July. Take gold and make from it a seal, as described above. Engrave thereon the form of a lion ... and while you are hammering it, say, 'Arise, lion of the tribe of Judah, and hasten to my judgement, my God, and to my plea, my God;' and 'distinguish my plea', etc., the psalm, 'Judge me, o God;, and distinguish my plea', etc.[27] On the side with the lion round the edge of the seal of Leo [engrave] 'Choel' and St James: and on the other side, round the edge, 'The lion of the tribe of Judah has been victorious, the root of David' [*Apocalypse* 5.5], 'Alleluia'. In the centre, engrave 'Heloi, Sadoi'. The special properties of this seal are, in general terms, that it has power over all pains in the stomach, the sides, the back, the kidneys, and excessive menstrual flow, the sun's heat, acute and very acute fevers, all imposthumes [purulent cysts or abscesses], and much else. It should be worn over the kidneys.

The seventh seal is that of Virgo. Take pure gold while the Sun is in Virgo, (i.e. 22 August). Make therefrom a round seal, as before with the other seals, and engrave on it the figure of a young girl while the Sun is in Virgo. While you are hammering, say as follows: the psalm, 'Arise, o Lord, help us and set us free according to thy name' [*Psalm* 43.2], and 'O God, we have heard thee with our ears', etc. [*Psalm* 43.26]. On the side with the young girl, round the edge, engrave 'Kyrie eleison' and St Luke; and on the other side, round the edge, 'The Holy Spirit will come upon you, and the power of the Most High will overshadow you' [*Luke* 1.35]; and in the centre, 'Pantuel, Emmanuel'. These are the special properties of this seal. It protects the wearer from stomach pain and colic, quickly relieves the trembling and re-occurrence of fever, and gets rid of intense, griping pain in the intestines and other parts of the body.

The eighth seal is that of Scorpio. When the Sun is in Scorpio, 22 October, take gold or silver and make a round seal. While you are hammering it, say, 'Arise, o Lord: the Lord is my glory: arise,' and the psalm, 'Arise, psaltery and harp: I shall arise early in the morning' [*Psalm* 56.9, Vulgate]; 'Take pity on me, o God, take pity on me, for my soul puts its trust in thee' [*Psalm* 56.2, Vulgate]. Engrave thereon the figure of a scorpion, round the edge, 'Day, Abel', St Philip, and on the other side, round the edge, 'I do not want the death of a sinner, but that he may turn and live.' In the centre where it has been enamelled, engrave, 'Peace'. Its general powers are these: it has power against quartan and quotidian fever, ill-regulated nerves, stomach, and bladder, and when dipped in a drink which is then taken with other remedies, it has power over epileptic fits. It is also good for enfeebling sicknesses, consumptive coughs, and all kinds of infection.

The ninth seal is that of Sagittarius: therefore on the day preceding 1 December, take pure gold and make therefrom a round seal. While you are hammering, say, 'Arise, Lord Jesus Christ, and meet me:' and, 'See, o Lord, God of powers, God of Israel': the psalm, 'Snatch me, o Lord, from my enemies' [*Psalm* 58.2, Vulgate]. Engrave thereon the figure of an archer while the Sun is in Sagittarius; round the archer, 'Scarphiel, Holy Spirit', St Jude; and on the other side, round the edge, 'Jesus, however, passing through their midst, went'; and in the centre, 'Sabaoth, Acatiathos'. It has power in general over epileptics and those possessed by demons, mad people, those suffering from gout and sciatic pains, fever arising from corrupt bile, and many other things.

[26] Perhaps *Psalm* 43.26 (Vulgate), 'Arise, o Lord, help us'. *Psalm* 18.2 (Vulgate), 'The heavens declare the glory of God'.
[27] *Psalm* 34.23 (Vulgate). The words 'lion of the tribe of Judah' do not appear in the psalm. *Psalm* 42.1 (Vulgate).

20 German weather magic. *Adjuration against a hailstorm* (11th century)

I mark you with the sign of the cross, o air. I adjure you, o Devil and your angels. I adjure you not to bring a hailstorm or any distress into this district, and not to have anything to say in the presence of God on the grounds that no one has spoken against you. May God speak against you, and the Son of God who is the beginning of all created things. May holy Mary speak against you.

I adjure you, Merment,[28] along with your companions, you who have been given charge of the storm. I adjure you in the name of Him who made heaven and earth in the beginning. I adjure you, Merment, by the right hand of Him who formed Adam, the first human being, in His own image. I adjure you, Merment, by Jesus Christ, the only Son of God.

I conjure you, demon and Satan. I conjure you that you have no power in this place or in this village either to do harm or to cause damage, to send a storm, or throw down very violent rain.

[28] A spirit-name perhaps based on Latin *murmurant*, 'they whisper, speak quietly', referring to the way in which magical practitioners sometimes voiced their adjurations or spells.

21 Christ as a sorcerer. Anon.: *Christ Before Pilate: The Dream of Pilate's Wife* (1463–77)

[*No. 30 in the York cycle of mystery plays. Mystery plays were dramas on Biblical themes, written to be performed in the form of circulating pageants.*]

Son: [Your wife] beseeches you as her sovereign to save that innocent man. Condemn him not to death, for fear of vengeance.
Pilate: What? I hope this is the man you have dragged hither.
Caiaphas: Yes, my lord, the very same one. But this is merely a joke. He has performed this trick[29] by witchcraft. He has sent

some fiend of his with a message and warned your wife before he went.

Pilate: Dear me! That man cannot have been sent unjustly. This is absolutely certain, and the truth should be sought.

Anna: Yes, through his guile and falsehood and fiend-craft he has performed many a wonder where he walked openly. Therefore, my lord, it would be lawful if his life were taken from him.

29 Sending a dream to Pilate's wife.

Hostile magic, demons, and witchcraft

22 Necromancy. *The Trial of Gilles de Rais* (1440)

[*Also known as De Retz, 1404–40. Marshal of France and close associate of St Joan of Arc in her campaign against the English occupiers of her country. De Rais was arrested for necromancy, sodomy, heresy, and murder in 1440. He was found guilty and hanged on 20 October that same year. There is no reason to suppose that the verdict was necessarily incorrect. The examples of ritual magic and blood sacrifice of various kinds contained in this collection illustrate clearly enough that some people were perfectly prepared to take part in elaborate magical ceremonies in order to obtain that which they could not get by other, natural means.*]

Items from the indictment.
15. The city and diocese of Nantes, crying out and lamenting the loss and death of their children, innocent sons and daughters, claim that they had been taken by the said Gilles de Rais, the accused, Gilles de Sillé, Roger de Briqueville, Henriet Griart, Etienne Corillant alias 'Poitou', André Buchet, Jean Rossignol, Robin Romulart, someone called 'Spaden', and Hugues de Brémont: and by them had their throats inhumanly cut, had been slaughtered, dismembered and burned, and tortured in other ways: and that by the said Gilles, the accused, the bodies of these innocents were sacrificed to demons: that he had invoked evil spirits and sacrificed to them: and that with these innocents, male as well as female, while they were alive, sometimes after their death, and also when they were dying, he had scorned the natural vessel of the females, and with the males had horribly committed the sin of sodomy or the sin against nature, and committed sexual acts in other ways.

The prosecutor says, and intends to prove if necessary, that about fourteen years ago the said Gilles de Rais, filled with an evil spirit and forgetful of his salvation, had, alone and in company with the above-named persons, taken several innocents, male and female, slaughtered them and cut their throats. Then Gilles de Sillé, Etienne Corillant alias 'Poitou', and Henriet Griart had burned to ashes the bodies of these children and scattered the ashes in strange and hidden places: had committed the sin of sodomy or the sin against nature with those innocents, and in a degrading fashion had committed sexual acts in other ways.

16. In order to clarify the preceding declarations and articles, the prosecutor says and intends to prove that Christians who wish to be admitted to the fellowship of the angels are not permitted to indulge themselves in sexual acts, but should have God before their eyes by baptism, consecration, and reception of the Catholic faith, turn aside from the vanities and errors of deceitful souls, and put their hope in the Lord our God and his sight, with all their heart, intelligence, and feeling ... . The said Gilles de Rais, however, who received the sacrament of baptism and confirmation as the sign of a true Christian, renounced the Devil, his pomps and works, held firmly to the Catholic faith, and professed his faith in one holy Church, has fallen away therefrom. About five years ago in a certain lower room in the castle or fortress of Tiffauges in the diocese of Nantes, belonging to the wife of the said Gilles, several signs, circles, and characters were made by Monsieur Francesco Prelati, an Italian claiming to be an expert in the prohibited art of geomancy, and Jean de la Rivière.

In a certain wood near the said fortress of Tiffauges, Antonio de Palerne, a Lombard, someone by the name of Louis, and other magicians and invokers of demons, made divinations and invocations to evil spirits called Oriens, Belzebuth, Sathan, and Belial, with fire, incense, myrrh, aloes, and other odoriferous substances. The dormer windows of the said room were open. The people knelt down to obtain a response from the said evil spirits. The said Gilles, the accused, worshipped them and sacrificed to them, invoked them, and had them invoked. He made a pact with these evil spirits to have and procure by their means, if he could, knowledge, power, and riches. This is a true account of what happened.

17. On another occasion at about the same time, the said Monsieur Francesco, who was in Italy, was sent for by a certain Monsieur Eustache Blanchet, priest of the diocese of Saint Malo, and told to go

to the said Gilles to instruct him in the invocation of evil spirits. In a meadow about quarter of a league from the fortress of Tiffauges, at night, with fire and circle, he invoked the said spirits in the presence of Etienne Corillant alias 'Poitou'; and Gilles, the accused, gave Francesco a document written in the hand of the said Gilles de Rais to give to a spirit called Baron if he actually appeared at the said invocation and conjuration. The document said that Gilles would give the said Baron whatever he asked, except his soul and his life, and in exchange he asked of Baron knowledge, power, and riches. This is a true account of what happened.

18. On another occasion at the said time (that is to say, when he went to the Duc de Bretagne, together with the said Francesco, to Bourgneuf in the diocese of Nantes), in the house of the Dominicans made and had made several invocations and conjurations of evil spirits, with the intention and hope that the said Duc take Gilles into his favour.

22. About fourteen years ago, Gilles de Rais sent the said De Sillé, formerly his right-hand man, accomplice, factor, instigator, and support to several different places in the world to search out and see if he could procure any male or female diviners, invokers and conjurors of demons, who could get him money, reveal and disclose treasures, and instruct him in other magic skills, and by these means obtain great honours, and be able to capture and keep castles and towns. This is a true account of what happened.

23. At the said time, Gilles the accused sent Eustache Blanchet to Italy and to Florence to find invokers, conjurors [of demons], and diviners. Eustache found the said Francesco Prelati in Florence and brought him back to Gilles. This is a true account of what happened.

Francesco Prelati's deposition
Francesco Prelati examined and questioned on 16 October 1440, deponed that he originally came from the district of Montecatini in the Meluloe Valley near Pistoia in the diocese of Lucca in Italy. He said he was a cleric and had received the tonsure from the Bishop of Arezzo. Recently he had been a student of poetry, geomancy, and other sciences or arts, and was a capable alchemist. He believed he was about twenty-three years of age.
Item: he deponed that about two years ago while he was living in Florence in the house of the Bishop of Montefragilio, that is to say, of

Mondeni, there came to him a certain Eustache Blanchet, a priest, who knew about him through Monsieur Guglielmo de Montepoliciano. Thereafter Eustache and he saw each other often for some time, eating and drinking together, and associating in other ways. Finally, Eustache asked him, among other things, if he knew the art of alchemy and how to invoke demons. Francesco said he did, and Eustache asked him if he was willing to come to France. Francesco replied that he had a cousin called De Martelli who lived at Nantes in Brittany, and that he would be happy to go and see him. Then Eustache told him that in France there was an important personage – that is to say, the Seigneur de Rais – who very much wanted to have with him a man learned and expert in the said arts, and that if Francesco was learned and expert in them, and wanted to go to this Seigneur, he would find him very generous. So Francesco agreed to join this Seigneur de Rais, and during this occasion braved the weather and the journey to get there, bringing with him a book of invocations and alchemical arts ...

Item: At Tiffauges where he spent a certain time, he met a Breton who was living in Tiffauges in the diocese of Maillezais, in the house of Geoffroy le Comte, lord of the district, and cured the eyes of the lord's wife. This Breton found a book bound in black leather. Some of its leaves were paper, others parchment with rubrics written in red. The book contained invocations to demons, and several other items dealing with medicine and astrology. He showed the book to Gilles who looked at it and said he would test it or carry out an experiment with it and make these invocations: for which purpose, the Seigneur and the Breton spent one night after dinner. They had a light or torches made of wax and other things, and the said book which they brought with them. With the point of a sword, they traced on the floor of the large lower room in the castle of Tiffauges several circles with characters and signs in the fashion of armorial bearings. Gilles de Sillé, Henriet and 'Poitou', that is to say, Etienne Corillant, and Eustache Blanchet were present when the circle was made and prepared. After the circle had been made ready, along with its characters, and the fire had been lit, all the above-named, at the command of Gilles de Rais, left the room. Gilles de Rais and the Breton entered the circle and, at the angles near the walls, drew other characters, lit charcoal in earthenware pots, and on it sprinkled powdered magnetite, incense, myrrh, and aloes, which gave off odoriferous smoke. They stayed in the circle, sometimes standing, sometimes seated, sometimes kneeling down to worship and make sacrifices to the demons, for about two hours, invoking and intending to invoke the demon. Sometimes Gilles read from the book and waited for the demon he had invoked to appear. On this occasion, Francesco says, nothing happened.

Item: He says that this book contained the information that the demons had power to reveal hidden treasures, instruct in philosophy, and direct those who were asking questions. The words are: 'I conjure you, Baron, Sathan, Belial, Beelzebub, by the Father, the Son, and the Holy Spirit, by the Virgin Mary, and all the saints, to appear in our presence and speak to us and carry out our wishes.' Asked if he made offerings or gifts to the demons to make them appear, he said yes: a cock or a dove or a pigeon or a turtledove, to ask them not to harm the invokers and to make it easier to question them.

Item: He says that Gilles and he, on another occasion, proposed making an invocation in the same place with other things, namely, a stone called *diadokhos*[30] and a crested bird; and they did so, but left out the stone. He says further that Gilles and he made several similar invocations in the same place and in the same fashion.

Item: On another occasion, he and Poitou, Gilles's servant, with Gilles's knowledge, and on his instructions, in his name came out of the castle of Tiffauges one night with the said book, light (wax candles or torches), powdered magnetite, and other aromatics as before, in order to make an invocation to the demons. They arrived at a pond in a meadow which was in the direction of Montaigu. There they made a circle and drew characters as before, lit fire as before, and made their invocations. Francesco told Poitou not to make the sign of the cross, and then they entered the circle and stayed there without making the sign of the cross because it would prevent the demons they were invoking from coming. They made the invocations just as he and Gilles had done in the castle-room, waited for about half an hour, but nothing appeared. They did this near an old uninhabited house about an arrow's flight away, whither they retired when it started to rain and a very strong wind began to blow ...

Item: He and Gilles both made several invocations to demons which did not appear. Gilles asked Francesco why the demons they invoked had not appeared or spoken to them, and Francesco said it was because Gilles made promises to all the demons they invoked, but did not keep them. If Gilles wanted the demon to appear to him and speak to him, he would have to make him an offering of a cock or a hen, a dove or a pigeon; and if he had a strong desire for what he was asking, it would be important for him to offer up part of a child's body.

Item: After Gilles had been given this information, on one occasion he brought to Francesco's room a jar containing the hands, the heart, the

eyes, and the blood of a child, gave them to him, and then Francesco made an invocation to offer them to the demon if the demon came in answer to the invocation ...
Item: A little later, he and Gilles made an invocation in the said place (that is, the lower room in the castle), along with the ceremonies described above, with the intention of offering and giving to the demon the said hands, heart, eyes, and blood if he appeared. But no demon appeared, and later on, he believed, the hands, heart, and eyes, wrapped in linen cloth, were buried in consecrated ground near the Chapel of St Vincent in the castle of Tiffauges.
Item: He said he made several invocations in the said room, with fire in earthenware pots, a circle, incense, myrrh, and aloes, and as a result there appeared frequently – up to ten or twelve times – a demon called Baron who had the shape or appearance of a handsome young man aged about twenty-five ... Asked with whom and from whom and where he learned how to make these invocations, he replied, 'In Florence from Monsieur Jean de Fontanel, a physician, about three years ago.' Asked what happened on that occasion, he said that Monsieur Jean led him into an upper room in his house and there, in daylight hours, he made a circle and then an invocation as described above; and when he had done this, about twenty birds rather like crows appeared. The birds did not speak to them, and nothing else happened ...
Item: He said that the year Gilles was away in Bourges, he [Francesco] made an invocation to the demon in the room in Tiffauges, and Baron appeared to him in the form [of a young man wearing a violet-coloured silk cloak]. The demon brought and gave Francesco a black powder on a piece of slate, telling him to send it to Gilles in Bourges. Gilles was to put it in a silver jar and carry it on his person, and his affairs would then prosper ...
Item: Francesco made a pact with Baron in Gilles's name and at Gilles's command, that each year he would give Baron three people to eat at three solemn festivals. Gilles did so on All Saints' Day last, but then failed to do so again, and Francesco and Gilles supposed that this was why Baron refused to appear to Gilles.

This is what the said Francesco deponed after diligent questioning on every article of Gilles de Rais's indictment. He knows nothing more.

---

[30] Pliny the Elder says it was like a berlyl, *Naturalis Historia* 37.157.

23 Politically inspired necromancy. Enguerrand de Monstrelet: *Chroniques* (referring to 1407)

[*French historian, died 1453.*]
[*Part of a speech delivered by Jean Petit, Professor of Theology in the University of Paris, in the presence of Charles VI and his Council on 8 March 1407, attacking the late Duc d'Orléans for having tried to murder the King in a number of ways, including hostile magic.*]

[pp. 291–2] Any subjects or vassals who intentionally plot against the health of their King and sovereign lord with a view to making him die from a wasting disease because they covet his crown and sovereign power; who have consecrated (or, to speak more appropriately), have desecrated swords, daggers, cutlasses, or knives, rods or rings made of gold, and dedicated them by necromancy in the name of demons, making invocations with characters, acts of witchcraft (*sorcellerie*), charms, superstitious practices, and acts of harmful magic, so that they can first be thrust and plunged through the body of a dead man hanging upon a gibbet and then into the dead man's mouth, and left there for several days in great abomination and horror in order to complete these acts of harmful magic; who wear both this and a piece of cloth tied or sewn with pubic hair and filled with powder made from some of the dead man's bones; anyone who does this commits not only a human treason in the first degree, but is also traitorous and disloyal to God, his creator and his king: and as an idolater and corrupter and cheat of the Catholic faith, is worthy of a double death – that is to say, of the body and of the soul – even when the said acts of witchcraft, superstition, and harmful magic fail to have their intended effect on the King's person through the means and treachery of the said conspirators …

[pp. 298–9]. Now I must show that the late Louis, formerly Duc d'Orléans, was so inflamed and smitten by greed to obtain empty honours and worldly riches for himself and his children, and so steal from our lord King and divert to himself the very high and most noble lordship and crown of France, that he plotted and studied through greed, trickery, acts of witchcraft (*sortilèges*), and wicked devices to destroy the person of our lord King, his children, and his descendants; and so much was he smitten by greed, tyranny, and temptation by the Enemy from Hell, that like a tyrant to his king and sovereign lord, he committed the crime of divine and human treason …

(pp. 300–4) In order to make the person of our lord King die through a wasting disease and in a way which would be so cunning that no one would notice how he was doing it, he deployed so much assiduity and so much money that he won over four people – an apostate monk, a knight, an esquire, and a valet.[31] To them he handed over his own sword, a cutlass, and a ring to be dedicated and consecrated (or, more properly, to be execrated), in the name of devils from Hell; and because acts of harmful magic of this kind can be successfully performed only in solitary places far from people, they brought these objects to the Tower of Montjay near Lagny-sur-Marne, and took up their lodging there for several days.

The apostate monk, who was in charge of this diabolic operation, made a number of invocations of devils several times a day for several days, two of which I shall describe for you. These he did between Easter and Ascension on a Sunday, very early in the morning before sunrise, on a mountain near the Tower of Montjay. First, near a bush he made a circle, wrote a number of characters, and performed other superstitious actions necessary to such evocations of devils; and while he was making his invocations, he stripped to his shirt, knelt down, and drove the points of the sword and the cutlass as far as they would go into the ground, and put the ring in the middle of the circle. Then he said several prayers invoking the devils. Immediately two devils came to him in the shape of two men clothed in what seemed to be greenish brown, one named Hermas, the other Astramein. He welcomed them and bowed very low, the kind of reverence one would make to God our Saviour. When he had done this, he withdrew behind the bush. The devil who had come for the ring picked it up, removed it, and vanished. The one who had come for the sword and cutlass stood by the circle, took the cutlass, waved it about in various ways, and then laid it down near the circle and did the same kind of thing with the sword: after which, he vanished, as the other had done. Straight after this, the monk came to the circle and there found the cutlass and sword lying flat. He picked them up and found that the point of the sword was broken, a token of what had happened to it. He found the point in some powder where the devil had put it and hidden it. He then waited for half an hour after which the other devil who had taken away the ring returned and gave it back to him. The ring was conspicuously red, a shade of scarlet as it seemed at that time of day. The devil said to him, 'It's done except that you must put it in the mouth of a dead man according to the way you know.' Then he vanished.

The monk mended the sword-point and then, in order to complete their acts of harmful magic, the monk, the esquire, and the valet came by night to the gibbet of Montfaucon near Paris, took one of the recently hanged corpses, lifted it down from the gallows, and slung it on a horse to take it to the Tower of Montjay. But because they realised there was not enough of the night left to take it thither, and daylight was approaching fast, they returned to the knight's house in Paris and put the corpse in a stable. Then they placed the ring in its mouth, and stuck the sword and cutlass in its body, up the anus as far as the chest; and there the objects remained in great abomination and horror for several days just as the devils had ordered. After this sword, cutlass, and ring had been thus dedicated and consecrated (or, to speak more appropriately, execrated), they were given back to the Duc d'Orléans to do and accomplish acts of harmful magic upon the person of our lord King, so that the Duc might attain his wicked and damnable purpose. The [magicians] also gave the Duc some powder made from the bones and pubic hair of the hanged man to carry about his person. These bones, wrapped in cloth, the Duc wore for several days between his flesh and his shirt, tied to an aglet in his shirt-sleeve; and he would have worn them even longer had it not been for a most honourable knight, related to both the King and the Duc, one of the Duc's principal servants, who forcibly removed them and took them to the King in the presence of several people who are here now. Because this knight had brought the bones to the King and revealed other things belonging to the Duc d'Orléans, the Duc conceived such a great hatred for him that he persecuted him and destroyed his honour and livelihood, even though he was his own relative and a relative of the King.

[31] *Valet* may also refer to a youth, possibly of noble birth, an official in a noble household, and an esquire.

24 Demons cause illness. Guibert de Nogent: *Monodiae* (c.1115)

[*French Benedictine historian, 1053/5–1124. Abbot of Nogent. In addition to the* Monodiae, *which constitutes his autobiography, he also wrote an historical work,* Gesta Dei per Francos *(c.1108), an account of the Jerusalem expedition.*]

Book 2, chapter 6. At Saint Médard there was a man who had the office of [night-watchman] in the abbey. He spent a small part of the night on top of the fortified gate which is on the same side as the fish-pond, shaking rattles, talking aloud, and taking several drinks (as watchmen do),[32] and then, when he had finished, he came down to take a walk at the water's edge. While he stood there, three creatures looking like women appeared to him and while he listened, one of them said, 'Let's enter into this man.' The second 'woman' answered, 'He's poor. He couldn't keep us warm and comfortable.' The third 'woman' replied, 'There's a cleric here, Hugo, fat and rich with grease. He has an abundance of goods. He is the kind of man who would feed us well.' While they were fading away, the man recovered himself and realised that the three of them were rather well-known types of fever, who, with their absurd curiosity, looked down on him as a poor man, and were now making their way to someone who was scarcely able to use up his various meats and possessions. Therefore he did not wait for the dawn, but went to the monks who were nearest to him, found them, told them what he had seen and heard, and asked them to send someone to Hugo to find out how he was. Someone was sent, and Hugo was found to be suffering from the very high temperature of more than one fever. From this, one comes to the conclusion that such types of illness are provided by evil spirits under God's adjudication.

[32] *Cornua* refers to drinking horns. The plural form makes me suggest he had more than one drink. *Cornua* can also mean 'hunting horns', but one asks oneself why he should have more than one with him. 'Rattles' poses the same kind of question, of course, but his having more than one of these relatively small objects is perhaps a little more believable than his having more than one hunting horn with him.

25 Witches' acts of harmful magic. Johannes Nider: Preceptorium divine legis (c.1437)

[*Dominican theologian, diplomatist, and reformer, c.1380–1438. He was an active and influential participant in the Council of Basel (1431) and was sent therefrom to preach against the Hussite heresy in Bohemia. His best-known work is* Formicarius *(1437), which contains much information on diabolical activity, which helped to form contemporary and later views on witches and witchcraft. The Latin vocabulary for magical practitioners was very wide and gives a notion of the particular activity in which the person specialised or in which she or he was engaged at the time of the recorded incident. Translating all these as 'witch' is extremely misleading unless the context makes it clear that the person is conforming to what was later understood as a conventional 'witch'. This picture, however, did not become relatively fixed and therefore 'conventional' until late in the sixteenth century.*]

[1.11v] They do not do these without an intermediary, by performing an unmediated action peculiar to acts of harmful magic, but by the agency of evil spirits who have had an uninterrupted sight of acts of harmful magic in accordance with the pact they have made with workers of harmful magic [*malefici*][33] from the beginning of the world and the time of ancient idolatry and who know what kind of effect they ought to provide to carry out the witches' intention. For example: the broom a female witch [*malefica*] plunges in water to make rain does not cause the rain. It is the evil spirit who has seen such things before and, provided God gives him permission, has the power over all physical things, and over the air, the winds, and the clouds to succeed in making such things happen. The female magician [*maga*] may well give a sign with her broom, but it is the evil spirit who makes the phenomenon happen; and so it rains because of what is done by the evil spirit to whom the female magician is in bondage because of her wicked promise and activity, and has given herself over to worshipping him or to other things.

[33] Note, both male and female practitioners are covered by this term.

26 Witchcraft and marriage. *Summa Parisiensis* [Commentary on the *Decreta* of Gratian, Causa 33, question 1] (c.1154–9)

The first question is whether a woman should be separated from her husband because they cannot have sexual intercourse; for when the Lord listed the reasons for repudiation, He left out fornication as the only reason, and yet fornication is not an impossibility. Therefore it is obvious that a woman should not be repudiated because she is frigid or cannot have sexual intercourse. Some authorities say that a marriage can be dissolved because of such inability, to the extent that when a wife has been repudiated because of her frigidity, her husband may contract a marriage with someone else. Therefore one must specify whether the inability came before the marriage or after. Likewise, one inability has natural causes, another is accidental. When either of these inabilities precedes a marriage, it is a cause for dissolution. If it follows, provided the parties contracted the marriage legally, it does not dissolve it at all. In the case of one person, such an inability happens naturally; in another, there is an outside cause. If the inability is produced by male or female witches (*sortiarii*), the marriage can be dissolved and another contracted while the repudiated wife is still alive. If it is produced by some other cause, the husband cannot enter into another marriage, if the parties were legally contracted in the first place. A natural inability is different; for if the inability is caused by nature, the marriage can be dissolved but the husband will never be able to contract marriage with another woman afterwards. If he does, both he who swore to the marriage, and those who swore along with him, will be held guilty of the crime of perjury; and if the woman marries for a second time, she will be removed from her second husband and restored to her first.

27 A lying witch. Marie de France: *Les Fables* (1189–1208)

[*A French woman living in England, possibly Abbess of the convent in Reading.*]

No. 48: *Le voleur et la sorcière*. This is the story of a thief who was stretched out asleep under a bush. A witch (*une sorcière*) came across him, sat down beside him, and woke him up. She started to advise him to carry on with his trade, saying that she would help him wherever he went. There was no need for him to be afraid at all (she said), as long as he was willing to ask her. So the thief was without fear.

One day, he happened to be arrested while committing a robbery. His neighbours discovered him and told him he would be hanged. He sent for the witch and summoned her to ask her for advice. He asked her to help him. She told him not to be afraid, to have confidence, and be absolutely at ease.

When they were near the gallows, the thief called her over. 'Madam', he said, 'rescue me!'

'It's all right', she said, 'don't be afraid. I'll certainly rescue you.'

When they put the rope round his neck, and he called out from the other side a third time to the witch to remember how she had reassured him under the bush, she replied deceitfully, 'Ever since that time I have been helping you, supporting you, and advising you. But now I see you are behaving in such a way that I cannot give you advice. Think about what you are going to do, because you won't get any advice from me!'

This provides a lesson for everyone. God forbids us to give credence to prediction or to witchcraft; for whoever trusts them will be betrayed. One's body is put thereby in torment, and one's soul in great danger.

28 An incubus and the use of apotropaic magic. *Acta et processus canonizacionis beate Birgitte* (c.1391)

[*An incident dating to 1372. The testimony of Count Nicholas of Nola.*] He said that a certain woman by the name of Picziolella, one of his vassals from Nola, who had once been the wife of Spiczochus: a woman with a good reputation, advanced in years, not in the least beautiful, was being vexed almost every night by a foul spirit. When she was starting to be overcome by sleep, a big strong man would suddenly burst in upon her and have sex with her in such a fashion that all the signs of this vile business used to remain and be obvious after the deed was done. (According to the woman's opinion, the spirit was substantial enough to be touched, but she was quite unable to recognise him because he would always put out the light before having sex.) The woman began to have grave suspicions about some of her neighbours, but each of them justified himself by means of sworn assertions and excuses validated by an oath. The woman started to reinforce her doors, and to invite those of her female neighbours who were married to help her at night to stop the violence, and see if they could recognise her assailant. They kept each other awake, but when sleep did overcome them, it happened as before and, while the act was taking place, she could not call out to the sleeping women. So, thinking that the female sex was inadequate for her defence, she invited a suitable young man into the house, and he lay in bed with her daughter. The young man fought strongly against sleep and made the women keep awake, too, and so passed the whole night unsleeping, so to speak. But, in order to show that he was stronger than all of them, the spirit entered the house with a loud noise, put out the light, induced fear in everyone and sent them to sleep as well, and then, while the woman's helpers were lying stretched out on the ground, he had sex with the foresaid woman as usual.

The woman began to realise she was dealing with a foul spirit. She turned to God, went to confession several times, and also received the body of Christ. But even this did not stop the foul spirit from troubling her. So at some people's suggestion, she turned to magical incantations, carried written characters,[34] and did other things which soothsayers (*arioli*) suggested (intending to deceive her). She also carried round in her hair an amulet made of characters, which a priest, Raimundo by name, from Lauro in the diocese of Nola, had shown her; and so that the woman might become credulous and in consequence condemn herself, the spirit began to trouble her much less frequently, although she did not lead her life free of his attentions, which is what the woman very much wanted.

Now, this woman had been for a long time a very close, respectable friend of the foresaid witness [Count Nicholas] and, hoping that perhaps he might be able to provide her with the means of freeing herself from her harassment, she revealed to him, with tears and sobbing, the things which had caused her to be wretched. When he heard this, the said witness was unhappy and astonished, and while he was not able to offer any help, he did discuss the strange phenomenon and the woman's misery with Brother Alfonso who was then in Nola. Count Nicholas, who was very sad about her wretchedness, on the said Brother Alfonso's advice, sent her to Naples to Madam Bridget in order to ask for her prayers, and Madam Bridget disclosed her interest, as the woman herself later recounted to Count Nicholas. First, Madam Bridget asked the woman if she had on her person anything which had been put together by the art of magic. This the woman absolutely denied. Madam Bridget replied that, by the grace of God, she knew much that was hidden. 'What you say is not in the least true. You have in your hair things which a Christian is not permitted to wear.' The woman was astonished, confessed she had told a lie, and threw away the amulet (*fascinum*). Madam Bridget then told her to go to confession, make a true repentance, and receive the body of Christ the following morning. She also told her to fast, and then she herself prayed to God. Once the woman had heard Mass and received communion, she was very little troubled thereafter: for which she gave thanks to God and returned to Nola with joy.

[34] I.e. words or signs or pictures intended to act as a magical protection.

29 The witch as vampire. Etienne de Bourbon: *Anecdotes historiques* (early 13th century)

[French Dominican, 1190/5–c.1261]

No. 364. The Devil makes sport of us by means of witches [*striges*] when he transforms himself into the likeness of some woman riding a wolf and with God's permission and through the necessary circumstances of their parents' lack of faith, kills small children (in the bodily sense). In connection with this, I have heard that in Brittany a certain woman happened to lose two children after each had completed one year of its life. Women told her that witches were doing this by drinking the children's blood. She believed them and told them that when her third child came to the end of its first year, she would keep watch during the whole night of the last day of the year, and place on top of the child a small iron lid she used to cover her pot when it was on the fire, so that when the witch came, he or she would imprint his or her likeness in the warm metal and thus be identified next morning. This she did and about midnight saw an elderly woman, one of her neighbours, riding upon a wolf and entering by the door which was fast shut. She approached the child's cradle. The child's mother pretended to be asleep. [Suddenly] she snatched up the iron lid and thrust it against the witch's face; whereupon the witch, with a very loud shriek, beat a retreat. When morning came, the woman summoned her neighbours and the bailiffs of the village, and laid a complaint before them. They went to the elderly woman's door and found it bolted; and when no one came to open it, they broke it down and arrested the elderly woman who had a burn-mark on her cheek in testimony [of her guilt]. Placing the iron lid on the wound proved that imputing the crime to her proceeded from the truth. But the elderly woman denied everything, saying that she knew nothing about the alleged offence. Hearing this, the Bishop found out the woman's complicity in the crime and called upon the demon who had been the agent of this deed to show himself and explain what had been done. Then the demon changed himself into the likeness of the elderly woman and, at the Bishop's insistence, removed the burned skin from her face in front of everyone, and placed it upon his own; and thus by word and deed, he laid bare for everyone both his deception and its cause.

---

30   A witch in battle. *De gestis Herwardi Saxonis* (late 11th/early 12th century)

[Section 25] [King William's soldiers, seeking to enter the Isle of Ely along a causeway in their pursuit of Hereward], put a woman who uttered prophecies (*phithonissa mulier*) on a fairly high place in their midst so that, defended on both sides, she might exercise her art freely. Se climbed up there and held discourse for a long time against the island and its inhabitants, [prophesying] their destruction many times over, making images to bring about their downfall, and showing her naked buttocks whenever she came to the end of her speech and her incantation. She went through this abominable process three times, as she had said she would, and then behold, the men who had concealed themselves in a marsh among the reeds and sharp thorn-bushes which were everywhere, left and right, lit fire there. Whereupon, hastened by the wind, smoke and flames sprang up in front of [the Norman] camp. The fire spread about two furlongs, racing hither and thither among them, a frightful sight in the marsh, and the roaring of the flames made a terrifying sound with the crackling twigs of the brushwood and the willow trees ... [The Normans fled, some being drowned in the swamp, others felled by Saxon arrows]; and among them, the woman of the abominable art, frightened out of her wits and overwhelmed, fell to the ground and broke her neck.

---

31   The witch as a subject for humour. Etienne de Bourbon: *Anecdotes historiques* (early 13th century)

[*French Dominican, 1190/5–c.1261.*]

No. 52. There is a story about an elderly witch [*sortilega*] which says that when she heard a bird called the cuckoo saying 'cuckoo' five times on 1 May, she was quite convinced she would live at least as many years as that. So when she became seriously ill and likely to die, and her daughter advised her to repent and make her confession, she said it was not necessary because she still had five years to live; and when it reached the point when she could not speak properly and received the same advice again, she said 'cuckoo' five times; and when she could not speak at all, she raised five fingers and, while she was doing so, died.[35]

No. 361. Two women came to a female diviner. One came because she wanted a male child, the other because she wanted to make a certain person fall in love with her. The divineress said they should sleep overnight in her house. While they were doing so, she got up in the middle of the night and invoked a demon by moonlight: and when the other women looked out from the bed-clothes to see what was happening, they saw the demon come to her like a disgusting ghost and ask her what she wanted. She told him what the two women had asked her to undertake, and he replied he would bring her a jar, and whatever he might have put in it, she should give to them. He pee'd in the jar and then left. But the women, hearing and seeing this, fled terrified early next day, not waiting for a reply [to their requests].

[35] The Latin word for 'witch' is important for this joke. *Sortilega* strictly speaking refers to someone who casts lots in order to be able to foresee the future.

32 Blackening people's reputations. Etienne de Bourbon: Anecdotes historiques (early 13th century)

[*French Dominican, 1190/5–c.1261.*]

While I was making inquiries about heretics in Comté de Forez, a priest took me to his parish where he laid accusations against a number of people, saying that in a house in which he used to stay, there was a large, bare table. Many people from his village and other distant places – and he gave their names – used to come there, and when they were seated at their empty places, a small black dog would come, jump upon top of the table, raise its paw, and wheel round in a circle on the boards. Immediately the table was filled to overflowing with all kinds of dishes, and the people imagined they ate and thereafter withdrew to a rocky place, after which they went their various ways. But after I had spoken to one of them, a man of good reputation and, I believed, of good life, I found nothing about him to make me think he was involved; and so I am of the opinion that it was an illusion created by the Devil, and that the transformations were done in order to blacken the reputation of virtuous individuals.

33 Flying to the Sabbat. Martin le France: *Le Champion des Dames* (1440)

[*French diplomatist and poet. Secretary to the anti-Pope Felix V. The* Champion *is a dialogue in defence of women against the denigration of allegorical characters such as 'Badmouth' and 'Evil Thinking' who produce many of the standard complaints against women.*]

[*Relating the testimony of a confessing witch.*] Let me tell you, I have seen in a document how, since she was sixteen, if she was not mistaken, on certain nights of the *Valpute* she went to see the vile synagogue upon a stick.[36] A troupe of two thousand old women were there together, having a fortunate view of the Devil in the shape of a cat or a goat. They kissed him frankly on the arse in sign of homage, renouncing God and His high power quite openly. There they did various things. Some learned from the Devil perverse arts and sorceries with which they did several evil deeds. Others took pleasure in dancing, and many took pleasure in eating and drinking. There, they found in abundance more than one could believe. The Devil often preached to them, and he had very harsh, angry words with anyone who wanted to repent. They were beaten without respite. But to all those who were willing to consent to his pleasures, he promised, without a word of a lie, the fulfilment of all their desires. This Devil went round among the people in the form of a cat and, like a judge or an advocate, listened to all their requests. Each person paid him the same respect as should be given to God. The false knave also brought happiness to one and all by his words and looks.

Let me tell you that when they parted, each man took his woman, and if a woman was without her share of a man, a devil arrived for her. Then each person went away like a wind on his or her little stick. Such power Satan gave them, this wicked villain.

Likewise, the old woman told us that when homage was paid to the Devil, he brought them an ointment composed of various poisonous substances, which destroyed many people – more than a hundred so far – made them go mad, and disfigured many a handsome, pleasing innocent. Likewise, the evil creature repeated that by means of a powder which she blew [into the air], she made a storm arise, which ripped the heads off corn and vines, blew down saplings and trees, and had devastated a countryside. If anyone grumbled against her, he suffered a storm at once. More than six hundred had deponed, without being put to torture, that they had fabricated the hailstorm over the mountains of Esture and, contrary to nature, made rain and wind crash down where they wanted; and the devils made them do many other wicked acts.

Even more forcibly she said – and this I find quite repugnant – that the Devil turned into a man and engaged with her in the heat of lasciviousness. O God, how horrible! Just God, what a noteworthy couple! O just God Jesus, what heresy! The woman is married to the Devil!

---

[36] Valpute. The Sabbat was often called a 'synagogue' at this period. Later on, this designation fell out of common use.

34 The Sabbat described during a witch-trial. Jacques du Clercq: *Mémoires* [adapted], relating to 1460

[*c.1420–1501. Advocate and councillor to the Duc de Bourgogne.*]

Chapter 3. About All Saints' Day, 1459 a young woman by the name of Deniselle, aged between thirty and forty (a woman of foolish life), was arrested in the town of Douai at the request of the Inquisitor resident in Arras, Pierre-le-Brousart, a Dominican and Master of Theology. As soon as Deniselle was arrested, she was brought before a number of town officials and lawyers of Douai, and there she asked what they wanted of her. They answered they would tell her in due time, and made no other reply except to ask her, as though jokingly, if she knew a hermit called Robinet de Vaux. As soon as she heard this, she said, 'What's this? Do you think I'm a witch [*vauldoise*]?'– as was told and testified to me. After she had had the law of Douai explained to her, this Deniselle was brought prisoner to the Bishop's prison in the city of Arras. The reason Deniselle was arrested was that the Inquisitor had attended the general chapter which the Friars Preacher hold every year and which [this year] had been held at Langres in Burgundy. During this chapter of the Dominicans in the said town, the person known as Robinet de Vaux had been named as a witch [*vauldois*]. He was a native of Hebuterne in Artois, and behaved and dressed in every way like a hermit; and this Robert had said that several persons, male and female, were witches [*vauldois*] and had named, among others, Deniselle resident in Douai, and Jean Lavite, called 'silly abbé' ...

Deniselle, put in the Bishop's prison, was interrogated and several times put to the torture in the presence of the Bishop's representatives; Master Pierre de Hamel, archdeacon of Ostrevan; Master Jean Thieubault, canon and law-officer; Master Jean Pochon, also a canon; and Master Mathieu du Hamel, the Bishop's secretary and canon of Arras; and Master Jacques Dubois, Doctor of Theology, a canon and dean of the church in Arras, aged between 24 and 25, thrust himself into their company in order to interrogate the said Deniselle. It was this Master Jacques who took particular pains to interrogate Deniselle about witchcraft (*vaulderie*). Deniselle was subjected several times to torment and torture, after which she confessed she had taken part in a Sabbat[37] where she had seen a number of people, and among others the said Master Jean Lavite, the silly abbé, who was a painter and used to live in Arras, although she did not know where he was living now.

Then the Inquisitor said he knew he was living at Abbeville en Ponthieu; and the Inquisitor went there, arrested him, and brought him back to the Bishop's prison in Arras on 25 February that same year. As soon as the silly abbé was put in prison, fearful of confessing something which could get him into serious trouble, he had the idea of cutting off his tongue with a small knife; but when he felt the pain, he stopped cutting and simply gave himself a wound, hurting himself so badly that he could not speak for a long time. Nevertheless, they did not hesitate to interrogate him under torture and by other means, because he knew how to write and made his confession in writing.

This silly abbé confessed he had taken part in a Sabbat and had seen a good many people there, whom he named in full – people of every rank, nobles, churchmen, and other men and women. Among others he named Huguet Camery, known as 'Paternoster', a barber; Jean le Febvre, sergeant-at-law in Arras; Jeanne Dauvergne, dame de Noeuves in Arras; and three prostitutes, Belotte, Vergengon, and Blancqminette. Consequently, the said Huguet, Jean le Febvre, and the women were arrested and put in the Bishop's prison in Arras. After this was done, the Bishop's representatives saw that the business was getting out of hand and considered releasing without punishment all these men and women arrested as witches; and in fact they would have released them at Easter, when Master Jacques Dubois objected to their release and put himself in opposition to them and to the prisoners. Also opposed was Brother Jean, Bishop of Varut [Baruth], a Franciscan, a Doctor of Theology, and suffragan bishop of Arras. After this, the Dean of Arras went to Péronne to Jean, Comte d'Estampes. The person who enabled the Dean to get an audience of the Comte, and spent time with him, was a man called Jean de Meurchin who was completely blind. As soon as the Dean had spoken to the Comte, the Comte came to Arras, summoned the officials, and ordered them to do their duty anent the prisoners, otherwise they themselves would be arrested. Then he left them and went back to Péronne.

Chapter 4. [*After Deniselle, the abbé, and those he had named had confessed to taking part in a Sabbat*] the Bishop's representatives sent their confession to Cambrai to seek advice about what they should do from Master Gilles Carlier, Doctor of Theology, aged 72 or more, Dean of the Church of Notre Dame in Cambrai, with the reputation of being one of the most famous churchmen in Christendom: and Master Grégoire Nicolaï, canon and representative of the Bishop of Cambrai, a very noble cleric, people said. These respected clerics looked at the prisoners' confession and sent back their opinion in writing to the officials [in Arras]; and notwithstanding it does not survive, it is said nevertheless that their opinion was that if the prisoners wished to take back their confession this once, they should not be put to death, provided they had not committed any murders or maltreated the body of our Lord Jesus Christ (that is to say, the sacrament of the altar). The Bishop of Varut and Master Jacques Dubois were completely opposed to this opinion, because they thought that those who had confessed to taking part in a Sabbat should die, along with those whom they had accused, provided the prisoners had not named them under torture or in any other way, and that there were three or four witnesses against them. The Dean and Bishop took all this trouble so that every prisoner might be burned and suffer pain thereby.

The Dean said, and swore to the truth of what he was saying, in every gathering he joined – and plenty of people heard him say it – that a third of Christendom and more had taken part in a Sabbat and were witches. He knew more than he could say, and if he could say it, people would be very frightened. Moreover, he said that all those accused of being witches were witches and that they could not have been accused if they had not been witches. When anyone – cleric or layman – argued with him, he said they should be arrested on suspicion of being witches; and anyone who agreed with his opponents or made some reference to their opinion, he said should be arrested on suspicion of being witches. He also said that before any of them burned, when it came to the point of death they would take back everything they had said and that the Devil made them do this so that they might be damned in Hell. In all this, the Bishop of Varut agreed with him and supported him and said he was speaking the truth. Moreover, he said he believed there were bishops, not to mention cardinals, who had taken part in a Sabbat, and other important people, too; and that there were so many of them that if they could have some king or great prince as one of them, they would rise up against all those who were not of their number and be very powerful in their despite, and inflict injury and annoyance on all who were not of their company.

Before he was consecrated, this bishop had been a penitentiary of the Pope in Rome during the year of pardons, that is 1455, which is why people said he must know a lot; and the Bishop had such a great imaginative faculty that when he saw people, he would pass opinion whether they had taken art in witchcraft or not. The Bishop and the Dean used to say that as soon as a man was arrested for or accused of witchcraft, no one should help him or come to his aid, whether father, mother, brother, sister, or any other relative or friend, on pain of being arrested as a witch and they said further that on the assumption that these friends and relatives knew perfectly well their kinsfolk had been accused of witchcraft, they could not be allowed to escape. In short, they laboured with all their power, intelligence, and strength to make sure that those who had been and could be arrested were burned, be they noble, rich, or poor.

They did such a good job that there was a further arrest for the same crime, someone called Jennein de Vevry, a timber-merchant, married, forty years old; and once again the Comte d'Estampes wrote to the representatives of the Bishop of Arras, asking them to shorten the prisoners' trial. Therefore these officials, who were completely persuaded by the advice of the Bishop of Varut and the Dean of Arras, brought together all the clergy of Arras among whom were Dom Jean Barré, Prior of Saint-Vast, Doctor of Theology, and other clerics such as the canons of Arras, chaplains, Dominicans, Franciscans, Carmelites, and lay clerks such as Master Gilles Flameng, an advocate in Beauquesne, Master Mathieu Paille, also an advocate there. To these clerics were shown the completed depositions and trial-papers of Deniselle, Jean Dauvergne, Belotte, Vergengon, Blancqminette, the silly abbé, and Jean le Febvre. Jean le Febvre did not stand trial because before he was interrogated or put to the torture, on the night before sentence was passed they found him in prison, hanged by the point of his hood;[38] and no one can ever know for certain whether he hanged himself or whether he was hanged for fear he might accuse more people.

After these trials were over and the clergymen had delivered their opinions, the next day (9 May) the silly abbé, Deniselle, Belotte, Vergengon, Blancqminette, and Jean Dauvergne were let out on to a high platform specially built in the courtyard of the Bishop's palace – Jean le Febvre being carried because he was dead – and there they had mitres put on their heads, each mitre carrying the painted figure of the Devil depicting the way they had confessed to paying him homage, facing him on their knees. Master Pierre Le Brousart, Doctor of Theology, Dominican and Inquisitor, gave a public sermon to everyone present – there were so many people, it was extraordinary, for they had come from all the villages round Arras and ten or twelve more places in the neighbourhood – and the said Inquisitor explained that those he named had taken part in witchcraft, and then he described the manner in which they had done so.

When they wanted to go to a Sabbat [*vauderie*], they smeared a tiny wooden rod, their palms, and their body with an ointment the Devil had given them, and immediately they would fly away whither they wanted over cities, woods, and water. The Devil carried them to the place appointed for their assembly, and here they all found tables set out and laid with wine and food. They also found a devil[39] in the shape of a goat, dog, or monkey, but never a man. They sacrificed to him, paid homage to him and worshipped him, and several of them gave him their souls and more or less all (or at least some part of) their body. Then they kissed the devil in goat shape on his backside, that is, on the arse, with lighted candles in their hands, the silly abbé being the person appointed to guide them and be master of ceremonies in charge of the homage when they were new to the Sabbat. After they had made their homage, they trampled on the cross and spat on it to show their contempt for Jesus Christ and the holy Trinity, and then displayed their arses to the sky and the vault of heaven to show their contempt for God. After they had drunk and fed well, they all had sex together – the devil, too, in the shape of a man and a woman. The men had sex with the devil-as-a-woman, and the devil-as-a-man with the women. There, too, they committed the sin of sodomy, and buggery, and so many other crimes so absolutely foul and shocking, as much against God as against nature, that the Inquisitor said he would not venture to give them a name in case innocent ears were alerted to such base, shocking, and cruel crimes.

The Inquisitor also described how they would make the ointment they used. When they went to receive the sacrament (the sacred Host or precious body of our Lord Jesus Christ), they would take it, put it in a pot with some toads, and leave it there until the toads had used it. Then they would take the bones of Christians who had been hanged, and make powders out of them; after which they would sear and kill the toads, and make the ointment out of these toads and the bone-powder, along with the blood of young pure children, and herbs, and other things. The foresaid abbé had made some of this ointment. The Inquisitor added that during their assembly the Devil preached to them, forbade them to go to church, to hear Mass, or take holy water, and said that if they did so to show that they were Christians, they should say, 'May this not displease our master.' They were not to go to confession, he said, and there was no other life save that we are living now; they did not have a soul; and if ever anyone who had taken part in the witchcraft and been to the Sabbat wanted to renounce it and repent, the Devil would beat him or her with a bull's pizzle in such a way that they were bruised and cut all over. The Inquisitor said they had held their assembly in the Forest of Mofflaines, quite near Arras; in the Forest of Maugart, half a mile from Arras; and in Hautes-Fontaines-lez-Arras whither they had gone on foot and in broad daylight after dinner.

All this was said and explained by the Inquisitor who asked each of [the accused], one after the other, if this was true. They answered that it was; the abbé and everyone confessed it publicly. After their confession, their sentence was delivered in French and in Latin (that is, they were relaxed to the secular arm as rotten and unworthy to be members of Holy Church), and all their inheritances confiscated to the use of their feudal lords, and their moveables to the Bishop. Deniselle was handed over to justice in Douai, the abbé to the city magistrates, and the four women and Jean le Febvre to justice in Arras. The women were quickly led into the town-hall of Arras where they and Jean le Febvre were sentenced by the magistrates to be burned and their bodies reduced to powder. As soon as the women heard their sentence, in desperation they began to shriek and say to Master Gilles Flameng, an advocate who was present and who had assisted at all their interrogations, whether under torture or not, 'Ha, false, underhand traitor! You have deceived us! You told us if we confessed what they said to us, they would let us go, and we would have no other penance than to go on pilgrimage six, ten, or twelve miles away. You know, wicked man, you have betrayed us!' Then, in public, they said they had never been to a Sabbat, and that they had confessed to going because of torment and torture, and because of the inducements and promises of Master Gilles and others who had interrogated them. They said a lot more, but it did them no good at all; for they were handed over to the executioner and quickly taken to the place of execution in Arras, where their bodies were burned and reduced to powder; and while they were being led to their deaths, and right up to the point when they surrendered their souls, they said publicly (and did not recant) that they had never been to a Sabbat, and that what they had confessed had been because of torment and torture, and because people had given them to understand that if they did not confess, they would be burned.

From the time sentence was pronounced right up to their deaths, they displayed all the behaviour a good Christian should display. They made their confession, they recommended their souls to God, they asked the people to pray to God for them, they asked those who knew them to have Masses said for them, and died in this condition, saying they had never been to a Sabbat and that they did not know what a Sabbat was. These words and this behaviour of theirs made the people think deeply, and gave rise to muttering. Some said it had been wrong to put them to death; others, that the Devil had ordered them to speak so, and made them recant so that they might be damned. As far as all that is concerned, I leave it to God who knows everything. Deniselle was taken to Douai where the city magistrates condemned her to be burned; and so she was. She too said she was wrongly put to death, and said everything and behaved in the same way as the others had done until they died. The city magistrates also condemned the silly abbé to be burned on the same day [the ecclesiastical court] passed its sentence and he was the first to be executed at the Bishop's court. He too said everything and behaved the same way as the others, and more. He said they were wrong to put him to death, and his last words as he was being bound to the stake to be burned were these, in Latin: 'But Jesus, passing through the midst of them, went away.'[40] This abbé was sixty or seventy years old, and a painter. He was welcome all over the place because he was a fine speaker and composed songs and ballads which he recited in public; and in particular because he had made a number of compositions and ballads in honour of the glorious Virgin Mary, for which several people held him in high regard. But every time he recited or read one of these compositions or ballads in honour of God and Our Lady or any of the saints, when he had finished he would take off his hat or hood and say, 'May this not displease my master,' as a number of people testified. I do not know what this means.

The men and women who had been denounced as witches by those already under arrest, and were executed at the request of the said Inquisitor were: someone by the name of Thomas who trimmed clothes with fur; someone called 'Little Henriot' who ran a gaming-house; Jean du Bois, resident in Wailly; someone called Jacques Molnier, a cook; Master Robert le Jeune, knight, Governor of Arras; Colin de Bullecourt; the wife of a saddler (she was called Franche-Comté because she had married a herald of this name); Colette Lestrevée, a prostitute; a girl called Printemps Gay, a prostitute; a girl called Catron alias 'La Gringaude', a prostitute; a girl called 'La Parqueminière', a prostitute; and another girl called Jeanne le Lucque, also a prostitute.

[37] Literally 'had been in witchcraft'. So the term *vaulderie* is being used here and later in the passage to refer to the witches' meeting as well as to what they actually did there.

38 The *chaperon* originally covered the head and shoulders, with a hole cut to accommodate the face. It often had a very long point which here seems to have served the function of a rope.

39 Not, therefore, necessarily Satan himself. The French demonologist, Pierre de Lancre, later addressed the question of how it was possible for Satan to be present at every one of the thousands of Sabbats held throughout the world, *Tableau de l'inconstance des mauvais anges* (1612). It is clear from his lengthy description and discussion of the Sabbat that the presiding demon might be any one of a large number of principal evil spirits.

40 *Luke* 4.30. The context is worth noting. Jesus is preaching in the synagogue of Nazareth, with the message that no prophet is accepted in his own country; at which the congregation angrily seizes him and tries to lynch him. Jesus, however, escapes their murderous intent.

35 A lawyer's reservations about the Sabbat. Ambrosius de Vignate: *Tractatus de hereticis* (c.1468). Adapted

[*Italian jurisconsult, Doctor of civil and canon law, teacher in Padua, Bologna, and Turin. He presents here two questions related to a particular case involving witches, and argues both sides of the question.*]

[*He has been asking a series of questions. 1. Which type of faithlessness is worst of all? 2. What kind of people are heretics? 3. What kind of people blaspheme? 4. Is the practice of hanging divine names round one's neck illicit? 5. Is divination by lots illicit? 6. Is it permissible to practise divination? 7. Is divination done by invoking demons licit? 8. Is divination by the stars licit? 9. Is divination through dreams licit? 10. Is divination via augury and similar observations of exterior things licit? 11. Should male and female casters of lots* (sortilegi) *and diviners* (divinatores) *be subject to the judgement of inquisitors? 12. A question on witches who attack children* (lamiae) *and witches who fly through the air* (striges) *and their transgressions.*]

So what do we say about women who confess that during the night they gad about over long distances in an instant, enter other people's locked and barred bedrooms with the help of their instructors the demons (so they say), have conversations with these demons, pay them regular amounts of money, and at their persuasion (so they day) deny God and the Virgin Mary, trample upon the holy cross: and with the demons' help (so they say) kill children, kill adult men and women, and make them fall into various illnesses, and say they do many things such as these: and that sometimes they change themselves into the shape of a cat, and say that the Devil changes himself into the shape of a dog or some other creature? Are these, and things like them, either consistent with fact or believable?

I have dealt with this case quite often, in fact, and one such among others has come my way. A certain accused party voluntarily confessed that he belonged to the sect of 'Masked Ones' (*masci*) or workers of harmful magic (*malefici*). He inculpated other men and women, saying that they were members of the same sect, that they went about at night, and that at places where three roads or four roads meet, or at the junctions of roads, they would go running about all over the place, doing many wicked things. Because of this man's deposition, the inquisitor into heretical depravity arrested some women and imprisoned them. A number of them confessed, of their own free will, the things I have been describing and others of a like kind. Some who denied them were put to the torture and during their torments confessed.

In regard to this case, since it actually happened, I thought there were two things, in the main, which required investigation. First: were the things to which they confessed possible, consistent with fact, and believable, or not? Secondly: can one suppose it possible that the confession of the man who had confessed of his own accord, and those of one, two, three, or four women who were deponing similar things, provided evidence sufficient to warrant torture?[41]

Regarding the first article – that they talk to demons, go about with them, do business and perform similar acts of harmful magic of this kind with their cooperation – it is alleged and appears after due consideration that such things are possible. For first of all, it is deemed by St Thomas Aquinas in [*Summa Theologiae*] 2.2, question 95, article 4 that it is possible to enter into a pact, either tacit or overt, with evil spirits. Secondly, St Augustine says in *De doctrina christiana* Book 2, 'Whatever emerges from an association between evil spirits and human beings is superstitious,' etc. Therefore this kind of stupid woman can have association and traffic with evil spirits. [*Further references given.*]

Likewise, that it is possible for an evil spirit to talk to such women or men when they invoke him is proven because the Lord asked the demon, 'What is your name?' and he replied, 'My name is Legion, because we are many,' etc. as it is written in *Mark*, chapter 5 [v.9]. [*Further references*] Likewise, in *John* chapter 8 [v.44] it is said that when the Devil speaks a lie, he speaks from what properly belongs to him, because he is a liar and the father [of the lie]. Consequently, the foresaid women did not confess things which are impossible. [*Further references, showing that good angels are recorded as having spoken to human beings; therefore it is perfectly possible for a demon to do so.*]

From this it is clear that an angel can not only take on a physical body, but also, once it has done so, it can set in motion by the operation of the invigorating soul things which are alive, which nurture, engender, and sustain – all of which is understood by 'nurturing'. So if good angels can do this, so can demons.

If women such as those I have described both say and confess that the Devil has sometimes had sexual intercourse with them, this does not seem to be entirely impossible. In support of this, I refer you to what St Augustine wrote in *De civitate Dei*, Book 15, that he had heard from people worthy of belief that shameless, wanton gods associated with forests and uncultivated land (*sylvani*) and deities of the countryside (*fauni*), which we call 'incubi' and 'succubi', had appeared to women. For just as angels of light take on bodies made from air (from the higher and purer part of air) so angels of darkness take on bodies made from its lower, stinking part, as Aegidius[43] says in the eighth distinction of Book 2 of his *Sententiae*, and St Isidore in *De summo bono* Book 7, chapter 1, and as the majority of theologians agree. [*Further references*] Therefore it is possible that a demon appeared to these women, sometimes in the shape of a dog or some other animals (as they say). So they do not seem to have confessed impossibilities if they say they had a conversation with demons, saw them in human shape, had sexual intercourse with them, and were transported by them from one place to another, for example, from Paris to Rome. [*Further references to illustrate shape-changing.*]

The truth of the matter [however], argues the opposite – that the foresaid things are not possible because, as Damascenus says in Book 2, chapter 3,[43] an angel and a devil are incorporeal beings. Therefore it is a gross [error] to say that demons have hands or feet; likewise, it is obvious that demons cannot have sexual intercourse, even if with God's permission they take on bodies made from air, because it is physically impossible. Doctors say that semen is an overflow of the end of the digestive process; so those beings who do not undergo change in their nutriment do not emit semen. Likewise, that the Devil cannot speak and therefore that he cannot ask these women for payment, or tell them to deny God, seems to be proven in as much as even if [demons] were free to take on physical bodies, the things necessary to the formation of a voice do not exist in these bodies they take on. [*References in support of this.*] So although demons sometimes seem to speak in their assumed bodies, the sound is not that of their own voice, and indeed not, properly speaking, 'voice', but something like a voice; and although we may also say that sometimes they eat, it is not real 'eating', because even if we read that sometimes the good angels of light have eaten – as Aegidius whom I quoted above says in Book 2 of his *Sententiae* – it is not real eating because their assumed bodies lack the power of digestion.

[*Although we say that good and bad angels take on physical bodies by God's permission, they have no power to harm human beings unless God allows them to do so.*]

Moreover, I offer a rational proof that the demon does not appear to the person invoking him by an act of free will on his part, because if demons could do harm by an act of free will and, in the bodies they have assumed, persuade [people] in their wicked fashion, they would persuade not only women but men, too, to hold heretical opinions, abjure our holy faith and do all kind of evil things – something which does not happen as a general rule. Likewise, they would harm good, religious men – which they do not do, because it is certain that the good, the dutifully religious, and the just are safe from the attacks of demons; for, as St Jerome says in his *Life of Saint Antony*, 'The just man is not exposed to a demon.'

My general conclusion is that although *Job* [chapter 41] writes of the power of the Devil: 'There is no power on earth which is comparable to it,' nevertheless it is reined in by the power and goodness of God. [*Further references. The art of magic which claims to be able to change people's shape cannot do so in reality. The changes are not real but illusory, springing from deceptions by evil spirits.*] Therefore however many transformations and changes we read about in histories and poets, we must always understand that they take place only in appearance, not in reality, just as we see in lunatics and drunks who very, very frequently think that one thing is something else. It is not difficult, you see, as theologians maintain, for a demon (with special permission from God), to demonstrate that a human being can be an ox or a wolf, because he does not allow the truth of the matter to come as far as the eyes. Cecco d'Ascoli (a man who is said to have known the whole range of incantations of demons and their powers) because they were his very intimate companions,[44] maintains in his treatise on the sphere [of the world] that demons cannot turn the human body into that of a beast, and cannot do so because the dead rise again;[45] but demons can perform wonders through a power of natural things which is hidden from us but very well known to them. Demons can also do other things which may seem to be miracles, and this can happen in two ways. One method involves the inside. Demons can alter the image people present to others, and even their physical senses, so that something appear to be other than it actually is and this is sometimes said to happen through the powers of other physical things. In the second way, the demons can do this from the outside. A demon can assume an aerial body, made from air, and the shape of someone who is dead, and under this form appear to the living. By these means demons cause their illusions to happen. [*This explains the apparent changes in appearance found in Classical literature, the Bible, and the Church Fathers and their prohibitions against the art of magic. Examples given.*] Therefore I conclude that it is impossible for a person to be changed into an animal or into a brute beast by the art of magic. [*Miraculous changes, however, are a different matter because they are real, not illusions. Examples given.*]

Now, then, I have earned the right to pass to the second article of the above-mentioned case. It frequently happens, in fact, that some people who say they are friends[46] accuse other men and women of participating in the society and the Sabbat by going around with demons and [the witches'] instructors. Can one suppose it possible that this kind of testimony from male and female friends who talk stupidity of this kind is sufficient evidence to warrant torture? [*It may be argued in favour if one admits the evidence of excommunicates, associates, and participants in the crime and if one agrees that only slight circumstantial evidence is necessary in crimes of heresy: for both of which points legal references are provided.*] Even if it be said that this kind of associate does not furnish full proof or sufficient evidence for torture, some of the women mentioned in the aforesaid case confessed, were put to the torture either in threat or in practice, and afterwards held to their confession both after the pain had finished and outwith the place of torture. Therefore it seems they can be condemned as a result of their confession. [*References given.*]

The contrary may be argued and the negative proponed in the above-written case, that when the women confessed as they did, their male and female associates were not adequate to provide proof, nor was the circumstantial evidence sufficient to warrant torture. This is proved, first because this crime of heresy is among the greatest crimes, and therefore when it is a question of a greater crime a greater prejudice,[47] greater and more unambiguous proofs are required. [*Legal references given.*]

Likewise, these male and female associates say they were participants in the crime. Therefore it does not seem as though one should believe them. [*Legal references which say that such a confession is not sufficient to lead to torture. Moreover, one cannot presume that torture will lead to confirmation of facts or any reasonable conjecture one may have had beforehand*], because what some of these men and women confess is impossible – namely, that they turn themselves into cats or other dumb animals and, as has been said already, it is impossible for one created being to be changed into another except by the Creator alone.

[41] The Latin formula for asking this question presupposes that there is a fairly strong possibility the answer to the question will be 'No'.
[42] Egidio Colonna, died 1316. Italian Augustinian and Archbishop of Bourges.
[43] St John of Damascus (c.675–c.750), Greek theologian. This reference is to his *De fide orthodoxa*.
[44] Italian poet and scholar, 1257–1327, the nom de plume of Francesco Stabili. He taught astrology in various places, including the University of Bologna, but was condemned as a heretic in 1324. His treatise is a commentary on the *Sphaera mundi* by the English astrologer, Joannes de Sacro Bosco.
[45] I.e. in their human form and not in that of an animal.
[46] *Socii et sociae*. The emphasis upon males as well as females is maintained throughout all references to 'friends' or 'associates' in this context.
[47] I.e. pre-judgement of his or her case in a negative light.

Prohibition, reservation, and scepticism

[*Any act of magic was a potential threat to the state because it indicated that an individual was seeking to exercise power beyond the boundaries apparently set by nature. It was also feared that this attempt was likely to involve the help of non-human entities. Many of these acts also consisted of malicious attempts against life or property or both, and consequently involved breaches of the civil or criminal law. Hence the interest taken by secular authorities. The following examples are drawn largely from German sources and stop at about the tenth century. But obviously this does not represent the end of secular concern. The fourteenth century, for example, saw a rash of cases in Ireland, France, and the Papal Court, in which charges of hostile magic were brought against very highly placed individuals, in what were clearly politically motivated attacks upon them. As in the case of Gilles de Rais, this does not mean to say the charges were necessarily false, but their appearance does mean that various secular as well as Church authorities were obliged to deal with the practical problem of an offence which had its roots in preternatural causes.*]

Secular

36 Pactus legis Salicae (6th century)

Text 19. *Acts of harmful magic.* If anyone performs acts of harmful magic (*maleficia*) against another, or gives him a herbal drink with the result that he dies, and this is proved against him: let him be adjudged liable in the sum of 8,000 denarii which makes 200 shillings.

64. *Poisoner/Worker of poisonous magic.* (1) If anyone calls another 'poisoner/worker of poisonous magic' (*herburgius = veneficus*), i.e. 'witch-carrier' or 'someone who carries a cauldron in which witches (*striae*) do their cooking, and cannot prove it: he must be judged liable in the sum of 2,500 denarii which make 62.5 shillings. (2) If anyone calls a freeborn woman 'witch' (*stria*) or 'prostitute', and cannot prove it: he must be judged liable in the sum of three times 2,500 denarii which make 187.5 shillings. (3) If a witch eats a person and is proved to have done so, he or she must be judged liable in the sum of 8,000 denarii which make 200 shillings.

37 King Rothair: Edictus (643)

No. 197. *The abominable crime.*[48] If anyone has the guardianship of a freeborn girl or woman and calls her 'witch' (*striga*) – that is, a female magician (*masca*)[49] – he is to lose his guardianship unless he is her father or brother. She is to have the right of entrusting herself and her own property, in accordance with her wishes, to her relatives or to the Court of the King who must then have her guardianship at his command. If the man denies that he accused her of this crime, he must purge himself; and if he does purge himself of the offence, he may have the guardianship on the same terms as he had it before.

No. 368. *Single combat.* No one who takes part in single combat may take it upon himself to have on his person, when going to engage another man in fighting, herbs which relate to acts of harmful magic,[50] or anything else which is similar: only his weapons which have been agreed upon. If there is a suspicion that he is secretly wearing such things, he is to be searched by the judge, and if they are found on him, they must be ripped out and thrown away. After this search, the person engaging in single combat should put his hand into the hand of one of his relatives or a fellow freeman and, by way of making atonement, say in front of the judge that he does not have on his person anything which pertains to acts of harmful magic. Then he may go to the ordeal.

No. 376. Let no one presume to kill someone else's *aldia* [half-free, half-slave woman] or female slave as if she were a witch (*striga*) – popularly known as a female magician (*masca*) – because in no way should Christian minds believe that a woman can eat a living human being from the outside inwards.[51] If anyone presumes to carry out such an unheard of and appalling act in future: if he kills an *aldia*, he must pay 60 shillings on account of her legal position and, in addition, add 100 shillings in recognition of his responsibility – half for the King and half for the person whose *aldia* she was. If she was a slave he must pay as decreed above on account of her legal position, (if she was a house-slave or a field-slave): and in addition add 60 shillings in recognition of his responsibility, half for the King and half to her owner. If a judge ordered him to carry out this wicked deed, the judge himself is to pay the above-written penalty from his personal property.

[48] The Latin of these three texts is full of variants. I have chosen those which appear to make most sense.

[49] *Masca* means 'mask' or 'nightmare', and is probably derived from Arabic. Some sixteenth-century descriptions of witches' gatherings describe the participants as wearing masks or, at any rate, have their faces covered.

[50] The text has *ad maleficias* which is a mixture of *maleficia*, 'acts of harmful magic', and *maleficas*, 'women who work harmful magic'. The former seems to be more satisfactory in this context.

[51] *Intrinsecus*, which may also mean 'from the inside outwards', as though the witch were a kind of grub.

38 *Leges Visigothorum*: King Flavius Chindasvind (c.644)

[*Visigothic King in Spain, 642–53. Strongly opposed to all forms of divination and magic. He re-enacted the legislation of Alaric II (484–507) against such practices, and added laws of his own.*]

People who are not allowed to testify. Murderers, workers of harmful magic (*malefici*), thieves, criminals or poisoners/workers of poisonous magic (*venefici*), rapists or perjurers, those who have gone to casters of lots (*sortilegi*), and diviners (*divini*), shall in no way be permitted to testify.

If a freeborn person consults soothsayers (vaticinatores) *about someone's health or death.* Whoever consults prophesiers (*arioli*), those who interpret signs and portents (*aruspices*), or soothsayers (*vaticinatores*) about the health or death of the ruler or anyone else, together with those who give replies to people who consult them: if they are freeborn, let them be flogged and then reduced to slavery along with confiscation of all their possessions, or let them be sentenced to perpetual slavery by the King and given to anyone, as the King directs. If their sons have joined their parents in committing a crime such as this, let them be punished with a similar sentence. But if they have had nothing to do with their parents' crime, they will secure their complete and unconditional right to the rank and full possession of property their parents have lost. Slaves should be subjected to a variety of tortures and then sold for transference overseas, so that the severity of their punishment may not offer them justification; for the outrageous way in which they have behaved, and the monstrous way in which they have transgressed make them answerable [for their actions.]

The persons of judges or anyone else who consults diviners or pays attention to auguries. Just as one does not lay hold of truth by asserting a lie, so it does not follow that one can track down a hidden truth by means of deceit. All truth comes from God, and deceit comes from the Devil because the Devil himself was a liar from the start. Since each thing has its principles, therefore, what need is there to allow truth to be investigated by someone's deceit? It is said that certain judges, who are devoid of the spirit of God and full of the spirit of error, because they cannot be subject to the investigation of a subtle and thorough inquiry anent the detestable utterances of diviners (*divini*), apply themselves to acts of maleficent magic. They think they cannot find out the truth unless they consult diviners and interpreters of signs and portents (*aruspices*) and thereby close the door on their discovering the truth, because they long to find out the truth by means of deceit. Since they are endeavouring to approve harmful magic (*maleficium*) through a diviner, and acts of harmful magic through divinations, they trap themselves into becoming the Devil's slaves.

Consequently, if any judge of any grade or rank tries to find out anything from diviners or such-like persons, or argues that they should be approved: and if anyone of any rank or character demands from such people responses concerning health or sickness, or believes they may be consulted about any matters whatsoever, he or she is to be considered liable to give satisfaction according to the law which, in Book 6 of this work, under section 2, paragraph 1, ordains that those who try to consult any soothsayers (*vaticinatores*) about someone's health or death are to be pruned back by order of His Highness. Only those judges who have not tried to get to know diviners and people of that sort, but have taken vengeance on them and ground them to dust by seeking retribution in front of many witnesses, will not be held answerable according to the purpose of this law; that is, if they do not make inquiries with a view to doing something for their own benefit as a result of their seeking to know them, but make inquiries with the sole purpose of exposing them and then striking them down.

But because these days we know that those given over to auguries are for that reason hateful to God, therefore by particular legal ordinance we decree that, regardless of who they may be, anyone who happens to pay attention to augurs or auguries is to be punished by a public flogging of fifty lashes. Moreover, if they subsequently return to the sin they were accustomed to commit, they will be punishable by a similar sentence of flogging.

Poisoners/Workers of poisonous magic. Of the various kinds of crime, those which do harm are to be visited with a range of different penalties. Thus, first of all, here is the immediate punishment which will be inflicted on freeborn persons or slaves who are poisoners/workers of poisonous magic (*venefici*): namely, if they have given anyone a drink with poisonous ingredients and the person who has drunk it dies as a consequence, they are to be punished by a most shameful death attended by continuous tortures. If, on the other hand, the person lives in spite of his having drunk from the poisoned cup, the person who gave it to him should be given over into his power so that he may do with him whatever he wishes according to his own pleasure without hesitation.

Workers of harmful magic and those who consult them. Workers of harmful magic (*malefici*) or storm-raisers, who by means of certain incantations are reputed to discharge hail-storms upon vines and crops: or those who throw people's minds into confusion by the invocation of demons: or those who sacrifice at night to demons and with wicked intent invoke them through vile invocations: whenever they have been found or exposed by the local judge, administrator, or procurator, they should be flogged in public with two hundred lashes, have their heads shaved to their disgrace, and be compelled against their will to make a circuit of ten properties in the neighbourhood, so that others may take warning by their example. But so that they may not be allowed to do such things by going to places further afield, a judge should either have them fetched back and given clothing and something to keep them alive, so that they may not have an excuse to harm the living: or he should send them into the presence of the King so that he can give a clear ruling about what he wants done with them. Those who are found to have consulted such people are to receive two hundred lashes at an assembly of the people, so that those accused by someone guilty of a similar offence may not remain unpunished.

39 Harmful magic. *Lex Ribuaria de maleficio* (c. 7th century)

(1) If a man or Ripuarian woman kills anyone through an act of harmful magic (*maleficium*), he or she must pay the legal money-equivalent of that person's life (*werigeldus*). 2. But if the person does not die and suffers change or weakness to his body, which demonstrably stems from this [act of magic], he must be judged liable in the sum of one hundred shillings, or he must take an oath with six people.

40 King Liutprand: *Laws* (727)

No. 84. If anyone forgets his fear of God and resorts to male or female prophesiers (*ariolos aut ariolas*) who provide divination or respond to any kind of question by consulting the organs of animals, he must pay to the royal treasury half the price someone would have to pay if he had killed him; and he must also do penance in accordance with the requirements of canon law. Likewise, those who in the manner of peasants pray to a sacred tree and worship fountains, or commit the sacrilege of making an incantation, must in similar fashion pay half their worth to the royal treasury. Anyone who has knowledge of a male or female prophesier and does not reveal them or conceals those who go to them, and does not reveal them, must undergo the abovewritten penalty. Anyone who sends his male or female slave (*servum aut ancillam*) to these male or female prophesiers in order to get some replies from them, and it is proved against him, must pay the abovewritten penalty. If any male or female slave goes to a male or female prophesier without their master's permission, simply on their own authority, in order to obtain responses in a similar fashion, then their master must put them up for sale outwith the district; and if their master fails to do this, he must pay the abovewritten penalty.

41 King Childeric III: *Capitularia* (742)

[Died c. 751. King of the Franks, last of the Merovingian dynasty. He took no active part in the events of his short reign, and was ousted by Pépin, the father of Charlemagne.]

Capitulare 1, section 5. We have also decreed that according to canon law, each bishop with the assistance of his registrator who is the defender of his church, should take care in his diocese that the people do not turn God into a heathen, but that they reject and spit out every piece of heathen filth, whether it is profane sacrifices to the dead, casters of lots (*sortilegi*) or diviners (*divini*), phylacteries and auguries, incantations, offering sacrificial victims (which stupid people do according to pagan ritual right next to churches, in the name of holy martyrs or confessors, thereby provoking God and his saints to anger); and that they diligently stop pagan customs, whether those sacrilegious fires known as *netfyres*, or anything else whatsoever.

42 Charlemagne: *Capitularia* (873)

[742–814. King of the Franks and then, from 800, Holy Roman Emperor.]

Title 45, chapter 7. Because We have heard that people who work harmful magic (*malefici homines*) and women who cast lots (*sortiariae*) are increasingly found throughout many places in our kingdom, and that through their acts of harmful magic (*maleficia*) many people have already been made sick and even more have died: and since, as holy men of God have written, it is the function of the King to remove wicked people from the land, and not allow workers of harmful magic and workers of poisonous magic (*venefici*) to live: We expressly command that every magnate in his territory employ great zeal in searching out and arresting such people. If men are found guilty thereof, or women, let them be destroyed as the law and justice say they should be. If they are named or suspected but have not yet been found guilty of these offences, or they cannot be found guilty thereof by truthful witnesses, let them be put to an ordeal so that God may judge them: and so let them be either set free or condemned by that judgement of God. Not only the perpetrators of this evil, but their friends and accomplices, male or female, should also be destroyed so that the knowledge of such great evil may perish from our territory along with them.

43 Early English Laws (9th and 10th centuries)

(a) The laws of Edward and Guthrum. *Concerning workers of magic, diviners, perjurers, etc.* If workers of magic or diviners, perjurers, or those who cause death by magic or poison: or filthy, corrupt, manifest adulteresses be discovered anywhere in the country, let them be driven out of the land, and let someone cleanse the people; or let someone totally destroy them, unless they desist and earnestly repent.
(b) On witchcrafts. And we have said with regard to acts of witchcraft, casters of lots, and deeds which cause destruction, if someone is killed as a result and [the perpetrator] cannot deny it, he will be liable to forfeit his life.

If he wishes to deny it, and turns out to be guilty in the three-fold ordeal, he will spend 120 nights in prison. After that, his sons/male relatives may take him thence, give the King 120 shillings, recompense the [dead] man's sons/male relatives, and stand surety for him that he will desist from such acts in future.

Ecclesiastical

[*The concern of early Church authorities was largely that expressed by St Augustine, to condemn and eradicate remnants of pagan religious practice which were regarded as diabolical in origin and idolatrous in consequence. Penance for varying lengths of time is thus regarded and recommended as appropriate punishment for those convicted of using magic or, indeed, astrology. Succeeding Church Councils issued condemnations of both; and then at the end of the ninth century, Regino of Prüm (died 915) produced a handbook of canon law containing sections on magic and the related sciences. The well-known* Canon Episcopi, *which throws doubt on the claim by certain women that they rode out at night as followers of the pagan goddess Diana, comes from Book II of this manual. As well as suggesting that the ride is an illusion, however, it also observes that the various types of magic were actually invented by the Devil. So the text neatly illustrates the ambiguous attitude of the Church towards magic at this time. With the growth of concern over heresy from the twelfth century onwards, however, the Church began to see magic and heresy as two faces of the same coin, and thus to regard magical practitioners in a new and harsher light.*]

44 Dionysius Exiguus: *Canones* (6th century)

[*Scythian theologian, mathematician, and astronomer, floruit sixth century. Traditionally regarded as the inventor of the Christian calendar. He records the decrees of earlier Church Councils.*]

Canons of the Council of Ancyra. No. 23. Those who seek out readers of lots (*sortilegi*). Those who pursue auguries or divinations according to pagan usage, or invite people of that kind into their homes in order to seek responses to questions by means of the malefic art, or so that they may purify their homes, are to live under a five-year rule [of penance] according to the established rules of penance.

Canons of the Council of Laodicea. No. 26. *Exorcists who have not been ordained by a bishop.* Those who have not been ordained by a bishop cannot perform exorcisms either in churches or in private houses.

No. 35. *Those who worship angels.* Christians must not abandon God's Church and go and summon angels and make assemblies. They know perfectly well these things are forbidden by decree. Therefore if anyone is found devoting him or herself to this secret idolatry, let him or her be anathema, because he has deserted our Lord Jesus Christ, the Son of God, and handed himself over to idolatry.

No. 36. *Those who make use of enchanters and phylacteries, i.e. magical bindings.* Those who hold sacred offices, or are clerics, must not be magicians (*magi*) or enchanters (*incantatores*), or make phylacteries, which for some time have been proven to be chains for their souls; and we order that those who use them be expelled from the Church.

45 Council of Orléans (511)

No. 30. If any secular priest or monk believes that divination or prognostications should be regarded as authoritative, or that anyone should be encouraged to consult the lots falsely known as 'saints' lots', he is to be excommunicated along with those who believe in them.

46 Council of Auxerre (c.573–c.603)

No. 4. It is not permitted to pay attention to casters of lots (*sortilegi*) or prognostications (*auguria*), or to a diviner (*caragius*), or to the lots popularly known as 'saints' lots', or to lots made of wood or bread, unless the person does whatever he wants to do in the name of the Lord.

47 Council of Paris (829). Adapted

Section 69. There are undoubtedly perpetrators of various wickednesses, individuals whom the law of God has repudiated and condemns, and because of those various crimes and enormities the populace is scourged by famine and plague, the standing of the Church is weakened, and the kingdom exposed to danger. Although they have been adequately execrated in holy sermons, we have realised that it is necessary to require that people be forewarned against them in every respect by our admonition and exhortation, and spread far and wide the knowledge of their wickedness. There are also those who carry out various acts of pollution. Several people are guilty of these in very different ways with men and animals, whereby, in as much as they sin against nature, they commit a grave offence, provoking the incomparable affection of the most merciful Creator [to turn] to bitterness ...

There exist also other very pernicious evils which it cannot be doubted are remnants of heathen religious practice: such are magicians (*magi*), prophesiers (*arioli*), casters of lots (*sortilegi*), workers of poisonous magic (*venefici*), diviners (*divini*), those who pronounce incantations (*incantatores*), and interpreters of dreams (*somniatorum coniectores*). Divine law commands that they be punished irrevocably. [*Leviticus* 20.6–8] says, 'The soul which has turned to magicians and prophesiers and has fornicated with them, I shall turn my face against it and kill it from the midst of its people. Sanctify yourselves and be holy, because I am the Lord your God. Keep safe my commands and do them, because I am the Lord who sanctifies you,' and elsewhere, 'Do not permit magicians and prophesiers and workers of harmful magic to live on the earth.'[52]

Now, there is no doubt – and many people know this – that because of some tricks and illusions of the Devil, certain individuals' minds are so tainted by drinks intended to provoke love, by victuals, and by amulets tied about their person, that in most people's judgement they have become insane, seeing that they are not aware of their own behaviour which causes people to insult them. For they say that by their acts of harmful magic they can upset the air and send hail-storms, predict the future, take away fruit and milk and give them to others: and are said to accomplish innumerable things by such methods. When it may be discovered that they are people of this sort, whether men or women, they are to be chastised severely by the vigorous instruction of the Prince, since they are not afraid to serve the Devil by means of a crime which is both abominable and reckless ...

Consequently, all Christians must clearly understand these points and pay heed with the utmost seriousness in case they do such things by accident and thereby forfeit the other good deeds they do and thus cut themselves off from the kingdom of God.

[52] This may be an expansion of the Vulgate *Exodus* 22.18, 'You will not allow workers of harmful magic to live,' Englished by the Authorised Version as the famous precept, 'Thou shalt not suffer a witch to live.'

48 Pope Leo IV: *Letter to the Bishops of Britain* (848/9)

[*Benedictine monk, reigned 847–55. He was particularly occupied in asserting ecclesiastical authority against the Emperor Lothair, fortifying Rome against feared Saracen attack, and restoring discipline to the Church.*]

Concerning the search for divinations or acts of harmful magic (*maleficia*), We have what has been written in the sacred Canons, and quote it word for word as follows: 'Those who seek out divinations and follow the example of the heathen, or bring people of this kind into their homes in order to ask something or take vengeance on someone by means of the art of harmful magic, are to do penance for five years.'[53] Consequently, when it comes to things such as these, we decree that the various employments of lots whereby you separate everything out in your prognostications are nothing more than what the Council Fathers condemned – divinations and acts of harmful magic. For this reason, we want them condemned altogether; furthermore, we are unwilling that such people be called Christians, and we debar them under the interdict of a formal curse, so that they may be cut off [from the Church].

[53] Council of Ancyra (314), chapter 23. Compare the slightly different wording recorded by Dionysius Exiguus above.

49 Herard, Archbishop of Tournois: *Capitularia* (858)

Chapter 1, no. 3. The unfamiliar, strange names of angels and other sacred beings should not be said aloud. Workers of harmful magic (*malefici*), those who chant incantations, diviners, casters of lots (*sortilegi*), interpreters of dreams, those who cause storms, amulets to cure agues, women who work poisonous magic (*mulieres veneficae*), and women who fabricate various extraordinary phenomena, should be forbidden and subjected to public penance.

50 *Council of Worms* (May 868)

Chapter 42. *How those who are accused of a crime may clear themselves.* If a bishop or a priest has been charged with a criminal offence – that is, murder, adultery, theft, or the practice of harmful magic – he must celebrate Mass every day, say his private Mass in public, administer the sacrament, and show himself to be innocent of every charge against him. If he does not do this, he is to be considered excommunicate for a period of five years, as the ancient Canons have decreed.

51 Instructions about the punishment of workers of magic. Pope Benedict XII: *Letter,* 7 April 1338

[*French Cistercian, reigned 1334–42. One of his principal concerns was to reform undesirable practices among the clergy. This letter is addressed to Guillaume Lombard, Provost of the church of Barjols in the diocese of Fréjus.*]

We have observed, not without horror and detestation, that Katarina Andrieva of St Paul Lofrech, and Simona Ginota of Baigneaux, women belonging to the diocese of Viviers, were arrested there not long ago and referred to the Apostolic See because, stirred up by a devilish spirit, they gave themselves body and soul to this same devil by offering him an annual rent or render of corn to be paid at set times, and by the dreadful commission of certain other superstitious and damnable acts in word and deed with this same devil. Therefore, because We wish that things of this and a similar kind be uprooted from the territory of the faithful, and that the said women be straightened out by the file of justice[54] on account of their outrageous deeds, We command you at your discretion in the case of these women and of others, as it shall seem expedient to you for the more complete tracking down of the truth of this business, to make diligent attempts to get the truth from them with respect to the general points and the details; and if you find them guilty of the foresaid crimes, you are to take pains to punish and correct them, and impose penances upon them, as justice requires – but in a spirit of mercy, in as much as their contrition merits and you acknowledge their return to a rational frame of mind.

[54] That is, they are to be treated like pieces of metal which have acquired excrescences or distortions, and need to have these filed away by an expert craftsman.

52 Synod of Salamanca, 2 May 1451

[*Decision of Bishop Gonzalo de Vivero.*]

No. 14. Because We are informed that certain people belonging to our diocese and its villages, men as well as women, are not observing the Catholic faith as they should (fearing neither God nor the risk to their souls which are much more precious than their bodies), and go or venture to seek advice from lot-casters (*sorteros*), male and female witches (*fechizeros e fechizeras*), and female diviners (*adevinas*), who are servants of the Devil, seeking advice about their health and a cure for their illnesses, and asking about their business and other things; in consequence there is no doubt that any such people (i.e. those who go for the foresaid or any similar reasons, seek out, or consult the said lot-casters, workers of harmful magic [*maleficos*], witches, diviners, and enchanters [*encantadores*]), have incurred the penalty of greater excommunication for that same deed, in accordance with what has been established by a constitution of [Cardinal Vallisoleti in 1322].[55]

Therefore, since this is a very great sin and a type of heresy, in that it resembles the worship of idols according to the usual ill-considered and futile practice of the heathen and pagans, as written records tells us: and because it also stands condemned in canon and civil law: wishing to remove this error of the people who have been entrusted to Us, by following the said constitution of the said Cardinal, We order and ordain that no one, man or woman, from our diocese and bishopric, of any rank, dignity, or condition whatsoever, be rash enough to go or venture to ask or seek advice from the said lot-casters, workers of harmful magic, male and female witches, enchanters, and diviners, either by themselves or by sending others, or by letter, or by any other means whatsoever, in order to get someone or some persons to make charms (*fechizos*) or harmful spells (*malefiçios*) of any kind, on any pretext or excuse: or ask for such people, or seek remedy or advice about anything he or she may want done or taken care of, because these people are the Devil's slaves and do not possess the ability to give good advice, or provide a reliable, beneficial remedy, and it must also be presumed that such people are strangers to our holy faith and to the company of our holy Mother Church; and if any person or persons disobey or act against this holy instruction and ordinance, We desire that by this same action they fall under the said sentence of greater excommunication.

Furthermore, We command all ecclesiastics, priests, and chaplains of this city and our bishopric, by virtue of holy obedience, that on great feast days they publicly proclaim excommunicated by the said sentence of greater excommunication any of their male and female parishioners whom they know, in ways susceptible of proof, are considered and believed to be diviners, lot-casters, workers of harmful magic, male and female witches, or get and procure any harmful spells or works of harmful magic of any sort, or try to ask for advice; and any of their male and female parishioners who rent their houses to such people, allow them to live there, or show them kindness, or give them advice or assistance, in public or in private. Henceforth let them not be absolved or receive the benefit of Holy Church until they amend themselves by the repentance warranted by such a great sin, and therewith give evidence of our absolution or what We have power to do in such a case. Furthermore We command, on pain of excommunication, all the ecclesiastics, chaplains, and priests of the entire said bishopric, and all our other subjects, both clergy and secular, who know the persons guilty of the aforesaid sin, to inform and notify Us and our successors in our said diocese, so that We may denounce them, and have them denounced and publicly declared excommunicate before the people and their neighbours when the Hours are said each Sunday and on the Feast of Nine Lessons, so that [the people] may distance themselves from such a grave sin. If, in the meantime, any of the said workers of harmful magic, lot-casters, enchanters, male and female witches aforesaid be found guilty and die in their perfidy and malice, We order that they not be given church burial or receive any rite or benefit of Holy Church.

⁵⁵ Canon law stipulated two grades of excommunication: lesser, in which a person was deprived of the sacraments, and greater, in which he or she was entirely cut off from the Church and its members.

53   Condemnation of magicians in Lombardy. Pope Alexander VI: *Decretal* (1501)

[*Spanish Pope, reigned 1492–1503. During the 1490s, Pope Alexander faced a challenge from a Domincan friar, Girolamo Savonarola, who prophesied doom for a corrupt Church and preached a return to asceticism in private and public life. Unacceptable practices, therefore, were in Alexander's mind, for more than one reason. This decree is addressed to the inquisitor Brother Angelo di Verona.*]

Since We have heard that various persons of both sexes in Lombardy are providing a [public] service by means of incantations of various kinds and diabolical acts of superstition: causing many dreadful crimes by their acts of poisonous magic (*veneficia*) and fatuous practices; ruining people, beasts of burden, and fields; and introducing various moral lapses from which great scandals are arising: because of the pastoral duty entrusted to Us by reason of our high office, We have issued a decree to suppress crimes of this sort and, in as much as We can in company with God, to take measures to deal with the scandals and lapses aforesaid. We therefore commission and order you and also your successors in Lombardy, in whom We have full confidence in the Lord in these and other matters, to make diligent inquiry by yourselves (and in company with respectable, trustworthy people whom you may choose), against these persons of each sex, and to punish and suppress them, with justice as your method. So that you may be able the better to carry out this commission, We grant you by these presents full and entire authority against them, Apostolic decrees and ordinances, indults and ordinary concessions perhaps made for the time being, and anything else to the contrary, notwithstanding.

54   Qualified scepticism. Michael Italikos: *Letters* (mid 12th century)

[*Byzantine teacher of rhetoric and philosophy at Constantinople, where he also taught medicine. He died some time before 1157.*]

[31]. To Tziknoglos. My very dear brother, I am asking you about your most admirable sister. How is she, and did that man who was taking it upon himself to use the arts of magic accomplish anything – or rather, after he had done his business, did it help? Did he discover any solution for her stubborn illness? For my part, I have no hesitation in calling the illness a most savage beast; and if he has not yet begun to use his craft, I hope he does not begin, for Christian laws reject the use of such things.

My very dear friend, I have no doubts about this at all, and I know a lot about such things – indeed, not one of the people who are concerned with this burden knows as much. I have read a good many books about these things by Chaldaeans and Egyptians, Proclus the philosopher's tireless efforts concerning the sacred art which is also known as 'the art of magic', everything by the two Juliuses, Apollonius of Tyana and the most learned Africanus; and I have also extended my eagerness for such knowledge to the daft babbling of the old women of the crossroads,[56] and anything else going round the common people. But God knows I have gained nothing thereby which I may not tell other people, nor have I stood by patiently when I have seen anyone else doing something unutterable; and yet I am in possession of charms, binding-magic, and a good many useful symbols which contain unspoken commands, and cures for stinking viscera, and relief for swellings. But I have not acquired any of these for my own benefit, nor have I ever had any faith in them.

On the subject of your most admirable sister, however, know that I should myself have made use of one of these things described as 'marvellous' by the babblings of the Chaldaeans did I not know that all those who pay heed to such things are, one after the other, people of the most abominable kind, and that a just and proper reward awaits them after they die. So I asked one of them to do me a favour, and have discovered something to appease 'the beast', something handed down from one of the ancients skilled in the craft. I shall describe it to you when we next meet, because it would take up too much space were I to write it down. If that man has started to do what he promised – well, as you know, when you told me about him I rejected the idea at once and predicted that his help would be of no use at all. But because we are dealing with a woman, I have relaxed my standards a little. Let us hope that produces no immediate cries of grief! I should like to be told if anything useful comes out of this jugglery.

[56] I.e. professional diviners.

55 Reservations about magic. Barsanuphios: *Letters* (6th century)

[*Egyptian recluse, died c.545. His responses to questions, together with those of another recluse, John 'the Prophet', were gathered by an anonymous monk and published.*]

753. Question: When my animal is ill, is it unacceptable to use incantations to help it?
Answer: Incantations are forbidden by God. One really must not use them, because disobeying God's command means that one loses one's soul. So use the remedies and treatments of veterinary doctors, because that is not a sin. Sprinkle holy water on it, too.

755. Question: Since going to a diviner [*mantis*] is contrary to what God wants, if I see someone going to such a person at any time, isn't it my duty to tell him not to go?
Answer: If he is your friend in Christ, it is your duty to say to him, 'Brother, you are harming your soul and you are angering God who forbids this activity.' If you don't give him your speech, he will see [the diviner]. If he is a passer-by, you have no need to do anything unless he asks you about this matter, and in this case you should tell him the truth. If you don't do so, judgement will follow. For when Saul went to see the necromancer[57] and questioned his son Jonathan, he forbade him to go there and condemned him for doing so. If the person concerned is someone over whom you have authority, it is your moral duty to reprove him and correct him if he disobeys you.

[57] *Engastrymythos*, meaning 'ventriloquist'. This refers to a person taken over by a god who then proceeds speak through the human's mouth. The obvious example from Greek and Roman religious history is the Pythia, the priestess of Apollo at Delphi. The reference here is to the so-called 'witch of Endor', 1 *Kings* 28.7–25 (Vulgate), 1 *Samuel* 28.7–25 (AV). 'Witch' here is a misnomer, since the woman was asked for a prophecy and called up the ghost of Samuel to provide the answers Saul required.

56 Types of magical operation. Guillaume d'Auvergne: *De universo* (first half 13th century)

[*French theologian and Bishop of Paris. He died in 1249.*]

Second part, part 3, chapter 22, adapted. There are three types [of magical operation]. One type is done by nimble manual dexterity as, for example, moving things or transposing them from one place to another. This is popularly known as 'sleight of hand' or 'transference', and causes great astonishment until people find out how it is done. The second type consists of things which are merely apparent and not at all real, such as making objects disappear or appear. It includes a certain kind of lamp or light, such as the lamp made from wax and a snakeskin impregnated with sulphur. If its candle is lit in a place where there is no other light shining, instead of husks and rushes on the floor, separate stalks and separate rushes will be seen as snakes wriggling through the house. The reason for this is that a variation in colours caused by the powdered snakeskin will produce a green colour similar to that of the rushes and the stalks, and the movement of the flame will make them seem to jump about and wriggle ...

Now, I have told you elsewhere that after a slight, moderate infection of the instruments of sight, or of the imaginative faculty, the sufferer will think that everything is black or has a sharp point,[58] or that it is shaking and receding into the distance. Other deceptive tricks of this kind are very common, as is the juggling deceit [*praestigium*] whereby someone thinks his hand is a donkey's foot and therefore blushes for shame when he takes it out of his pocket. (Perhaps you remember reading about it in books of experiments.)[59] If this is done by technical skill or human dexterity, it is done without the assistance of evil spirits. Have no doubt it is done in the way I have described above, whether by using a lamp or sprinkling something on top of the hand. There is also a trick in which water or streams appear when actually there is no water unless something is given to the spectators, internally or externally. It does not seem possible that an optical illusion causes this kind of deceit to happen, and yet in books of experiments practitioners are urged to employ certain things which do not seem to have any power at all to induce this kind of apparition...

Now, here is the Devil's deception in operations of this kind: he encourages people to use therein things which have no power at all to bring about the intended result. I say they are employed for his service and worship, not to help the operation along or give it some support. For these things have no power whatsoever. But it is not inherently impossible in nature that some things are unable to exert their power against or over others as, for example, in the case of the diamond and the lodestone; for because of, and in the presence of the diamond, the lodestone is unable to draw iron to itself. (Mind you, it is perfectly possible to be of the opinion that this does not spring from the power of domination which a diamond has over a lodestone, but comes rather from the character of the lodestone which singles out the diamond and accords it precedence over itself; but when the diamond is taken away, the iron comes running to the lodestone.) ...

Even more extraordinary is what experimenters have put in their books about the snake – that it binds male and female workers of harmful magic [*malefici*], and male and female magicians [*magi*], so that when it is present, all their deceitful tricks [*praestigia*] cease working, and their incantations lose their power. They say the same of quicksilver, too, if it is enclosed between two knots of a reed. Now, the most extraordinary thing about these last two [examples] is that the snake does not seem to have power over malign spirits or over things which are used in incantations of this kind; and as for quicksilver, what power can it be thought to have whereby it restrains incantations and the deceits of evil spirits? ...

So you should give particular attention to this point: there are many secret, amazing powers in things, which we cannot put our finger on, such as the power of freshwater crabs to drive away moles from gardens and meadows in which they have been hung up (as experimenters tell us, with fewer than ten individuals denying they have such power). But why is it that the moles run away, since they do not see the crabs suspended from a nail, or detect them by one of the other senses, when they themselves are hidden deep in the earth? So I say that if experiments lead us to believe that the plant known as a 'peony' has great power against malign spirits which, according to demoniacs who wear it hanging round their neck, it puts to flight – if this is so, we should not find it improbable that a snake (which is, after all, a living creature), has the power to impede anything done by male or female workers of magic [*magici*]; and consequently when it comes to quicksilver whose innate qualities and ways of working are extensive and astonishing, intelligent people should not find it incredible that quicksilver has some power against malign spirits or over things which are employed in magical operations.

[58] *Acutus*. The word also means 'high-pitched' or 'shrill' when applied to sounds.
[59] A reference to *libri secretorum*, books which contained a mish-mash of recipes, formulae, and instructions on how to accomplish a wide variety of things – practical handbooks rather than revelations of esoterica.

57 Reservations about the worth of evidence relating to witchcraft. Ulrich Molitor: *De laniis*[60] *et phitonicis mulieribus* (1489)

[*Swiss jurisconsult, died in 1492. Molitor's little work is written in the form of a dialogue between Archduke Sigismund of Austria, Conrad Sturtzel, his secretary, and Ulrich Molitor himself.*]

Conrad: Common rumour has it that witches [*strige*] cause thunderstorms and hail- storms, and bring great damage to standing crops and to people; and certainly it has been found from confession made under torture that they have indeed done such things, and given a description of the way they have effected them.
Sigismund: I myself pay no heed to naked rumours. The common people are quick to follow gossip. But I shall not be satisfied by a confession obtained under torture, because fear of pain induces anyone to confess to something which does not exist or happen naturally. The truth is, we want to have a clear sight of anything we haven't seen with our own eyes by [relying upon] authority or conclusive reasoning, because a properly conducted argument bases its conclusions upon authority and reason...

Since we have been talking about perversion and disturbance of the elements, it is appropriate for us to ask if [witches] can inflict diseases on people, and especially on young children, and do them harm with the help of evil spirits.
Conrad: I have been told by a good many women how various diseases have happened to children lying in their cradles – one child's nose has taken on a distorted appearance, another's eye has been completely destroyed. When these accursed women were arrested, they maintained and acknowledged under torture it was because of the parents' spite that they had inflicted this kind of thing on the children with the help of evil spirits.
Sigismund: You have already heard [me say] I shall not be satisfied with confessions of such a kind, which have been wrung from people by fear.
The various harms and illnesses which are inflicted on adults and young children.
Sigismund: Can [witches] infect[61] a man living in the married state, and render him unable to have sexual intercourse?
Conrad: I have been witness to a number of good-looking colleagues who have exercised little or no power at all in intercourse. Indeed,

many were unable to know their own wives carnally, and maintained that this had happened to them because of an act of harmful magic [*maleficium*].

Sigismund: Oh, a good many men say a good many things!

Ulrich: Undoubtedly, the *Canons* agree on this point. They maintain that through acts of harmful magic it can happen that a man who is not frigid by nature is rendered incapable of sexual intercourse. Consequently, in the *Decretal* we have a particular chapter on those who are frigid and those who have been affected by acts of harmful magic (33, question 1, 'If through witches' [*sortiariae*]), in which Archbishop Hincmar of Rheims says: 'If God, who never makes an unjust decision, permits that intercourse does not take place because of witches and their maleficent arts practised in secret, according to the Devil's plan which he has made in advance, those to whom this happens should make a straightforward confession of all their sins to God and a priest with a contrite heart and in a spirit of humility.' Here is what the text [of the *Decretal*] says: 'By the Devil's fore-planning, intercourse does not take place and even though the *Canon* should be sufficient to put an end to this doubt – because the decisions of the *Canon* ought to have everyone's approval, as it says in the first chapter of the *Constitutions* – nevertheless, Doctors [of Theology] underline the point. Hence, St Thomas Aquinas in his *Sentences*, chapter 4, distinction 34, says: 'Because of an act of harmful magic, someone can be impotent with one woman and not with another.' Therefore Master Hostiensis[62] in his *Summa*, Book 4, rubric 17, 'Those who are frigid and have been subjected to harmful magic', said: 'Sometimes men are subjected to harmful magic [*maleficiantur*] in such a way as to render them through sorcery [*sortilegium*] impotent with all women save one. Sometimes, too, [a man] is so subjected to harmful magic that he cannot have sexual intercourse with his wife, but is able to do so with any other woman.'

Sigismund: These things trouble me because they are extraordinary. We are, after all, endowed by nature with the ability to have sexual intercourse, and for those of us who are not familiar with such things, it will certainly be a cause of astonishment that the Devil can impede the course of nature.

Ulrich: Yes, well, I myself, Ulrich, have been an ecclesiastical advocate at the law-court in Constanz for the past eighteen years, as indeed I still am, and I have had in my practice several cases of this kind of frigidity and harmful magic, in which women were coming before a judge and accusing their husbands of impotence.

Sigismund: So what was the decision in these cases?

Ulrich: The judges decided that the men so infected should present themselves to physicians sworn in before the court for this purpose, and submit themselves for medical examination.
Sigismund: What happened then?
Ulrich: A large number was examined by the sworn doctors of the court, and the doctors maintained that the men were not frigid by nature but had been subjected to harmful magic through sorcery.
Sigismund: What was the final decision [of the court] after this medical examination?
Ulrich: The judges ruled that the parties concerned must live together for a period of three years, during which they must try to have sexual intercourse. At the same time, they would be undertaking extensive fasts and giving generously to charity so that God, who is the founder of matrimony, might be pleased to take away the malefice which was afflicting them.
Do [witches] come to their feasts on the back of a wolf or on a pole which has been rubbed with grease? Do they eat and drink and talk together, and do they recognise each other?
Sigismund: I should be glad to hear your opinion on these points.
Ulrich: You know from what has been said before that sometimes when someone is asleep, and sometimes when he is awake, mental pictures may present themselves so forcibly that the person believes he is really and actually seeing them, or that he is causing them to happen in reality. You have also been told that sometimes the Devil brushes the surface of people's eyes and their other senses so that they maintain they are doing one thing or another. In order that you may understand the point I am making, I shall tell you an anecdote taken from the story of Saint Germain. It is said (anent our subject) that the saint was staying one night as a guest in a house, and after the main meal was over they started to lay the table again. Astonished, the saint asked his hosts for whom they were laying the table once more, and they said it was for the good men and women who come during the night. So St Germain decided to keep watch that night.

Lo and behold, he saw a large number of demons in the shape of men and women, coming to the table. Forestalling their departure, St Germain woke all the members of the household and asked if they recognised these individuals. He was told they were men and women who lived nearby. St Germain sent to each of their houses and lo! They were found in their beds. The saint then exorcised the demons who said they were malign spirits who used to trick people and make fun of them in this fashion. [*Other examples given.*]

Sigismund: What about the counter-argument which says that sometimes women who foretell the future [*phitonice mulieres*] believe they have set out for one place while actually they remain in their own house?

Ulrich: You have already been given examples of a person's frequently believing he is in one place when actually he isn't. So the point is well taken in *Canon Episcopi* 26, question 5, where it says: 'One should not forget to say that certain wicked women who have turned themselves round [to face] backwards behind Satan,[63] and have been led astray by illusions and apparitions produced evil spirits, believe and assert that they ride upon certain animals with Herodias and a numberless crowd of women, and cross over a wide-ranging area in the dead of a chosen night: or that they obey [Satan's] commands, as they do those of the Lady, and that on certain nights they are summoned to his service. If only these women had died alone in their treachery and had not dragged those they had initiated to the death which awaits people who do not keep the faith. For a very large number of people, deceived by this false view of things, believes it to be true, and by believing it stray from the correct faith.' This is what the text [*of the Canon*] says.

Sigismund: Can't everyone else ride and go from one place to another at night, as well as during the day? So what stops women of this kind [from doing the same]?

Ulrich: Oh, I am certainly not saying that this kind of woman cannot ride and go about perfectly well on a donkey, a horse, an ox, or a camel, the same as other people, and in a way which is entirely natural, too. But we are talking about *this* case which stretches beyond the normally accepted way people do things, in as much as people cannot usually cover ten or twenty miles in a single hour.

Sigismund: So, if they don't go from place to place and visit feasts, as was said in the *Canon*, how does it happen that people in other communities, whom [the women] have never seen before, recognise them?

Ulrich: The answer is clear from what I have already said. They perceive this because of images imprinted upon their minds or brought before their eyes by the agency of the Devil, and believe that they have recognised [them] because they have had the sensation of a physical reality.

Sigismund: How is it that women who work harmful magic [*maleficae mulieres*] maintain and believe that they are the ones who are doing such things as disturbing the air, summoning up storms, and inflicting illnesses on people?

Ulrich: Well, it has to be said they believe they do such things because they are stupid and deceive themselves by their own credulity.
Sigismund: In what way?
Ulrich: The Devil, you see, realises from the movement of the elements that a change in the air and storms are bound to happen, and so he will be able to foretell these more easily and more quickly than human beings can. Or when, with God's permission, some plague[64] or chastisement of sins is bound to fall upon the earth through the just decision of God, and the Devil is assigned by divine providence to carry out these punishments, then the Devil knows in advance that this plague/blow is going to happen. From that moment onwards, he interferes with the minds of harm-doing women of this kind. Sometimes he persuades them; sometimes he impels them into an act of retribution because of the spite which criminal women such as these harbour against a relative. He works upon them as though he were a teacher, instructing them how to summon up storms and disturbances in the air.
Sigismund: So what does he teach them, or how does he instruct them with the result that women of this kind summon up misfortunes and bring them to a successful conclusion by means of their harmful magic [*maleficium*]?
Ulrich: He adopts this course and teaches them to do something stupid and ridiculous, and something which has no relevance whatever to a real achievement of this nature.
Sigismund: But if it's stupid, why does he teach it to them? How comes it that after these women follow his instructions, such storms do approach and happen because they have willed it so?
Ulrich: Well now, look! The Devil foresees – either from the way nature and the elements are behaving, or because he has God's permission to do so – that a plague/blow is going to be imbedded in some country or other, and that he has been granted the power to make it happen, and that in consequence an event of this kind is going to take place. Nevertheless, so that this sort of criminal women may believe that they are causing such things to happen as a result of the Devil's teaching, the Devil instructs them that whenever they get flint-stones they should fling them behind their backs towards the west; sometimes they should throw sand from a rushing stream into the air; sometimes they should boil pigs' hairs in a jar; sometimes they should put logs or pieces of wood from one side of a trench to the other.[65] For the performance of these and other such nonsenses, the Devil imposes upon them all indiscriminately a particular day and hour, and these stupid women, having faith in the Devil's instruction,

do these and other things like them. So, after they have done them, there follow the storms, hail-storms, and other nuisances which the Devil knew beforehand were going to happen at this particular moment, as I said before; and these stupid, criminal women believe that these are the results of what they themselves have done, although their efforts cannot in fact produce a single drop of rain. Yet afterwards, these women honour the Devil and worship him and offer him sacrifices and large numbers of burnt-offerings, or something else. Who is so dim-witted as to be able to believe that from nonsense of this kind, and the stupid activity of women, a single huge blast of air may be set in motion (and the other elements, too), so that hailstorms and lightning flashes may be summoned up?

[60] The title means 'Those who tear flesh to shreds and women who utter prophecies'. Many modern references substitute '*lamiis*' (witches) for '*laniis*' (butchers), on the assumption that the latter was a misprint. Certainly the topics of the dialogue as a whole do not seem to warrant reference to violence of 'butchers' or 'renderers of flesh'. On the other hand, '*laniae*' is also used several times in the body of the text.

[61] *Inficere*. The verb also means 'to poison' or 'to impregnate with some substance', and so it suggests the witch has given him something to eat or drink, or has smeared something on his skin or clothing. This would make the witch specifically 'a worker of poisonous magic', *veneficus/venefica*.

[62] Henry of Susa (c.1200–71). He was called '[H]ostiensis' because he became Cardinal of Ostia in 1262. His *Summa aurea* (1253) presented its readers with a masterly integration of Roman and canon law.

[63] An apparent reference to witches' riding backwards upon a creature through the air on their way to a Sabbat. This is frequently depicted in art.

[64] *Plaga*. The word also means 'heavy blow' or 'open wound'.

[65] Or 'from one bank of a river to the other', but 'trench' seems to be somewhat more plausible in this context.

58 Proposed punishments for those found guilty of practising harmful magic in Catalonia. Anthoni de Balcebre: Document relating to witches in the Àneu Valley (1424)

[*On 26 June 1424 Anthoni de Balcebre, judge of the County of Pallars, submitted a set of proposals to Arnau Roger, Count of Pallars and other leading men of the Àneu Valley.*]

In the said valley there have been enormous crimes committed against God and the said valley: namely, that people go at night with the witches to the Devil and accept him as their lord, pay him homage, forsake the Lord God before night falls, take children from their mothers' sides and kill them by giving them *gatirnons* or *buxols*,[66] and give them poisons in various ways. All these crimes appear in the confessions of the accused themselves. In the face of these enormous crimes, measures need to be taken. The very honourable, magnificent, and eminent Master Arnau Roger, by the grace of God, Count of Pallars, summoned and assembled a judicial conference in the Castle of Valencia in the Àneu Valley. The following were also summoned for that conference: Arnalot of Miranda, Arnau of Sentolària, Guillem of Borén, Arnalot Moga from the court of the said valley, Arnalot of Mambilia of Àrreu, Guillem Moga, Ramon Tortura of València, Bernat of Guillamó of Sacalarre, and Ramon Jutglar of Son, and Pere of Perves of Sorpe. We shall speak about these crimes with the said Count. We shall make a schedule or schedules of the forementioned crimes and, if need be, make others while correcting and interpreting and perhaps rectifying some of those already written. The abovenamed, after taking counsel and after deliberation with the Count, will order and formulate the schedules as follows:

First, we establish and command that if henceforth a man or woman from the said valley be found going with witches at night to the Devil, paying him homage, accepting him as Lord, forsaking the name of God, pulling out hair or killing infants by day or night, giving them gatirnons or buxols and feeding them poisons: the men or women who commit these crimes shall lose their life and all their possessions, including land and furniture, all of which will be confiscated by the Count. The accused are to be executed as follows: they are to be put in a sack which will then be tied tightly and fastened to the tail of an animal. The accused will then be dragged to the place of execution where they will be burned to ashes.

(This pleases the leading men.)

Likewise, we establish and command that if the accused has not confessed, but actually did go to pay homage to the Devil and did forsake the name of God, and did accept the Devil as lord, he or she is to lose his life and possessions as laid out in the first schedule.

(This pleases the leading men.)

Likewise, we establish and command that if the accused confesses that he or she merely gave gatirnons and committed none of the other offences contained in the first schedule, he or she is to lose all his possessions including land and furniture, and may be sentenced to death according to the judgement of the Count and the court.

(This pleases the leading men.)

Likewise, we establish and command that if the accused confesses that he or she simply administered poisonous substances, but does not confess to the other crimes, even if it is not proven that the accused actually did administer poison, he or she is still to be executed by burning and his or her possessions are to be confiscated; and if it is the case that those who received the poison do not die therefrom, the accused are still to be executed with loss of all possessions, as if the victim had died.

(This pleases the leading men.)

Likewise, we establish and command that if any man or woman put poison under the door or in the keyhole of someone's house, or uses other acts of harmful magic to injure those in the house, he or she is to receive the death sentence, according to the judgement of the court, along with confiscation of all possessions.

(This pleases the leading men.)

Likewise, we establish and command that if any man or woman use a [magical] ligature on any other man or woman in order to impede or disturb a marriage so that the husband cannot have sexual intercourse with his wife: those who employ such a ligature or act of harmful magic shall be taken through the village and lose half his or her tongue without mercy.

(This pleases the leading men.)

[66] Both words are unusual. *Gatirnons* seems to be derived from "gatir" = to gobble up, devour, and may refer to pieces of meat taken off the bone. *Buxols* does not seem to appear in any other passage and both its etymology and its meaning are obscure.

Interpreting and Manipulating the Universe

Astrology

[*Astrology is a collection of complex disciplines involving a high order of mathematical ability –* hence mathematicus *means 'astrologer' rather than simply 'mathematician' – and seeks to draw logical conclusions from the observation of multiple celestial phenomena. Noting, for example, such unmistakable facts as the moon's effect on the tidal movements of the sea, encouraged astrologers to propose that the constant changes of the position of the planets in relation to each other and to the earth also had effects on everything below the moon's orbit, partly, at least, because the earth was unmoving and therefore incapable of avoiding any influences pouring down upon it. Even today, some of our vocabulary reflects this point of view. Influenza is an illness caused by unfavourable planetary influence, that is 'flowing upon or into'; a disaster is a malign star or planet; a lunatic is someone suffering under a hostile aspect of the moon and people are described as jovial, mercurial, or saturnine because Jupiter or Mercury or Saturn have affected their temperament or complexion.*

Only seven planets were recognised at this time – Mercury, Venus, Sun, Moon, Mars, Jupiter, and Saturn – and these moved around the earth through an imaginary belt known as the zodiac which was divided into twelve arcs, each of 30°. These arcs were allotted twelve signs – Aries, Taurus, Gemini, Cancer, Leo, Virgo, Libra, Scorpio, Sagittarius, Capricorn, Aquarius, Pisces – which actually refer, not to the zodiacal arcs or 'houses', but to twelve constellations through which the Sun passes during the twelve months of the year. A horoscope is a chart depicting the heavens at a given moment – let us say, the moment of birth – and therefore shows the interrelationship of the planets at that time. This relationship can then be interpreted, rather as though it were an individual diagnostic chart from which a doctor is able to say what illness is affecting a patient and so what cure or amelioration will be most effective.

Various branches of astrology dealt with somewhat different situations: genethliacal astrology, *which casts and interprets horoscopes for individuals based on the moment of birth;* horary astrology, *which casts a chart for the moment at which a particular question is asked and then interprets the chart in answer to that question;* judicial astrology, *which seeks to interpret the influences of the celestial bodies upon human affairs; and* natural astrology, *which calculates and foretells natural phenomena such as tides, eclipses, and so forth.*

Astrological techniques were inherited from the Greeks and Romans. Here, the key name is that of Ptolemy, a second-century AD Greek from Alexandria in Egypt, whose Almagest and Tetrabiblos were the great astronomical and astrological text books for the following thirteen centuries. The sophisticated mathematics of the former and the insistence of the latter that the astrologer must be an expert astronomer so that he can know the place and time of any configuration of the planets, not only enabled astrologers to produce more accurate and so more reliable horoscopes, but also provided a subtle defence of the discipline itself. During the 12th century, the discovery of 'new' Greek and Latin astrological texts in the Arab world, and the translation into Latin of the works of some of the great Arab astrologers produced further interest and further sophistication – so much so, indeed, that one might almost call the astrology of the High Middle Ages a Latinised Arab art.

Not everyone, however, approved or found it useful. St Augustine condemned it because it appeared to deprive human beings of free will. 'One should not exclude from this type of deadly superstition those who, because they pay attention to the day on which the person was born, are called genethliaci (or mathematici, as they are popularly known these days). For although they seek out the actual position of the stars at a person's birth, and sometimes even get it right, because they use that information to predict what we are going to do, or the outcome of our actions, they are making a grave mistake and are selling people who do not understand these things into wretched slavery. When a free man goes to an astrologer (mathematicus) of this kind, he gives him money in order to come away as the slave of Mars or Venus or, rather, of all the stars' (De Doctrina Christiana 2.21.32). This kind of fatalism, he said, provides the perfect excuse for anyone to blame his or her sins on fate. 'Everywhere people exclaim, "If it had not been the will of God, I should not have done it. Tell me what I can do to resist my destiny" ' (Enarrationes in Psalmos 58.1). So whenever St Augustine came across books on astrology, he had them burned. St Thomas Aquinas was broadly in agreement. 'No foreknowledge of the future can be had from scrutiny of the stars', he wrote, 'except that in which effects are known in advance from [natural] causes'. But, as with magic, compromise took over from disapproval in the realities of everyday life, because the urge to know the future was greater than the impulse to dismiss the art's techniques.]

1 The planets and their houses at the creation.
Pseudo-Bede: *De mundi celestis terrestrisque constitutione* (second half 12th century)

In the beginning of the world the Moon was in Cancer. Although she always portends good things by means of her relationship with other stars, if she has the Sun in Cancer with her, she particularly pours out increase and fattening of flesh to the highest degree, as is obvious in summer which abounds with flowers. But [in the beginning of the world] the Sun was found in Leo, and in this sign he marks his powers by dryness and heat. This is why the dog-days are hotter than others; the Sun is showing himself in his own house. (The dog-days are so called from the 'Dog Star' into which the Sun is entering at the time.) Mercury, since it is the lowest of all [the planets], achieved the first election [*favourable conjunction*], and elected Gemini from [the houses] preceding Cancer, and Virgo from those which come after Leo, for this reason – so that there it might portend, as a principal (not an accessory), whatever it might wish to do. If, however, another planet had entered its house to seek lodging there, Mercury would say it was willing to defer to that planet in colour and effect. Since Venus is in the next position, she elected Taurus from the preceding houses and Libra from those following, and did so for the same reason, so that she might reveal her effects in those signs. But if an evil planet were to enter therein, she would want to oppose it and diminish its power by means of her own favourable influence. If she encountered Mercury in particular, she would want to hasten her favourable effects. Although she portends a great deal of good in her relationship with other stars, she offers especially a most delightful pledge for a happy marriage. [In order to portend its effects to best advantage], Mars too elected Aries and Scorpio wherein it portends very great enmity, and indicates the scorching heat of war in particular. Jupiter elected Pisces and Sagittarius. His effect is modified by hostile planets and increased by favourable. When he is with Mercury, he hastens the indications of his own benevolence, and he arranges a happy outcome for kingdoms. Saturn obtained two houses next to each other, Aquarius and Capricorn. With good planets, he is quite gentle: with bad, he is rather severe. When he is with Mercury, he is rather quick to be cruel, and among evil figures it abounds with coldness and excessive harshness.

2 Interpreting celestial phenomena. Giovanni Villani: *Croniche Fiorentine* (early 14th century)

5.20. On 22 June 1192 the whole face of the sun was darkened. This lasted from a little after three until nine. According to what learned astrologers said, this was a sign that something very new was going to happen in the Christian community.

6.27. On 3 June 1238 there was a total eclipse of the sun from about the ninth hour. It lasted a good many hours, turned day into night, and obscured the stars. Consequently many people, not knowing how the sun and the other planets behave, were very astonished. Because of this unaccustomed event, many men and women in Florence turned to confession and penance through great dread and fear. It was said by astrologers that this darkness announced the death of Pope Gregory who died the following year,[1] the overthrow and overshadowing suffered by the Church under the Emperor Frederick, and great suffering for Christians, as indeed followed.

8.48. In September 1301 there appeared in the sky a comet trailing great streams of smoke. It appeared in the evening, towards the west, and lasted until January. Learned astrologers said that it signified future dangers and damage to the province of Italy and the city of Florence. This was especially so because the planets Saturn and Mars were twice in conjunction, in January and in May, in the sign Leo: and the moon was darkened in January, likewise in Leo which is assigned to the province of Italy[2] ... They particularly noted that this comet signified the arrival of Charles de Valois who was the cause of many rebellions in the province of Italy and in our city of Florence.

[1] Gregory IX. He actually died in 1241.
[2] As its particular sign of the zodiac. Countries, districts, and cities, as well as people were subject to the influence of individual planets.

---

3 Astrology and free will. Albertus Magnus: *Speculum astronomiae* (c.1260)

[*German Dominican, c.1200–80). One of the great scholars of his time. He published extensive paraphrases of works by Aristotle as well as works of his own. Because of his fame, he later had many treatises attributed to him. The authorship of the* Speculum *has been the subject of much controversy, but the most recent authoritative scholarship seems to have established that it actually was written by Albertus himself, although perhaps with some collaboration.*]

Chapter 14. Now I come to interrogations and those questions which deal with the present, and [whose answers] do not appear to involve doubt, such as inquiry about someone who is absent, is he alive or dead? or about rumours, are they true or false? and a letter you have received from someone or other, has it come from (let us say) a King or from someone else? and a woman we know has given birth, is her child male or female? and a man who claims to practise alchemy, is he a genuine practitioner? Whether the answers to such things are true or not is determined in part by the nature of things, and it is not in the least extraordinary if they are signified by way of the sky.

Those questions relating to the future, however, naturally involve an element of doubt and we do not need to ask questions about things which are inevitable or impossible. Some questions about what may happen in the future carry a greater doubt than others, or those which are about things completely subject to free will. Some things are possible and future, and yet a person's free will cannot stop them from happening. For example, a question about the price of corn: will it be high or low this year (although, to be sure, this can be discerned from the cycle of the year)? Or: will someone enrich himself by his skill in alchemy, or from commerce? Or: will an individual obtain this or that office in Church or state? Things of this kind befall a person according to what is signified in his or her birth horoscope ...

There are two types of questions about things which are future and possible, and which are subject to free will. There are questions of fact: what will happen in regard to so-and-so or such-and-such? There are questions asking for advice: which is better for me to do, this or that? Questions asking for advice do not nullify free will, but rather steer and direct it as, for example, a question about a business dealing, do I benefit thereby or not? Or: which of two things is better for me to buy? Or: concerning a journey I intend to make, is it better for me to go or put it off? To argue against such things will be to argue against free will rather than for it, because the need to seek advice and do business is one of the more pressing *conditions*. To determine how questions of fact can co-exist with free will, however, is very difficult. For example, a question about a large sum of money the questioner is seeking, will the other person give it to him or not? In this case, if it has been signified a thousand times that he will *not* give, he will nevertheless be *able* to give it; and likewise, if it has been signified he *will* give, he will always be able *not* to give it, otherwise he would not be in possession of the freedom to choose; and no astrologer will have made the dogmatic statement, 'he will give', only that 'according to the horoscope made at the time of the inquiry, it is signified that he will give.' There still remains the question about what is signified – will it happen? For if it is not going to happen, the horoscope reading is wrong. But if it *is* going to happen, therefore it cannot *not* happen, or the consequence will not be a matter of chance. For with respect to that which is going to happen conditionally, and about which it is true to say it is going to happen, before it actually does happen, it is always possible that it does happen or that it does not. But when it does happen, it can no longer not happen. Thus, it can accurately be said that something *is* white now and that it *was* white before, but it is a non sequitur to say that it is *going to be* white. Therefore when it *was* white previously, it could not *not* be white; and yet at the same time, since it cannot *not* be so, it *is* white. Everything is contingent, whether it had its origins in more things or fewer or both. Before it exists, it can always exist or not exist, as I have said, although certain things do not have those potentialities in equal measure. But when it does exist, it then returns to the nature of something inevitable, not because it was inevitable before but because, when it does exist, it exists inevitably ...

With respect to the things God does through the agency of the sky, a meaningful sign in the sky is nothing other than divine providence;[3] and when it comes to those things among which we have pride of place, there is also nothing to prevent the sky's containing, not the cause, but a meaningful sign. For when someone is faced by a dilemma offering various possibilities, God knows from eternity which one he or she is likely to choose. Consequently He has been able to signify (if such has been his wish), in the Book of the Universe, meaning the sky, what it is He knew; and if He has done so, it is then determined that free will and divine providence are completely compatible with the astrological signification at the time of the question. So if it is not possible to deny the fact that divine providence is compatible with free will, neither will it be denied that the answers given during the inquiries are compatible therewith.

[3] Bearing in mind the literal meaning of *providentia* = foresight.

4 Astrology and religion. Albertus Magnus: *Speculum astronomie* (c.1260)

Chapter 12. You will find elegantly expressed in Albumasar a testimony of faith and eternal life which is not gained except by faith.

It is in his sixth tractate, section 26, where he explains why the ninth house is the house of faith.

'The ninth house is also called the House of Pilgrimage, of the Journey of Faith and of Good Works, because of its reversion in the direction of Jupiter,' etc. Further on he says, 'Jupiter and Venus are [the planets] of good luck, or two types, one referring to luck in this world, the other to luck in the next. Luck in the next world is more deserving than luck in this – something which is a matter of faith. Now, because Jupiter represents greater fortune than does Venus, it has acquired a signification with regard to faith (through which one looks for the more deserving luck of the next world); and Venus has acquired a signification with regard to the fortunes of this world which derive from games, joy, and happiness.'

So what merit is there in his book which deals with these things? But we must also ask, what merit is there if he wrote at the start of it that the birth of Jesus Christ by the Virgin was depicted in the sky, with an express mention of [Jesus's] name by the angel of the annunciation? For in the sixth tractate, section 1, in the chapter entitled 'The ascension of images', he says, 'The images which ascend with the Virgin appear to do so in her first aspect, that of the young virgin called *celchuis dorastal*. She is a beautiful, decorous, pure virgin with luxuriant hair and a beautiful face. She has in her hand two ears of corn, and is sitting on a canopied chair. She is giving suck to a child, feeding him with milk, in the place called *Abrie*. Certain people call the Christ child "Jesus" which, in Arabic, is *eice*. There ascends with her a man sitting on the same chair, and there ascends with her the planet of the Virgin.'

Nowadays we know that the Lord Jesus Christ was born under the ascendant of this part of the sky (i.e. Virgo), and that the amount of the orbit of the eighth sphere at the time of the Nativity, which had to be subtracted from the position of the planets found in the astrological tables of that time was, according to the most reliable calculation, 8 degrees, 37 minutes, 2 seconds. This was not because the most desired of children, who had created all the stars themselves, was lying underneath the orbits of the stars or was subject to their determination, but because (since He stretched out the sky like a parchment, forming the book of the universe, and disdained to make something which was incomplete) he did not wish [his book] to be without its letters and those things which are written in the book of eternity in accordance with providence. This was the most felicitous thing before [Christ] was born of the Virgin, and therefore it was through this that intimation was given to humankind of a man both natural and real who was not born according to nature – not because the figure in the sky was the cause of his being born, but rather a signification of his birth; or (to be more accurate), He himself was the cause whereby the manner of his extraordinary nativity was to be signified in the sky.

5   Jesus in the stars. Hermann of Carinthia: *De Essentiis* (1143)

[*Scholar and translator, especially from Arabic. Floruit 1138/43. He concentrated particularly on works of geometry, astronomy, and astrology, and was an important figure in the transmission of Arabic learning to the west.* De Essentiis *is his own work of philosophy, a discussion of the fundamental elements of creation.*]

Book 1(59r.F-G). [*The truth about Jesus Christ's divinity has been revealed clearly enough, even for non-Christians.*] Abu Ma'shar includes in his treatise on astrology a point taken from the Persian astrologers Hermes and Astalius. In my translation of that same book, this appears as follows: 'In the first decan of Virgo appears a young girl. In the Persian text, this is SECLIOS DARDAMA, which in Arabic becomes ADRE NEDEFA, and we understand it to mean "spotless virgin". She is seated on a golden throne,[4] holding in her hand two ears of corn, and is suckling a child and feeding him with milk. [She appears] in a region whose name is *Hebraea*, and the child has been given the name *Jesus*.'

I think the Magi read this passage, saw his star, and realised who he was. This in particular demonstrates the blindness of the Jews, since the truth of Jesus Christ was signified in advance both in the contemplation of nature and in the procession of the ages, to a people one might go so far as to call ignorant. There can be no doubt the astrologer saw the whole situation quite plainly. How extraordinary that he was able to announce something he saw would happen beyond the natural course of events!

[4]   Reading *aureatum* for *auleatum*.

6   Planetary powers seen in natural objects. Pseudo-al Majriti: *Ghayat al-hakim* [*Picatrix*] (mid 15th century)

[*The genuine al-Majriti was a Spanish Muslim scholar who was born in Madrid and later moved to Cordoba. His special interest lay in mathematics.*

He died in c.1004/7. Picatrix *is attributed to him. Its original title,* Ghayat al-Hakin fi'l-Sihr *means 'The Goal of the Learned in Magic'. It deals with talismans, amulets, and astrology, and its appearance stimulated debates in c.1300 among scholars over the use of therapeutic amulets.*]

3.1. Here I shall speak more seriously about the effects and powers each separate planet has in itself with respect to the effects and special capabilities of necromancy.

Let me begin with Saturn. SATURN is the origin of the powers of retention, and it can be seen in abstruse branches of learning, in those dealing with the law, in seeking the causes and roots of things and their effects, in speaking wonders, and in knowing the profound, secret properties [of things]. Among languages, it has a particular relationship with Hebrew and Chaldee; among the external parts of the body: with the right ear, and with the internal, the spleen – the origin of melancholia which conjoins every part of the body; among laws: it is associated with those of the Jews; among cloths: all those which are black; among technical skills: working the earth, ploughing, digging, extracting minerals and working them, and the building trade; among tastes: things which have a bad taste; among places: black mountains, dark streams, deeply dug wells, and desert places; among stones: the *aliaza*, and all black stones; among metals: lead, iron, and all those which are black and stinking; among trees: elders, oaks, carobs, palms, and vines; among plants: cumin, rue, onions, and any plant which has very large leaves; among spices: aloe, myrrh, and similar things such as white lead and the colocynth [*bitter-apple*]; among smells: cassia and storax especially; among animals: black camels, pigs, monkeys, bears, dogs, and cats; among birds: all those with long necks and a loud voice, such as cranes, ostriches, the *duga*, and the crow, and all living things which grow underground, and all tiny, dead, stinking animals; and among colours: any shade of black and any spotted colour.

JUPITER is the origin of the power of increasing in size, and it can be seen in laws and legality, in the branches of knowledge which deal with legal proceedings, quick-wittedness in getting petitions granted, reparations, and the retention of property. It also keeps one safe from fatal illnesses. It is associated with wisdom, philosophy, and the interpretation of dreams. Among languages, it is associated with Greek; among the external parts of the body, with the left ear and among the interior, with the liver whereby temperaments and the humours are purified; among laws: unity; among cloths: those which are white and valuable. Among skills to be exercised and not to be exercised: giving orders, putting right the law and pieces of merchandise which are elegant and highly polished; among tastes: things which are sweet; among places: oratories and all well-lit, clean, sacred places; among stones: the emerald and all white and crocus-coloured stones, such as crystal and any shiny, white stone which is regarded as precious. Among metals: tin and tutty [*zinc oxide*]; among trees: those which bear nuts, (especially hazel nuts), pines, pistachios, and all those which are fruitful and bear fruit and bark; among plants: white mint and all those which are fruitful and have a good smell; among spices: crocus, yellow sandal, moss, camphor, amber, and mace; among living creatures: all animals which have a handsome appearance and are classified as creatures whose appearance usually makes them suitable as sacrifices, and all animals which are inoffensive, smooth, and glossy, such as camels, wethers, stags, and gazelles. Among birds: any bird which is pleasing to look at and brightly coloured, such as peacocks, cockerels, mountain doves, and quails; among tiny living things: those which are useful, such as silk-worms and the like; and among colours: red inclining to white.

MARS is the origin of the power of attraction, and it can be seen in the branches of learning which deal with nature, surgery, the care of animals, extracting teeth, letting blood, and circumcising. Among languages, it has a special relationship with Persian; among external parts of the body, with the right nostril, and among the internal, with secretion from the liver whence bile and heat descend, the impulse to anger and battles. Among laws: those dealing with heretics and the revision of a single law; among cloths: linen, hare-skins, and dappled skins; among technical skills: forging iron, making weapons of war, and theft; among tastes: hot, dry, and bitter; among places: army camps, strong defensible places, battle-fields, places wherein fire is kindled, animals have their heads cut off, and wolves, bears, and wild beasts congregate, and places where judicial sentences are carried out. Among stones: *alaquech* and all dark red stones; among metals: *azernech* (that is, the red colouring matter of gold), sulphur, *naft*, glass, and red copper; among trees: any which is naturally hot, such as the pepper, pine, scammony, cumin, cochineal, spurge laurel, euphorbia, geranium, and trees which provide good kindling. Among spices: all those whose constituent parts do harm and kill anyone who eats them, because of the surpassing heat they have in them; among smells: red sandalwood; among living creatures: red camels and all animals which have big red teeth, wild animals, and animals which cause damage; among small animals: those which do harm, such as scorpions, mice, and the like; and among colours: red in particular.

THE SUN is truly the light of the world whereby the world is governed, and it is the origin of the power of generation. It can be seen in philosophy, auguries, and the interpretation of judicial decisions. Among languages, it has a special relationship with French, and one also finds it partnering Mercury in a relationship with Greek. Among the external parts of the body, with the eyes, and among the internal, with the heart which rules over the various parts of the body and is the source of heat, granting life to the whole body. Among laws: the law of non-Christians and those who call upon the planetary spirits; among cloths: those which are valuable and thick, embroidered with gold; among tastes: those which are concentrated and sweet; among places: great, royal, beautiful cities in which kings live, and places which are situated in a lofty position and are prizeworthy. Among stones: the ruby and *largonza*; among metals: gold; among trees: those which are tall and beautiful, such as tall, well-sited palms; among plants: the crocus and the rose. It also partners Saturn in emmer-wheat, cereal grain, and olives. Among spices: aloe wood, sandalwood, lac, and all spices whose constituent parts are hot and pungent; among smells: the best aloe wood; among beasts: those which have value and are brave such as a human being, cattle, horses, camels, rams, cows, and any animal which is big, strong, and powerful. Among birds: those which usually belong to kings, such as hawks, falcons, and eagles. It partners Mars in peacocks; it also has power over large snakes, and shares bears with Mars. Among colours: it has a particular relationship with the appropriate shade of red, and with golden-coloured crocus.

VENUS is the origin of things which have a strong taste. She can be seen in grammar, and the art of poetic metres, sounds, and short songs. Among languages, she has a particular relationship with Arabic; among the external parts of the body, with the right nostril, and among the internal, with the vagina, the channel from which semen is ejaculated, and the stomach whence proceeds the power and savour attached to eating and drinking. Among laws: with the law of the Saracens; among cloths: all those which are dyed or painted; among technical skills: all those connected with painting and drawing, the sale of pleasant-smelling spices, playing musical instruments in such a way that they are good to listen to, singing, dancing, and making strings for musical instruments. Among tastes: any which are sweet and taste good; among places: those which are unhealthy, places wherein people are accustomed to sleep, and in which people dance, places of laughter where people sing and make a noise, places of ladies and comely women, as well as places where eating and drinking take place. Among stones: pearls; among minerals: lapis lazuli and *almartach*; among plants: all those which have a good smell, such as the crocus and *arhenda*, roses and all flowers which have a good smell and taste, and are pleasant to look at; among spices: balsam and the wholesome grains of *juleb* which are very fragrant, musk, and amber; among living creatures: women, camels, those animals which are rather beautiful, and all animals which are beautiful and physically well-proportioned, such as *alguazels*, cattle, *algazels*, and hares; among birds: all those which are beautiful and shapely and have a good singing voice, such as partridges, larks, and the like. Among tiny creatures: those which are brightly coloured and pretty; among colours: the blue of the sky, and the colour of gold shading a little towards green.

MERCURY is the origin of the power of understanding. It can be seen in the process of learning [different] branches of knowledge, the arts of reasoning, dialectic, grammar, philosophy, geometry, astronomy [*i.e. astrology*] along with its determinations, geomancy, the *ars notoria*,[5] the interpretation of birds according to the way they chatter, interpretation of the Turkish languages and those of other peoples. Among the external parts of the human body, it has a special relationship with the tongue, and among the internal, with the brain and the heart whence emanate the faculty of comprehension, the powers whereby beings are arranged in order, and the memory of things concerned with sensory perception. Among laws: anything illegal, inquiries into what laws are for, special regard for the laws of the philosophers and those which deal with sensation; among cloths: linen; among technical skills: those of predicting, versifying, carpentry, geometry, explaining dreams, tracing outlines, drawing shapes, and any technical skill which uses a minutely thorough, logical ingenuity; among tastes: bitterness; among places: choosing where a home should be, and places in which precise workmanship is done, the sources of waters, streams, lakes, and wells; among stones: all those which have been shaped and engraved; among minerals: quicksilver, and all those which are found in high places and worked in elevated spots; among plants: reed, silk, linen, pepper, any tree with a sharp taste, such as those which consist of gum; among things which have a pleasant fragrance, those with medicinal and caring properties, such as ginger, spikenard, and the like; among living creatures: human beings, small camels, *azebas*, *rumas*, monkeys, wolves, and all animals which are fast jumpers and runners and feed on every kind of wild beast by stealth. Among birds: those which are nimble in flight, which apparently do everything using their senses and their intelligence, and which have pleasant voices; among tiny creatures: those which move nimbly, such as ants and the like; and among colours, sky-blue and a slight mixture of different colours.

THE MOON is the planet which receives the powers of plants and pours them upon the world. She is the origin of power in nature. She can be seen in geometry and arithmetic, in the weight and capacity of waters when they are gathered together, in the profound branches of knowledge – necromancy, medicine, and investigations into both these and antiquity. Among languages, she has a special relationship with German; among the external parts of a person's body, with the left eye, and among the internal, with the lung whence comes breathing. Among laws: [those dealing with] praying to idols and images; among cloths: animal skins and towelling; among technical skills: polishing, selling skins, making coins, and sailing; among tastes: things which lack taste, such as water; among stones: seed pearls; among metals: silver, and those which are white in substance; among trees: sweet flag, reeds, any tree which is white and smells good, anything growing in the earth whose stalks do not grow vertical, all very small plants, all cabbages, lettuces, and the like, and all pasture. Among places: sources of water, lakes, marshes, places with snow and water of any sort; among spices: those which look after the early stages [of an illness] and those which are medicinal, such as cinnamon, ginger, pepper and the like; among living creatures: those which grub around and are of a reddish hue, mules, donkeys, cows, and hares; among birds: any which are nimble in their movements, all animals born in the air and living therein, and all water-birds which are white in colour. The moon also has a special relationship with white snakes; and among colours, with a colour made up of crocus and red.

[5] A magic technique which seeks knowledge from God by the use of invocation of angels, characters, signs, and prayers. It was particularly popular during the Middle Ages, and books dealing with it often ascribed its origins to Solomon.

7 Human character in relation to Mars and Venus.
Anon.: *Ovid Moralisé* (early 14th century)

Book 4. 1488–1528 (On Ovid: *Metamorphoses* 4.169–89). Mars is a planet which wanders, full of a choleric disposition. He is dry and burning. From this, legend quite rightly depicts him as master-god of battle, and as harmful and ruinous if he is predominant [in the horoscopes of] those who are bold, those who are undisciplined, and those who are prone to anger.

Venus is a peaceable planet, moist, warm, of good disposition, full of grace and good will. Those in whom the blood predominates, and who are moist and warm because the humour stinks on account of the heat, desire the work of lust, if they are naturally given to love. They are also gentle and kind and courteous. Consequently, those who are lustful are like Venus in their behaviour. She is called 'goddess of [more than one] love'.

When Mars travels through the sky at the lowest point of his orbit, and Venus is at the highest point of hers, if there is nothing in between which parts or separates them, Venus becomes bad, loses her graciousness, and her customary humour. All this can be seen as a result of the sun which reveals them.

Vulcan takes them in what they are doing. Vulcan is the immoderate and violent passion which increases and grows through the conjunction of these two planets. He diminishes Venus's love, her worthy moderation, her graciousness, and her good will, and makes off with them. The result is that she commits adultery and brings shame [on herself and her husband].

8 The planetary interaction of Saturn and Jupiter. Marsilio Ficino: *De vita libri tres* (1489)

[*Italian scholar, 1433–99, leader of the Platonic Academy of Florence. He revived an interest in Plato to counter what he regarded as the antireligious tendencies of contemporary Aristotelianism. His translations of Plato were immensely influential.*]

Book 3, chapter 22. You really must not neglect the power of Saturn. The Arabs say that of all planets, he is the most potent: that (obviously) planets subordinate their power to the planets they are approaching: that all the planets approach him rather than the other way round: and that planets in conjunction with him behave in accordance with his particular character. He is the 'head' of the widest orbit among the planets. (Obviously, any planet is the 'head' and 'heart' and 'eye' of its own orbit.) Saturn is also closest to the numberless [fixed] stars, and very like the Primum Mobile in that the circle he travels is a long one. He is the highest of the planets, and this is why people call the man on whom Saturn has breathed auspiciously lucky. Although most people are afraid of him because they think he is far removed from the common life of humans, nevertheless they think he is favourably disposed to that common life at any time he has his fullest power and dignity in his ascendant, or Jupiter (who tempers him) is in a favourable aspect with him or receives him with particular benignity within his sphere of influence.

In general, however, his influence[6] when taken up at an unseasonable moment in matter, especially dense coarse matter, becomes like poison, just as rotting or burning turn an egg poisonous. This is why some people are born or end up foul, indolent and cowardly, morose, envious, and open to foul demons. Avoid any traffic with these people, and keep your distance. In other respects, Saturn's poison lies hidden and indeed asleep, in the same way as sulphur when it is kept away from a flame. In living bodies, however, it often flares up and, like sulphur which has been set alight, not only burns fiercely but fills everything round it with a noxious vapour and poisons anyone near it. Against his influence (which is alien to all human beings alike and, so to speak, unharmonious), Jupiter arms us by the distinguishing characteristic he has by nature, by foods and medicines which self-evidently belong to him, by images (so people think), and by habits, particular activities, pursuits, and practices properly pertaining to him.

[6] *Influxus*, literally 'his flowing upon, in the manner of liquid'. The word has thus a much more physical connotation than its pale English derivative.

9 Planetary influences on the processes of birth. Michael Scot: *Liber phisionomie* (1209)

[*Scottish mathematician, physician, and scholar, c.1175–c.1234.*]

Chapter 10. The horoscope of infants enables us to say whether, once they have been conceived, or born alive, they will die in the womb or while they are being born. So we know there is a great deal going on in the horoscope because of the activity of the planets whose disposition [in the heavens] organises things below in many different ways. Consequently we say that in the seventh month [of pregnancy], the Moon adds a lot of moisture to the solid lump of humours, which holds in position any embryo in a woman's womb; and once this softening process has taken place, the humours descend to a lower position so that the sediment of those [humours] which lay stagnant in the womb can rise up and come out through the mouth of the uterus, either together with the embryo or after it has come out. All this happens as a result of the activity of the Moon which governs every male and female. So, while the Moon operates in accordance with the regular principles of nature the foetus comes out gingerly from the loins and passes into the light of the temporal world. Therefore we say that if anyone is born before the seventh month, [a full-grown foetus] does not come out from within, in as much as the planets have not all performed their particular function in comparison with the vigorous action of the Moon ...

If it is born in the first month, nothing comes out except humour conjoined with a great variety of solidified matter [attached to] some threads. This is because Saturn is reigning at the time, and so everything the Moon has liquefied becomes solid.

If it is born in the second month, blood comes out in driblets mixed with solid matter. This is because Jupiter is reigning at the time and is dominant. His activity has already changed the aqueous humour into blood and into a large number of bits and pieces of flesh,[7] although these are not strong enough to form anything which can be considered to constitute a complete, solidified being.[8]

If it is born in the third month, it is rarely born alive because it is delicate and is easily ripped apart in the womb, and it does not have an ability to repair itself, even though it is alive. It is also suffocated by too much heat because in this month Mars is dominant, and this produces a small gangrenous concretion.

If it is born in the fourth month, it will come out alive, and if it is alive, it will die at once because it is delicate and because the Sun, which reigns over it, is far too hot.

If it is born in the fifth month, it may be alive, but when it does come out, it does not survive because Venus is dominant, and this planet is weak when it comes to females and to strength.

If it is born in the sixth month, it does not survive because Mercury is dominant and this is the planet of the strength of the community as a whole. Consequently, when [the foetus] is separated from the womb and enters into conjunction with the Moon which is weaker [than Mercury], it cannot survive.

If it is born in the seventh month, it survives perfectly well and is able to survive because the Moon is dominant, since through her dominance the sequence of the duties of the planets is fulfilled in a created being such as I have just been describing; and with this richly endowed sequence of the working of the seven planets, which happens at the end of the seventh month, the embryo is either born and survives or, if it is not born, the foresaid planets begin to rule over it in the aforementioned sequence.

   [7] *Membra*, meaning 'parts of the body'. The implication is clearly that the limbs and organs have begun to form.

   [8] *Creatura*. The Latin noun can be seen as a future participle cognate with the verb *cresco*, and describing something which is about to undergo the process of coming into being.

---

10 Interpreting Classical myths in the light of astrology. Giovanni Boccaccio: *De genealogia deorum gentilium* (1350–75)

[*Italian poet and scholar, 1313–75, best-known as the author of* The Decameron. *This work on the genealogy of the pagan gods was begun in about 1350 and Boccaccio continued to revise it and work on it until his death.*]

Book 9, chapter 4. What we call 'cupid' [i.e. lust] is a passion of the mind inflicted by exterior things ushered in via the physical senses, and rendered acceptable by the special quality of their intrinsic powers, for which the supracelestial bodies are responsible. For according to the interpretation of astrologers (as my respected friend Andalò used to maintain),[9] when it turns out in someone's horoscope that Mars is in the house of Venus, in Taurus, or in Libra, and is the signifier of the horoscope, and indicates this, the person born at that time will be lustful, a fornicator, someone who will take advantage of lecherous people, and a wicked person in relation to such things. In connection with this, in his commentary on Ptolemy's *Tetrabiblos*, the scholar whose name was Haly[10] said that whenever Venus and Mars are found together in someone's natal chart, one must attribute to him or her a disposition inclined to acts of promiscuity, fornication, and lust. He is driven by a specific inclination, with the result that as often as such a man sees a woman whose outward appearance delights him, the fact that she has pleased him immediately transports him in the direction of his inward sensory potentialities. First of all it comes to the imagination, and from there it is transmitted to consideration, and from these sensory locations it is carried to that type of capability which is the more noble among the apprehensible potentialities: that is, to the potential mind. This is the receptacle of types, as Aristotle says in his *De Anima*.[11] Once there, if the sufferer's willing disposition (which controls his freedom to reject an impression, or to retain it if it be approved) recognises and understands the impression, his memory confirms that this is something of which he approves, and the strong feeling, now called 'love' or 'lust', takes up its position in his sensory appetite; and various agencies work upon it there and sometimes cause it to become so great and powerful that it forces Jupiter to leave Olympus and take the shape of a bull.[12]

[9] Andalò del Negro. Boccaccio praises him as 'my honoured teacher', *Genealogia* 1.6; 2.7; 15.6.
[10] 'Ali ibn Ahmad al-'Imrani, Arab astrologer, died 955.
[11] 3.7 (431a–b) and 2.5 (417a–b).
[12] A reference to the rape of Pasiphäe by Zeus in that form. Boccaccio means that sometimes passion may grow so great that controlling reason is abandoned and is replaced by animal lust.

11 Medical powers of the planets. Marsilio Ficino: *De vita libri tres* (1489)

Book 3, chapter 10. It is necessary to remember that Aries is in charge of the head and the face; Taurus, the neck; Gemini, the forearms, arms, and shoulders; Cancer, the chest, lungs, trunk, and upper arms; Leo, the heart, stomach, liver, back, and posterior ribs; Virgo, the intestines and pit of the stomach; Libra, the kidneys, thighs, and buttocks; Scorpio, the genitalia, the vulva, and the womb; Sagittarius, the thighs and below the groin; Capricorn, the knees; Aquarius, the legs and shins; Pisces, the feet. Mindful of this sequence, you will take good care not to touch any part of the body with iron, fire, or cupping-glasses when the Moon is running her course under the sign of that part. For during that time, the Moon increases the humours in the part, and their copious flow prevents it from becoming stronger and overpowers the natural potency belonging to that part. But on such occasions you will follow the procedure, which yields good results, of soothing the part at the appropriate time with certain congenial remedies applied either externally or internally.

Now, it is useful to know which sign was in the ascendant at your birth; for this sign, in addition to Aries, denotes your head, and in this sign, the Moon looks upon your head with a specific aspect. Furthermore, when the Moon enters Aries, it is a good time for you to try the effect of going to the baths and getting yourself washed. When she enters Cancer, it is the right time to thin the blood; take the medicine first and foremost in the form of an electuary.[13] When she is in Leo, do not induce vomiting. The right time to use clysters[14] is when she is in Libra; in Scorpio, don't experiment with baths ... In Capricorn, it is harmful to take medicine, and likewise when she is in Aquarius. In Pisces, however, it does good ...

We ought not to fail to notice Ptolemy's rule about purging the stomach and bowels. 'I approve taking purgative medicine when the Moon is in Cancer, Pisces, and Scorpio, especially if the lord of the sign then in the ascendant is coming into conjunction with a planet which is passing beneath the earth. But if the lord of the ascendant is in conjunction with a planet occupying the mid-heaven overhead at that particular time, nausea and actual vomiting should be induced immediately.'

Finally, let me draw the conclusion, with Galen, that astrology is necessary for a physician. During his debate on critical days, he says that the opinion of the Egyptians is indisputable: that is, that the Moon indicates the mental and physical condition of a sick and a healthy person day by day, to the extent that if the rays of Jupiter and Venus are mixed with the Moon, each person is favourably affected; but if she is mixed with the rays of Saturn or Mars, the opposite will be true.

[13] A cordial consisting of the medicinal ingredient added to honey or syrup.
[14] Medicines introduced into the rectum to open and cleanse the bowels.

12 Advice to a King. John Lydgate: *Secrees of Old Philosoffres* (c.1450)

[*English Benedictine and poet, c.1370–c.1451. He wrote voluminously on a wide variety of subjects. This is part of his version of a book commonly attributed to Aristotle, supposedly giving advice to Alexander the Great.*]

To see to his physical health, the King must be determined to have someone who knows the firmament and is a man of experience therein, a good astronomer who knows the seasons of the year, such as, in his day, was Cyprian, a philosopher and a man of experience. He knew the orbits of the planets and the way they are arranged relative to each other; he knew about moist and dry, hot and cold, the annual changes and the cycle [of nature]. He was experienced and daring when it came to the manifold orbits of the planets, the cycle of the elements, and the changes of times and the proportions and combinations of the elements. In particular, in astronomy, he knew the [proper] time to sleep or wake according to the regulation of philosophy, so that in no way should the King have an excess of either. The King must also forego all surfeit, and if he is given to any kind of excess, the astronomer must advise the use of leeches to modify his pleasure.

Saturn is slow, Mars melancholy, and the Sun causes a disposition to be happy. Mercury helps in public speaking, for in the Moon there is no stability. Fortune always moves quickly in duplicity. So a King places great reliance on other people to guide him through changes.

Astronomers who know secrets, physical health, how to diagnose sickness, the various causes of infirmities (among which fevers produce such great distress), aches, and gouts arising from excessive drinking: and be wary of the King's remaining awake for long periods when he should be asleep, for this is inimical to his health.

13 Astral and planetary magic. Marsilio Ficino: *De vita libri tres* (1489)

3.20. Astrologers are of the opinion that images intended to attract the favour of the gods have a power through which they change, in some fashion, the nature and behaviour of the person who wears them. They restore him (they think), for the better, so that he transcends [circumstances] as though he were someone else, or at least keep him in good health for a very long time. But harmful images (they say), have against their wearer the power of [a dose of] hellebore which has been taken over and above what medicine prescribes and the patient can withstand – that is to say, a power which is poisonous and deadly. But they say that images which have been fabricated and directed against another person, aiming to ruin him, have the power of a bronze concave mirror so accurately situated that, once it has gathered together and reflected rays directly back at him, they reduce him to ashes if he is close by, and if he is at a distance their force dazzles him and makes him blind and dizzy. Hence has arisen the story or belief which thinks that people, animals, and plants can be paralysed by the action of the planets, or waste away to nothing because of the devices[15] of astrologers and acts of poisonous magic by magicians. For my part, I do not really understand how images exert power upon any object which is not close to them, but I imagine they have some on the person who is wearing them. In my opinion, however, they do not have the kind of power many people claim they do – and it arises from the material which is used to make them rather than the figure depicted upon them – and (as I have said before) I very much prefer medicines to images.

Still, it cannot be denied that the Arabs and the Egyptians attribute so much to the statues and images they have made by means of their skill in astronomy and magic, that they think the spirits [*spiritus*] of stars are shut up inside them. Now, some people regard the spirits of the stars as wonderful powers belonging to celestial objects; others regard them as inferior but god-like entities [*daemones*][16] who are man servants to this or that star. So they think that whatever the spirits of the stars may be, they are grafted on to statues and images in just the same way as when demons [*daemones*] sometimes take over human bodies and use them to speak, move, move other things, and perform marvels. They think the spirits of the stars do similar things by means of images. They believe that the entities [*daemones*] who inhabit the cosmic fire are inserted into our bodies via fiery humours or humours which have been set on fire, and likewise via ardent dispositions [*spiritus*] and emotional states of this kind. Likewise, they think that the spirits of the stars can be inserted into images made of materials compatible with those spirits by means of rays caught at the right moment, suffumigations, lights, and vigorous chanting, and can work wonders upon the person wearing them or standing near them. I think this can indeed be done through the agency of demons [*daemones*], not so much because they have been confined in a particular material as because they take pleasure in being worshipped.

The Arabs record that when we fabricate images in the correct ritual way, if our spirit has been concentrating fully upon the work and the stars through our imagination[17] and emotional state, it is conjoined with the cosmic spirit itself and with the rays of the stars, through which the cosmic spirit acts; and when it has been conjoined in this way, it is also [conjoined] in the motive [for creating the image], with the result that the particular spirit of any star – that is, a power full of vital force, especially one which is compatible with the spirit of the operator at that moment – is poured into the image by the cosmic spirit through the rays.

They say that an operation of this kind is helped by suffumigations which are adapted to the stars, in as much as such suffumigations thus have a direct effect upon the air, the rays, the spirit of the person who has made the image, and the material of the image. I myself think that since odours are very similar in nature to the spirit and to air and, when [arising from the material which has been] set alight, compatible with the rays of the stars, if they belong to the Sun or Jupiter very strongly stir the air and the spirit to capture the qualities of the Sun or Jupiter dominant at the time at a favourable moment beneath [that planet's] rays. I also think the spirit so affected and endowed can, by some more intense aspect,[18] not only act upon its own body but upon a nearby body, especially one which is naturally in harmony with it but weaker, and can affect it by means of that characteristic they have in common. In my opinion, the rather solid material of the image can scarcely receive the slightest thing from the odours and the imagination of the operator; but the spirit itself can be so affected by an odour that the two things coalesce into one. This is obvious, because odour acts no further upon the sense of smell once it has been registered ...

Therefore I think that the concentrated attention of the imagination does not have power when one manufactures images or makes medicines so much as when one applies the former to one person or swallows the latter. So if anyone wears an image which has been ritually manufactured, as they say, or – and this point is certainly true – uses a medicine made in the same way, passionately hopes it is powerful, and believes this and hopes without the shadow of a doubt, then certainly he will derive an immense amount of support therefrom.

[15] *Machinae*. This word is rooted in physical objects – stage machinery, missiles, mill-stones. It thus implies that the astrologers are credited with using some kind of material contraption to work their intended harm. Optic glasses, well-known to Roger Bacon, for example, may have provided one such suspicious object.
[16] Ficino here uses the word daemon in its purely Classical sense of 'a spirit intermediary between divinities and human beings'. In the next sentence, however, he reverts to Christian, Mediaeval usage. Similar slippages or ambiguities can be seen in following sentences.
[17] That is, the particular faculty whereby we create closely detailed and visualised images in our head – an important magical technique.
[18] The power of individual planets is modified – either increased or diminished – by their positions relative to the other planets. This positioning is known as their 'aspect'.

14 Fraud. Roger Bacon: *Opus maius* (1266–7)

[*English Franciscan, 1210/15–c.1292. Imprisoned for heresy in 1277. Bacon prefaces the following passage with an explanation of how important mathematics are for both theological and secular learning, but, he says, theologians have not always distinguished between good and bad mathematics, forgetting that good 'mathematics' are derived etymologically from a Greek word* (mathesis) *meaning 'acquisition of knowledge', whereas bad 'mathematics' come from* matesis *which denotes* mantia, *i.e. 'divination'. The distinction is, alas, bunkum.* Mathematicus, *however, was used in Classical times as well as later to mean 'astrologer'.*]

Part 4, on judicial astrology. There are five kinds of magical art, namely, prophesying, astrology (*mathematica*), working harm (*maleficium*), trickery (*praestigium*), and casting lots (*sortilegium*). Astrology therefore constitutes the second part of the art of magic. This appropriates to itself a warped contemplation of the heavens by means of characters, magical chants, invocations, superstitious sacrifices, and various kinds of deceit. It states specifically that everything happens by necessity, nothing of its own free will and accord, nothing by chance or luck, nothing as the result of advice, from essential goodness: and so that the constellations may be able to help us more efficiently, it furnishes each constellation with its own invented written and pictorial characters, and other means of prediction. These things are overtly stated in books of magic. So this body of knowledge states that everything happens by necessity via the medium of the sky, and through this inevitability it presumes to make infallible judgements about all future things. But this astrology has been condemned not only by the saints but also by [natural] philosophers, as Isidore says in his treatise on astrology, adding that one part of astronomy is superstitious, namely, that which is magic and known as 'lying astrology' (*mathematica falsidica*).

[*Aristotle, Plato, and Pliny the Elder all condemn it. Cicero points out that it destroys true worship of the gods, does damage to the state, infects medicine, and undermines natural philosophy and all the worthwhile arts.*] Ptolemy, too, and Aristotle, Avicenna, Messehalac, Haly, and Albumazar, who have all spoken about this subject with greater authority than anyone else, do not say that things below [the heavens] are subject to untrammelled compulsion through the power of the sky, because free will is not subject to natural phenomena; nor do they think that [the sky's] judgement should be regarded as infallible ... So natural philosophers universally condemn the delusions of this false astrology.

Not only do they condemn it in essence (that is, because of the erroneous opinion astrologers have about the heavens), but because astrologers summon up demons to the aid of these activities in the sky by means of invocations and sacrifices – something which is entirely forbidden – and, regardless, spoil their investigations of the skies by the circles, figures, completely futile characters, ridiculous chants, and irrational prayers in which they put their trust. Moreover, they add to the fraudulence of their operations by collusion, darkness, bogus equipment (*instrumenta sophistica*), subtle hand movements whereby they know they can create an illusion, and, through these things in which the power of the sky does not play any part at all, do a great deal which stupid people find astonishing; and, what is more, they contradict themselves, because what they attribute to the sky in front of other people, they know among themselves is not true at all. Likewise, although elsewhere they put their trust in certain invocations, sacrifices, chants, characters, and various figures as co-workers with a constellation (in their opinion), nevertheless they frequently fabricate these things in accordance with the types of deception I mentioned earlier and, in the presence of those who believe them, ascribe a great deal to the constellation when this actually has no power – and they know perfectly well what they are doing. Therefore because of these stupidities, natural philosophers have condemned astrology, and both the saints and Catholic men have noted this and objected to astrology along with the natural philosophers.

But the principal reason of the saints has been that these astrologers have, from the beginning, impeded the entry of the faith into this world, because not only have they made errors in faith because they were soaked in this fantasy, and foisted their conventions upon the heavenly bodies – such as, because of celestial bodies what has already been said about compulsion, people become prone to anger or gentle, chaste or lascivious, and so forth – but they have ascribed Christ's miracles, which provide proof of the faith, to this astrology of theirs, saying that Christians are astrologers and magicians [*magi*] who lead people astray. For just as this demon-inspired cunning has enabled them to show off in front of people who are crude and unsophisticated, and imprison them in their errors, and so lord it over them: so they have made the deceitful suggestion that the Apostles, the martyrs, and all the others who have spread the faith did not perform true miracles with the help of God, but by the art of magic which they used [with no help] but their own.

15 Imperial acceptance of astrology. Niketas Choniates: *Historia* (early 13th century)

[The Emperor Manuel Komnenos] entertained the discreditable notion that the retrograde and progressive movements of the stars, their positions, the configurations of the planets, along with their approaches to each other and keeping their distance from one another, are intimately connected with good and bad fortune, and the incidents of human life. He also believed the rest of the things star-chatterers say when they make a pretence of divine foreknowledge and slip in (so that you scarcely notice) the phrases 'it was decreed by fate', and 'the ordinances of Necessity are unchangeable and unalterable.'

16 An Imperial sceptic. Anna Komnena: *Alexiad* (post 1148)

6.7.1–5. An astrologer (*mathematikos*) by the name of Seth, who prided himself that he knew a great deal about astrology, had predicted under the form of an oracular response that Robert [Guiscard] would die after he had crossed into Illyria. He wrote this response on a piece of paper, sealed it, and handed it to certain of the Emperor's close friends, instructing them to take good care of it for the time being. Then Robert died. Seth told them to break open the seal. The prediction ran as follows: 'A great enemy out of the West will die all of a sudden after stirring up many disorders.' Consequently, everyone was astonished at the man's skill and knowledge, for he had striven to reach the peak of his craft, and was now in possession of it.

Now, let me digress for a moment from the principal theme of this narrative in order to say a little about the nature of oracular responses. Divination is a fairly recent discovery. This craft was not known to ancient times. At the time of Eudoxos [c.408–355 BC], a man very skilled in astronomy, the rules governing oracular responses did not exist; Plato did not know this particular branch of knowledge, and even Manetho [floruit 280 BC], an influential astrologer, did not thoroughly understand it or investigate it accurately. They did not know how to cast a horoscope in order to be able to predict the future, how to fix the cardinal points, how to observe the way in which the whole [sky] is arranged, or how to do any of those things the discoverer of this system has handed down to posterity, which masked perfectly good sense to those who occupy themselves with this kind of nonsense.

I myself once engaged in this branch of knowledge in a small way – not to become mistress of it (God forbid!) but so that having gained a better understanding of its silly jargon, I might censure those who were devoting themselves to it. I do not write this to show off, but to demonstrate that under the Emperor [Alexios] many branches of knowledge had been given their head. He honoured learned men and learning itself, although it was plain he disliked and was disgusted by this mathematical discipline of astrology because, I think, it persuaded most of those who were somewhat naïve to lay aside their hopes derived from on high and gape at the stars. This was the occasion the Emperor made war on the science of astrology.

This, however, did not cause any dearth of astrologers during that period. Seth – the Egyptian from Alexandria whom I have mentioned already – was in full flower at that time and played a leading role in the secret rites of astrology. He was consulted by many people, and gave prophetic answers, which were very accurate. In some cases he did not need to use an astrolabe, but made his predictions by a form of psephophoria.[19] This required absolutely no magic at all from the Alexandrian, only a certain skill in calculation. The Emperor, seeing young people streaming to the man because they reckoned he was a prophet, put questions to him himself on two separate occasions. Each time the Alexandrian hit the mark in his response. Afraid that many people might suffer harm, and that everybody could become favourably disposed to the completely worthless and profane things offered by astrology, the Emperor banished him from the city and sent him to live in Rhaidestos, showing him consideration, however, in as much as his needs were plentifully supplied from the imperial storehouses.

Then, of course, there was Eleutherios, a man very skilled in dialectic, who was also an Egyptian. He was in the first rank of those who practised this branch of knowledge, and operated to the highest degree of genius, not stepping aside for anyone at all, even the foremost of the profession. Later on, a man by the name of Katanankes[20] came to Constantinople from Athens, taking first place from his competitors. Certain people asked him when the Emperor would die. He gave a prediction in accordance with what he believed, but his conjecture turned out to be false. It happened, however, that the lion which was living in the palace at the time, and which had fallen ill of a fever, after four days vomited up its life, and most people believed that this was the fulfilment of Katanankes's prediction. Quite a long time passed. He predicted the Emperor's death again and got it wrong; but on the very day he had predicted, the Emperor's mother, the Empress Anna, died. But even though he had made more than one prediction about the Emperor, and had made a mistake each time, Alexios was unwilling to remove him from the city because he had convicted himself, and the Emperor did not want to give the appearance of banishing him out of a feeling of resentment.

[19] Originally this referred to voting in elections. The process involved pebbles, possibly marked in some way. Seth's procedure may have been similar to casting rune-stones.

[20] Probably a professional pseudonym, since it means 'compelling force'.

17 Doubts about astrology. John Barbour: *The Brus* (1370s)

[*Scottish poet, c.1330–1395. Archdeacon of Aberdeen. Sometimes called the father of Scottish vernacular poetry. The Brus centres upon the Wars of Independence fought by King Robert I.*]

4.688–734. But many people are so curious and greedy to know things that through their great knowledge or else through their devilry, they make an attempt to have knowledge of things to come in these two ways: one of them is astrology whereby learned men who know how to do so may know planetary conjunctions, and whether the planets' orbit places them in a favourable or a hostile house; and how the arrangement of the sky as a whole can have an influence on things down here, on localities or on climates, [an influence] which does not have the same effect everywhere, but is less in some places and greater in others according to whether its rays are extended evenly or unevenly. But I think it would show great mastery [of his art] for any astrologer to say, 'This will happen in this place and on this day.' For although a man spends his whole life in studying astrology with the result that he cracks his head on the stars, the wise man says he could not make three [such] reliable days in the whole of his life and he would always have doubts until he saw how it turned out in the end. So there is no reliable judgement [in astrology]. Or if those who wish to study the craft of astrology were to know the details of every person's birth, and knew the constellation which gives them their natural dispositions which incline them to good or bad, so that through the knowledge of learned men or through their mastery of astrology they could tell what danger was coming to those who are naturally disposed to it, I believe they would fail to let them know what might happen to them. For whether a person is inclined to virtue or to wickedness, he can perfectly well hold his will in check, either because he has been brought up that way, or through an exercise of his reason, and turn himself completely in the opposite direction.

18 Condemnation of astrology and magic. St Alcimus Ecdicius Avitus: *Poemata de Mosaicae historiae gestis* (late 5th/early 6th century)

[*French scholar, died c.525. He became Bishop of Vienne in 490. Known as a man of learning, he converted King Sigismund of Burgundy in 516.*]

Book 2: *De originali peccato*.
For henceforth your posterity, with corrupted offshoot, has developed a wish to discover the future by means of illicit skills, and to give rein to the sluggish senses by secret rites, to investigate things high in the sky or drowned in the foul sea, and to burst open the secure laws of nature. To inquire now from the stars how anyone born under a star/planet may live successfully for the rest of his or her life; to learn from well-matched signs an outcome which is different. To attribute different fates to twins born at the same time in a birth which thrust them into the light at exactly the same moment, on the grounds that the movements [of the stars] were different. To say that each star has its own particular divine being which a young age has given precedence over the ancient stars which have been buried for such a long time in deepest night; and to distribute meaningless names throughout the immense sky. Who is able to say magic is fraudulent these days, while he is trying to master a secret power in the silence of his heart, and while he wants to achieve union with divine powers? Once upon a time, during the reign of an arrogant king, the law-bearing prophet [Moses] was demonstrating the novel wonders of a sign he had been commanded to produce and moved the magicians to envy, with the result that they tried to do the same and by their burning jealousy heaped up their own ruin.

If by chance true power were available to them, they would make haste to remove, not to accumulate prodigies which are comparable only to signs and do not equate with power; and because [the magician] cannot get rid of them, he endures them with an anger which is doubly great. This accounts for what the Marsi[21] can do by means of a much-commended chant when, using a silent art, they produce savage snakes and, keeping themselves at a distance, frequently urge them to fight among themselves. Then, so that each person may be fully conscious of the relentless water-snake [in preparation for] war, or detect the closed ears of the pitiless viper, he rattles the weapons of his secret chant within himself. Immediately the poisons are weakened by the word which grapples with them, and in a short time the disarmed snake is handled with impunity and only its bite, not its venom, is feared. Sometimes the person dies while he is chanting the spell, if the deaf snake has disregarded the crafty murmurs of the one who is seeking to bind him by a magical formula. Because they inherit this from their mother and first origin, and because they are thus skilled in the deceit and language of snakes, they do their reciprocal business under cover of speaking. Likewise, an anxiety about salvation is antithetical to those who are distressed by a foreknowledge of their allotted life-span, since they think that ghosts brought forth from their underground abodes hold converse with them and bring back information. But the spirit of error is in those who run wild, and furnishes useless innuendos in return for the responses for which [the ghosts] were consulted; and so that not a single one of these may be said with a word which is actually true, whoever has been deluded thereby and tries to find out something which is forbidden will be condemned to an eternal judgement.

[21] A people of central Italy, famous as magicians and snake-charmers.

19 Condemnation of judicial astrology. Girolamo Savonarola: *Trattato contra li astrologi* (1497)

[*Italian Dominican, 1452–98. Politician, religious reformer, executed as a heretic and schismatic.*]

Part 2, chapter 2. Divinatory astrology shows itself to be worthless, not only because the finest philosophers either did not deign to speak of it or did so only in derision, but also because, according to the basic principles and considered opinions of their philosophy, it has no right whatsoever to be called a 'type of knowledge'. This is evident first because all our knowledge starts with the senses. Through these the causal agencies based upon the senses are carried to the imaginative faculty, and from there to the intellect; and because the exterior sense recognises the causal agencies when these are present to it, there is no way we can get to know future causal agencies via the exterior senses. Again, we cannot recognise them through the interior sense (that is to say, the power of the imaginative faculty), because it turns out that the imaginative faculty recognises and looks again at the causal agencies based upon the senses when the sense-perception is absent, not present. Because the imaginative faculty as a whole originates in the sense-perception, however, and has no capacity to reason, it can recognise only those things which co-exist as conditions in the sense-perception. But future things, which were never present to the sense-perception, it cannot recognise in a future sense because the future does not fall within the sense-perception's ability to recognise [things]. Consequently, if the future is to be recognised, it must be so through the power of the intellect which talks of one cause in another and one cause understood by means of another. Since the future is not present to it, therefore it cannot recognise the future in itself. So if recognition needs the actual presence of things to be able to recognise them, it cannot do so unless it sees that these present things are going to come into being, as an effect proceeds from its cause. For example, if during winter you see trees as dry, your intellect enables you to recognise that this state of affairs will produce flowers, leaves, and fruit. Consequently from this you recognise these future effects, not in themselves, but from their cause (because of what reason tells you), and from your experience in times past.

Nowadays philosophers distinguish between causes and say that each cause always necessarily produces its own effect because it is argued that such an effect always necessarily follows from the cause. For example, granted that the sky moves as it does, every time there is an eclipse of the sun, there must be an eclipse of the moon. Therefore they say we can have a completely certain recognition and a true knowledge of such effects as these.

Some other causes do not produce their effects of necessity or on every occasion. But it is true that they do so almost always – as when the sun is in Leo and approaches the star known as the Dog Star: then it is very hot and the air seethes and boils. This does not necessarily happen every time, because there may be an occasion when, through some other arrangement of the elements, the air is temperate. But it is more or less always so. They say one can philosophise about these effects; and although one's recognition of them cannot be certain, nevertheless they are not excluded from 'knowledge' because one can be pretty certain to recognise them [for what they are].

Some other causes are indifferent about the effects they produce; that is to say, they do not determine one thing rather than another.

For example, a log of wood can be the material cause from which is made a table, a door, a post, or something else. It is not bound to produce one of these things rather than any of the others. Likewise, although free will is fixed with respect to its ultimate aim in general, nevertheless it is indeterminate in many things – whether to pick up a straw from the ground or not, whether to jump or not; and when it comes to things which are not its [ultimate] aim, it can be fixed in whatever part of its own nature it pleases. Therefore philosophers say that one cannot have any recognition of or reliable conjecture about these effects because they cannot be known in themselves, they are not of the present time or even present in their own causes. So because they are not determined by one [potential] role more than another, nobody can have any reliable recognition of them, and he cannot determine what, arising from such causes, he should follow. It is simply a matter of guesswork.

Some other causes produce effects which are not inevitable, do not always happen, and are not indifferent, but take place on very rare occasions – as when a woman gives birth to a monster – and, again, once cannot have either knowledge or recognition of this because reason tells us that similar things have happened in the past.

So observational astrology is a real branch of knowledge because it seeks to recognise effects from real causes, such as eclipses, the conjunctions of planets, and similar effects which always necessarily follow from their causes. Likewise, one can call 'art' or 'branch of knowledge' the astrology which seeks to recognise certain natural effects which more or less always proceed from how far or how near the sun is to us, or the conjunction, opposition, and movements of the moon. But divinatory astrology which rests entirely on effects which proceed indifferently from their causes,[22] especially in human affairs which proceed from free will and only on rare occasions proceed from their causes, is completely worthless and cannot be called either an art or a branch of knowledge.

[22] I.e. which are not determined in advance by the very nature of what causes them.

Alchemy

[*Alchemy sought to manipulate the hidden powers of nature to speed up natural processes. If everything sooner or later tended towards perfection – the seed became a plant, the baby an adult, the human soul locked in a physical body a non-material participant in the Beatific Vision – there was nothing to prevent human beings from trying to achieve that end more quickly than nature was likely to manage it, just as medicine sought to cure a disease or heal a wound by giving a push to nature. The physical transformation of metals, which is perhaps the most famous or notorious aspect of this art, was intended to provide a particularly vivid illustration of humankind's ability to manage this with some, or even complete success. The stages of the process were complex and involved breaking down matter in order to be able to reconstitute it. Decay, burning, and distillation were therefore three constant stages – each open to things' going wrong, as happens in any modern laboratory – but if the operation worked, the alchemist was rewarded with at least one of a number of products which had extraordinary powers. One was an elixir which could prolong life, give perfect health, and cure any disease. Another was the Philosopher's Stone, not actually a stone but a reddish-brown powder which had the effect of transforming immediately into a more perfect type any metal with which it came into contact during an alchemical procedure. Like any other technically based science, alchemy developed its own impenetrable jargon which practitioners liked partly because it helped preserve their art from ignorant amateurs, and partly because jargon flatters any specialist by casting an aura around his or her specialism and keeping the* polloi *bemused.*]

20 Technical terminology. Pseudo-Geber: *Summa Perfectionis* (early 14th century(?))

[*The real Geber was the eighth-century Arab alchemist Jabir ibn Hayyan. The author of this* Summa *adopted his name because of the Arab scholar's immense reputation.*]

(Chapter 40). SUBLIMATION is elevation of a dry substance by means of fire, which will cause [the vapour] to cling to the vessel used in this process. Sublimation is of different kinds according to the spirits which are to be sublimated. Some need a strong burn, some a medium, some a fire which lacks intensity. So, if one is sublimating arsenic or sulphur, they must be sublimated by a gentle fire because they have components which are very subtle and closely joined together, and these would rise as one with their gross components, their whole substance would be engaged, and no purification would take place. Indeed, they would turn black and be quite burned up. Consequently, so that a person can separate the impure, earthly substance, he must find the inherent qualities of two methods of proceeding: i.e. the ratio of fire, and purification along with a mixture of dross. This is because a mixture of dross takes hold of the gross parts, keeps them down low at the bottom of the *aludel*, and does not allow them to rise. Hence, the alchemist is obliged to apply fire to sublimation in three separate stages.

(Chapter 49). There were three reasons for the procedure known as DESCENSION. (a) When some matter is enclosed in a vessel called an alchemical *descensorium*, after it has become liquid it descends through the opening in the vessel, and by its descent we know that liquefaction has taken place. (b) [Descension takes place] so that it may preserve weak bodies from being burned up after they have been revived from their ashes.[23] When we try to revive weak bodies from their ashes, we cannot revive every single bit of them at one time, and if that component part we revived first of all is kept waiting until we have revived everything, most of it would vanish because of the action of the fire. Consequently it had to be arranged that when one part was revived, it was removed from the fire at once. This process took place in the *descensorium*. (c) The pure body in its liquid state descends and releases in the hollow part of the vessel all extraneous matter.

(Chapter 50). DISTILLATION is an elevation of watery vapours in the vessel used during this operation. There are various types of distillation. One uses fire, the other does not. There are two kinds of distillation using fire. One elevates into an alembic, the other descends and becomes the medium whereby oil is extracted from vegetable matter. Distillation was devised – and this is the general reason for any type of distillation – to purify something which has been liquefied from the dregs produced while it is being boiled, and to preserve it from becoming stale and foetid.

(Chapter 51). CALCINATION involves reducing something to powder via the medium of fire, and depriving it of the moisture which holds together its component parts. It was devised to destroy by fire the sulphurous quality which burns, damages, and contaminates. There are various types of calcination according to the variety of things to be calcinated: bodies, spirits, other things extraneous by their nature and used for various purposes. There are, for example, imperfect bodies which consist of two types: hard, such as Venus [copper] and Mars [iron], and soft, such as Jupiter [tin] and Saturn [lead], all of which are calcinated ... Calcination of spirits was devised to fix them better and make them more soluble in water.

(Chapter 52). SOLUTION is the conversion of something dry into water, and I maintain that one achieves a perfect solution every time by using distilled water which is very alkaline, bitter, and briny, without any impurity ... Everything one turns to liquid must have the nature of salt or alum or things which are closely related to them, because it is their nature which allows them to fuse before they vitrify ... Solution is of two kinds: one uses hot dung, the other boiling water, and they both have one aim and one effect. The method using dung is as follows: put the calcinated matter into a glass jar and pour over it a quantity of distilled vinegar (or the like), double the amount of water, close the top of the jar tightly so that the stuff cannot breathe, and cause it to dissolve under the warm dung. Then remove the solution by distilling it through a filter. If it has not dissolved, calcinate the material again and repeat the solution process until, by repetition of this procedure, the whole thing has been turned to liquid. The method which uses boiling water is quicker. Put the calcinated matter in a jar, as before, with vinegar, block the mouth of the jar so that the matter cannot breathe, and then bury it in a cauldron full of water and straw ... Then light a fire underneath until the water has been boiling for an hour, and when the matter has dissolved, distil it and keep it separate.

(Chapter 53). COAGULATION is the reduction of something which has been liquefied to a solid substance by depriving it of moisture. There are two reasons for using it. One is to harden quicksilver, the other is to separate elixirs from the water mixed in with them, and there are various types of coagulation according to the large number of things which are to be coagulated.

(Chapter 54). FIXATION is the appropriate adaptation of something which shrinks from fire to endurance of it. The reason for using fixation is so that any transmutation and alteration may last in its altered state and not undergo any change. There are various types of fixation according to the large number of things to be fixated – for example, certain bodies which are less than perfect, such as Saturn [lead], Jupiter [tin], Mars [iron], and Venus [copper] – and according to the diversity of their spirits which are, for example, sulphur and arsenic in one stage, quicksilver in another, and marchesite, vitriol, zinc oxide, and the like.

(Chapter 55). CERATION softens a hard substance which does not normally melt, until it becomes liquid. From this it is obvious that the reason one used this process was that because of its lack of moisture the substance provided no means of entry into its body whereby alteration could take place, and ceration would soften it until it turned runny and so offered a way in for alteration. Consequently, some people thought that oils, liquids, and water produce ceration; but that is a mistake, profoundly at odds with the principles of this technique which is based in nature, and which the clearly apprehensible ways in which nature works have shown to be wrong.

[23] *Calces.* This is a technical term referring to ashes produced from the burning of matter during the alchemical process of *calcination*, q.v.

21 Metals and minerals. Pseudo-Roger Bacon: *Speculum alchemiae* (pre 16th century)

[*Roger Bacon, c.1220–92, was a Franciscan scholar interested in a wide variety of different branches of knowledge, including mathematics, astronomy, optics, alchemy, and languages. Because of his eminence as a scholar, his name was adopted by the writer of this work on alchemy.*]

(Chapter 2). I am now going to explain fully the guiding principles in nature and the ways in which minerals procreate. First one should note that the principal minerals in mines are quicksilver and sulphur. From these are generated all metals and all minerals, of which there are many different types; but I maintain that nature always sets up as her objective and strives for the perfection of gold. Various chance occurrences, however, arrive unexpectedly and change the form of metals, as one finds quite frankly expressed in many books by alchemists. For pure and impure metals – for example, gold, silver, tin, lead, copper, iron – are generated in accordance with the purity and impurity of the foresaid quicksilver and sulphur; and I shall now tell you facts about their nature, that is, about their purity and impurity (or excess of dirt), and the thing which makes them deficient.

(a) Gold is a perfect substance,[24] generated from pure, fixed, bright, red quicksilver, and from pure, fixed, red sulphur which does not cause damage by burning or blistering. It has no deficiencies.
(b) Silver is a clean, pure, almost perfect substance generated out of pure, almost fixed, bright, white quicksilver and sulphur of a similar quality. It lacks a little fixation, colour, and weight.
(c) Tin is a clean, imperfect substance procreated from pure quicksilver fixed and unfixed, bright, white in its outward appearance and red in its hidden manifestation, and sulphur of a similar quality. It is deficient only in decoction or digestion.

(d) Lead is a dirty, imperfect substance procreated out of impure, unfixed, terrestrial, cloudy quicksilver, whitish in its outward appearance and red in its hidden, and partly combustible sulphur of a similar quality. It lacks purity, fixation, colour, and calcination.

(e) Copper is a dirty, imperfect substance generated from impure, unfixed, terrestrial quicksilver, burning an ill-defined red, and sulphur of a similar quality. It lacks fixation, purity, and weight, and has too much impure colour and an earthiness which does not burn.

(f) Iron is a dirty, imperfect substance generated from impure, over-fixed, terrestrial quicksilver which burns an indistinct white and red, and sulphur of a similar quality. It lacks smelting, purity, and weight, and has too much fixed, impure sulphur, and does not burn with earthiness.

(Chapter 3). All metals are procreated from quicksilver and sulphur. Their impurity and uncleanness damages them, and since nothing should be applied to metals, which has not been compounded from them or originated in them, one is left with the obvious conclusion that no external matter which has not originated from these two has either power or capacity to perfect them or to effect their further transmutation. Consequently, it is astonishing that anyone with any sense should base his purpose on things animal or vegetable (which are things far removed from what he wants), when he can find things mineral fairly close at hand. Nor is it in the least credible that any natural philosopher will practise his art on those remote objects unless he does it figuratively. But from the two foresaid substances come all metals. Nothing attaches itself to them unless it originates in them; and therefore by rights we are obliged to take quicksilver and sulphur as the basic materials of our Stone. Neither quicksilver nor sulphur generates a metal by itself alone, but different metals and different minerals are procreated in different ways from a commingling of both. Consequently everyone agrees that our Matter must be extracted from a mixture of those two substances.

Our culminating secret is most excellent and very well hidden.[25] It is from this mineral substance that something related to it and quite like it in nature should arise, and we are obliged to extract this very thing with a great deal of anxiety.

I maintain, therefore, that our matter be extracted first from vegetable substances such as herbs or trees or anything issuing out of the earth: in which event, this must first be turned into quicksilver and sulphur during a long decoction. But we are exempt from using either these substances or this operation, because nature produces quicksilver and sulphur for us. If we were to extract it from animal matter such as human blood, hairs, urine, excrement, hens' eggs – anything which comes out of living creatures – it would be necessary to turn these into quicksilver and sulphur by concoction, too, and we are exempt from doing this, as before. But if we were to extract it from median minerals such as all types of mercury, marcasite, zinc oxide, 'ink'[26] or vitriol, alum, borax, salt, and many other things, it would be necessary, as before, to turn them into quicksilver and sulphur by decoction: and we are exempt, as we were in the previous instances. If we were to extract separately any of the seven spirits[27] – quicksilver alone or sulphur alone – or quicksilver and one of the two sulphurs – either sulphur vivum, or orpiment, or yellow or red arsenic, or one which is similar – we should not perfect it at all, because nature never perfects anything unless each of a pair of substances is mixed equally with the other: and we are exempt from these, as in the foresaid cases of quicksilver and sulphur, in their inherent nature. Finally, if we did not extract them – which does not matter – we should have to mix them in accordance with the proper ratio, something unknown to the human intellect, and afterwards to decoct them to the point where they coagulate into a solid lump. Therefore we are exempt from recovering both (that is, quicksilver and sulphur) in their own inherent nature, because we do not know the ratio proper to each of their natures, and we come across bodies in which we do find these substances adjusted, coagulated, and joined together just as they should be. Keep this secret well hidden.

[24] The text has *corpus* which refers principally to the body of a human or an animal. The Latin therefore emphasises the link between the 'procreation' of metals and minerals, and the generative process in humans.
[25] A manuscript marginal note in the copy I am using says at this point, 'Here something lies hidden in the herb.'
[26] *Atramentum*. Ancient ink was made from soot and gum, but it is quite possible that the black substance here designated 'ink' refers to something else.
[27] *Spiritus*. The 'spirits' are here essences or distilled extracts of particular ssubstances, not incorporeal beings. See further document 26 below.

22 Why metals turn to gold. Pietro d'Abano: *Pretiosa Margarita Novella* (1330)

[*Italian physician and philosopher.*]

It should be noted that in the generation of metals, there are two kinds of moisture. One is viscous, external, does not come to a complete union with the earthy parts of the matter, and is inflammable and sulphurous; the other is a viscous, internal humidity, exactly alike throughout with the earthy parts, not inflammable, but incombustible because in all its smallest earthy parts it has been so strongly balanced and mixed together that the smallest part of one has become the same as the smallest part of the other, and they have turned into quicksilver by their own digestive process. Therefore the moist part does not abandon the dry part in the fire, nor vice versa. Either it withdraws from the fire with its substance intact, or it stays there intact: and it does this because the moist part does not adhere to what it touches. The earthy parts bind and temper it in equal measure. The dry part is not restricted to its own boundary, either, because the watery parts loosen and temper it in equal measure; and so the moist and the dry are balanced within [the matter].

So the first matter of all metals is moist, viscous, incombustible, subtle, assimilated to the subtle earthy part, strongly mixed in balanced fashion throughout its smallest parts in the mineral caverns of the earth. Their nearest matter is quicksilver which is generated out of their strong admixture. But it does not produce its essential self with the matter. Therefore discerning and most wise Nature has joined to it an appropriate agent, namely sulphur, so that she may change the form in the metal by a process of digestion and 'cooking'. For sulphur is a certain fatness of earth, generated, thickened, and hardened in its minerals by a controlled decoction. Sulphur is related to quicksilver as male is to female, and appropriate agent to appropriate matter. One type of sulphur can be melted naturally, another cannot; and according to whether nature has been willing to make it fusible, it joins fusible sulphur to them so that it may extract a like liquefaction from capacity of the matter. This is why metals liquefy in fire and coagulate when they are removed from the fire, although quicksilver is always naturally in a liquid state. But when nature has not wanted things to be fusible, she has added infusible but coagulated sulphur to them – for example, marchasite, magnesia, and antimony. The sulphur in marchasite is not fixed, and combustible, whereas in antimony it is fixed and incombustible …

Just as the elements are scarcely removed from the basic matter out of which they arise, and so are generated one after the other in turn, in a manner like that of a circle: so metals are generated, but in a somewhat different fashion … Metals are a different case because they are all imperfect in themselves, the sole exception being gold (when it comes to any stage of imperfection). So they are all organised [to tend] towards gold as to their final goal and do not revert after they have become gold. The sign of this natural transformation into gold is their being mingled in a single mineral followed by their successive stages of change. For if they were perfect and complete so that they had one nature and one completion which was defined and concluded – that is, they had already reached their final state – then undoubtedly they could not be converted into anything else unless they were first reduced to something which was not a metal ...

So nature adopts two ways of generating gold: one, first and foremost, through herself by generating gold in her own minerals and according to her own principles; the other – not first and foremost – through herself by first generating imperfect metals from these same principles in her own minerals, and then finally converting them into gold. Alchemy therefore follows nature in generating gold according to her second method, generating gold out of imperfect metals, just as nature does. It is not possible for alchemy to follow nature's first method.

23 Alchemical equipment. Pseudo-Geber: *Liber Fornacum* (15th century)

The furnace for calcination. The furnace for calcination should be square, four feet long, and three feet wide, and the walls should be six inches thick, as shown in the picture. Put silver [the moon], copper [Venus], iron [Mars], or anything else to be calcinated in earthenware dishes made of the very robust clay from which crucibles are made so that they can withstand the intensity of the fire until what is being calcinated is reduced to ashes. Calcination is the treasure-house of the process, so do not become tired of calcinating and pay attention to what I say in my books. By calcination imperfect bodies are purified, and by reduction what has been calcinated is turned into a solid mass. At this point, our 'medicine' can be projected on to them, and you may rejoice.

The furnace for sublimation. The furnace for sublimation should obviously be made according to the description in my treatise on the sublimation of spirits, which I published earlier with a full description, as above. During the sublimation of sulphur, you must make sure the cover of the sublimatorium has a large, unhindered hollow tube inside, like an alembic without the nose. Otherwise the sublimate would sink to the bottom of the vessel in the face of too much heat. At the end of the sublimation, the sulphur does not rise as far as the firing of the aludel unless it is squeezed out; and if the sublimate were to be held back further up in the tube while it was being poured gently, it would sink to the bottom once more along the sides of the vessel. Thus, one would find nothing had been sublimated, as experts have noted.

The furnace for descension. The furnace for descension should look like the one in the picture; and we, along with smelters of metal who employ cupels and 'cement', make remarkable use of it. All calcinated, cremated, dissolved, and coagulated bodies are reduced to a solid mass by the furnace – or, more precisely, the cupels and patens, earthenware vessels or crucibles in which silver is frequently poured in order to recover the saturated metal.

The furnace for smelting. The furnace for smelting, in which all bodies are gently smelted separately, is also the furnace much used by coiners. Brass, however, is not smelted in these furnaces; nor is it coloured with zinc oxide or calamine, as experts have noted. It looks like the one illustrated here.

The furnace for solution. The furnace for solution consists of a receptacle full of water, with pieces of equipment made of iron. These hold other pieces of equipment carefully fixed so that they do not fall down and so that they can catch the entire dissolution. The picture shows the shape of this furnace and its vessels.

The furnace for fixation, also called the athenor. The furnace for fixation is much like that for calcination, and should have a deep earthenware dish filled with sifted ashes. The vessel containing the matter to be fixed should be closely sealed and placed in the middle of the ashes; and the density of the mass of ashes below, above, and around should be four fingers thick, or as thick as is required for the matter you want to fix, because more fire is required in one fixing than in another. This is the furnace and this is the method which alchemists in ancient times used to achieve the Great Work, as has been accurately noted by those who undertake it. For those who would be investigators of the truth, I have demonstrated the point perfectly well in my books. The picture contains an illustration of the athanor.

LIBER FORNACVM
Furnus Calcinatorius.

bici fine naſo. Nam aliter deſcenderet totum ſublimatum ad fundum uaſis præ nimio calore. Nam in fine ſublimationis nō aſcendit ſulphur, niſi cum expreſſione, uſq̢ ad ignitionem aludelis, & niſi ſublimatum in cannali retineretur ſuperius cūm leuiter fundatur, deſcenderet iterum per uaſis latera, uſq̢ ad fundū, & ſic nihil inueniretur ſublimatū, ut notū eſt expertis.
De furno

1 Furnace for calcination

GEBRI. 187
Furnus Sublimatorius.

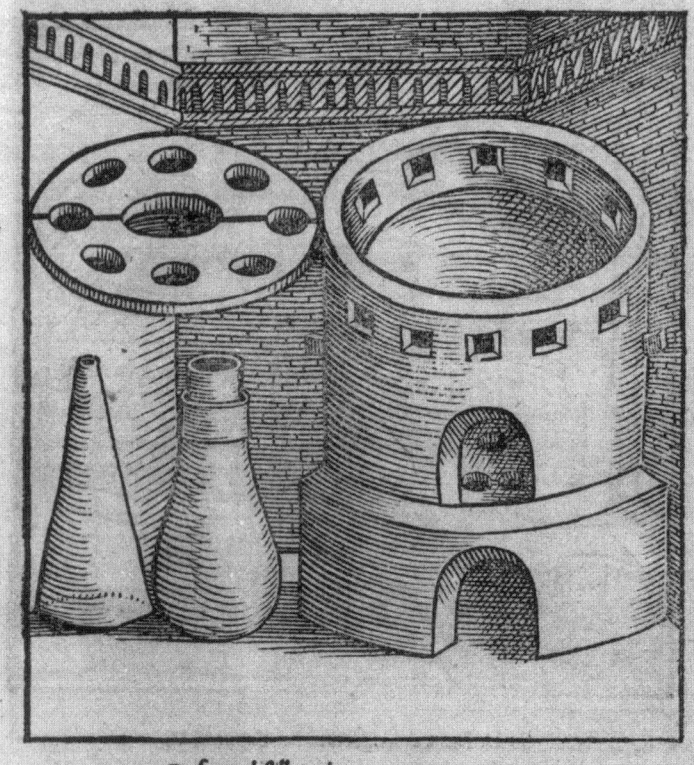

De furno distillatorio. Caput IIII.

FVrnus distillatorius est idem cum furno sublimatorio, fit autem uas distillatorium ad modum istius figuræ. Ignis autē administrandus est secundum exigentiam rei distillandæ. Modum autem sufficienter descripsimus distillatorium tam mineraliū, quám uegetabilum, in Summa nostra perfectionis.
A ij De furno

2 Furnace for sublimation

De Furno descensorio. Caput V.

FVrnus autem descensorius fit in hunc modum ? Et est apud nos inter fusores cineritiorum, & cementorum mirabiliter usitatus. Reducuntur aũt omnia corpora calcinata, cõbusta, soluta, & coagulata per hũc furnũ in solidã massam. Imò cineritia & cemẽta, & testę seu crusibula, in qbus sępius susum est argentũ ad recuperationẽ illius metalli imbibiti.

De

3 Furnace for descension

De furno fusorio.   Caput VI.

FVrnus fusorius, in quo omnia corpora leuiter funduntur per se, & est furnus iste multum usitatus inter fusores monetarios, nec non & aurichalcum in his furnis funditur, & tingitur cum Tutia uel Calamina, ut notum est expertis, & sic fit.

De fur-

4   Furnace for smelting

LIBER FORNACVM

De furno Solutorio.   *Caput* VII.

FVrnus diſſolutorius fit cum cacabo aquæ pleno cum inſtrumentis ferreis, in quibus artificioſe tenentur alia inſtrumenta, ne cadant, in quibus fit omnis diſſolutio, & hæc eſt forma furni & uaſorum, ut ſequitur.

De

5   Furnace for solution

De furno fixatorio uel Athannor.   *Caput* VIII.

Flat furnus fixatorius ad modum furni calcinationis, & sit patella profunda terrea plena cineribus cribellatis. Sit autem uas cum materia fixanda bene sigillatum in medio cinerum situata, sic quod spissitudo cinerum subtus & superius & in circuitu sit ad spissitudinem quatuor digitorum, uel secundum

6   Furnace for fixation

LIBER FORNACVM

secundũ illud, qp fixare desideras, Quia maior ignis requiritur in uno ɋ in alio fixando, Per hunc furnũ, & per hanc uiã peruenerunt antiqui philosophi ad opus magisterij, quod notũ est uere philosophantibus, quod per nos est satis monstratum sufficiẽter in libris nostris, illis qui fuerint ueritatis inuestigatores. Et hæc super est figura Athannor. Qui uero in huiusmodi potest magis ingeniari, nõ excuset se ab hoc, per nr̃am traditionẽ.
SECVN-

7 Athanor

24 An alchemical operation. Paulus Eck von Saltzbach: *Clavis Philosophorum* (1489)

Dissolve one measure of silver in two measures of nitric acid. Then take eight measures of quicksilver, and four or five measures of nitric acid. Pour them all together into the solution of silver, then place into slow-burning or completely cold ashes. In the first stage, you will see wonderful things. This is the Mercury principle of fixation or precipitation. Geber says, 'Fix a part, save a part for the ashes.'

The character of this operation. During the union of the waters, the waters are turbulent for a while at first, but once they have been well mixed, they become calm. Secondly: in cold sand, the matter builds itself up into the most delightful outgrowths, small eminences, and shrubs. Suddenly it bursts into movement and life, and stays the colour of metal, especially when you drain off the waters and pour pure water over it after the shrubs have grown. Thirdly: this matter coagulates in three days in a slow heat. Fourthly: the spirits do not separate or rise, because the water impedes their ascent. If anything does ascend, it collects on the surface of the water and descends again in the shape of a thin metal sheet. Fifthly: the ferment is united with the spirit via the 'medicine'. The body is reduced to its prime matter, i.e. into the water to which it is close in nature, that is, the principle of the mercury of fixation and the mercury of precipitation. Therefore the water should be drained off from the small eminences which should be allowed to dry slowly and then ground up and put in a Wallenburg vessel beneath a tap and a beam, and at first the surplus water will rise.

I opened the tap and wanted to reduce the sublimate overflow, but I saw that it smoked impatiently upwards in the vessel together with the spirits of the nitric acid. So I quickly covered them again by means of the tap and allowed them to stand thus overnight to fix them more effectively with their sublimate fire. This was done the following day. Once again I pushed the stuff which had risen down to the bottom [of the vessel], using a hare's foot for the purpose, and there they stayed for the major part of the rubification and fixation. The inside of the vessel just above the ashes turned red; in the middle it turned citrine, and above that, round the tap, it became light blue. At last, however, it turned red all over in the evening of the second day, (i.e. the Saturday after 'Invocavit'),[28] and I let it stand until the third Sunday (i.e. 'Reminiscere').[29] From one measure of silver and eight of mercury, I obtained four ounces of very good fixed precipitate, nearly a dram and a half; but because round the tap it was black and therefore useless, I threw it away.

[28] The opening word of the anthem for the first Sunday in Lent.
[29] Referring to the second Sunday in Lent.

25 Alchemical recipes. Arnaldus of Bruxella: *Alchemical manuscript* (transcribed at some time between 1473 and 1490)

[*Arnaldus was a publisher, regarded by contemporaries as one of the best of his period. He was thus a collector rather than an author of the following.*]

To change copper into very good gold: take hens and keep them cooped up so that they are unable to eat anything except pulse, i.e. lentils. Then take a small, trough-like vessel with a big lip to it, and put in fifteen of their eggs until they have formed little eddies. Then take them and put them in a separate, secluded place and let them stand until they are all reduced to a single [mass]. Then take [the mixture], put it in an oven, and let it reduce to ashes with heat sufficient for this purpose. From this powder you will make very good gold, if you know how to conduct the operation with true understanding.

To make silver from iron: take one *ligur*,[30] if you can get one which is alive, and one live toad. Put them together in a single jar so that one creature may eat the other. Seal the jar, but leave an opening in the top, through which you can see when the smoke ceases while they are being burned to ashes on top of a stove, and when the smoke stops, remove the jar from the fire. Throw some of this powder on to liquefied copper [sic], and it will be changed into silver.

To make silver from iron: another method on which great scholars are in agreement, having given some consideration to this craft, but have preserved only this [way of proceeding]. Take two toads which are carrying poison with them – you may actually have ten of them, or as many as you can find – take freshly gathered asphodels and a large quantity of white hellebore, and pound them really well. Then take a little vinegar and mix all these together in a rough pot; put the resulting mixture with iron, and if you add a little sublimated white sulphur, I guarantee you will be happy with it and that it will be happy with you.

[30] The word does not appear in any dictionaries.

26 The hidden spirit in sulphur. Anonymous manuscript: *Alchimiae tractatus* (14th century)

So when you ask what is the hidden spirit in sulphur and arsenic in solution, if you discuss the matter scientifically,[31] it is useful to note the distinction that we are employing two principal starting-points, namely, masculine and feminine; and we understand that herein their elements are also lying dormant in some fashion. This masculine and this feminine together give birth to our Stone. Although sulphur is masculine, in this place of whitening it will, because its nature is willing to do so, absorb and experience the form of a woman. So if you are a natural scientist, know that in this is hidden white quicksilver which we have extracted from our whitened mixture via the sublimated arsenic. This is the daughter and wife of sulphur, a viper who has killed her husband and enclosed herself in his stomach. So let a grave be dug and the woman buried with the dead man in horse-dung until such time as the principals be joined. The method of decocting this dung is to be found in the writings of natural scientists. The transfiguration which takes place in the dark is not achieved by an arrogant practitioner of the art, but if you enclose the horse-dung in both its physical and symbolical sense, you will undoubtedly deserve to be counted among the number of natural scientists. I say that the woman's stomach is full of poison. I call 'poison' sulphur which is not active but passive because in the first stage something which masters his wife and becomes masculine has lain down and been submissive, thus fulfilling the words of the philosopher: 'Nature contains nature, and nature overcomes nature and rejoices with it for ever,' if you understand correctly. The Roman natural scientist Morienus[32] makes it clear when he criticises those who make mistakes in this branch of knowledge. 'They will not arrive at the truth', he says, 'until the sun and moon are converted into a single body'. This is the extraction from sulphur of the spirit you sought. Don't you know that our Stone does not have an equivalent in earth? (Please notice that I am not using the word 'earth' in its conventional sense, but in ours: that is, the sense in which we natural scientists use it.) It is golden-yellow without and within, but when it is altered its body turns black and dark, like charcoal. The spirit removed from it, on the other hand, is white and liquid, like water. Its essence is reddish in colour, and it is by means of its essence that you restore the spirit of the Stone to life and make it rejoice; and you see it laughing because when the dead rise again, they live for ever. This was the spirit of sulphur which we extracted and returned again to itself, involving the sun during the process of resurrection.

You may proceed in the same fashion with arsenic, bearing this in mind – that obtaining the red tincture of sulphur is easy, obtaining the white one is more difficult; and that it is very difficult to achieve both the white and the satisfactory red tincture of arsenic. So that you may understand this, I tell you that there are things which work in successive stages until they turn into spirits and bodies. Secondly, I tell you that a medicine is held fast in a house of marble under their keys, and these keys are in their elements. If you are a natural scientist, I give you one key I call a sign, namely, a fall of water through the neck of a vessel which has a head like that of a man. So if you have scientifically investigated the loneliness of this man, you have found all the keys. The marble house is [made] of green jasper decorated with drops of blood, and it restricts the flow of blood. This red coral natural philosophers have recognised as they make a journey by sea. If you understand this kind of metaphor, you will realise that in scientific terms it has been drawn from arsenic. So you will conclude [that] the spirit hidden in sulphur and arsenic is a red and white tincture, [that] this tincture is defined in terms of yellowness, and [that] it corresponds to the yellow of the natural philosophers. If you want to secure the elixir so that it does not become unfixed, work it from the descent of the Sun towards the head of Capricorn until it rises into Aries; and render yourself safe, because at no time is it strictly secured. The man explains this symbol to you, saying, 'My son, receive a dog of the colours of air. Drink it from the water of the sea, because it will defend the elixir from the smelting of fire and its heat.' If, then, you have recognised the dog and the bitch, you may worthily be called to the succession of natural philosophers. If you have not, consult those who are more skilled [than yourself] and read the passage again so that you may learn from your mistakes; for the distinction discussed above, with reference to masculine and feminine, should be debated in a scientific fashion.

[footnote] 31 *Physice* = 'in a manner relating to the study of physical nature'. A similar implication has led me to translate *philosophus* as 'natural scientist' below, even though both translations carry unfortunate anachronistic overtones.

[footnote] 32 An Alexandrian Christian, the pupil of the third(?) century AD alchemist Zosimus. Morienus, in his turn, was said to have taught the Arab alchemist Khalid ibn Yazid (d.704 AD).

27 The need for secrecy. George Ripley: *The Compound of Alchemy* (c.1471)

[*George Ripley, died c.1490, was an Augustinian canon who studied alchemy in Rome, Louvain, and Rhodes. The following passage is taken from the introductory epistle to his work, and is addressed to King Edward IV*].

Once to your Lordship such things I did promise,
What time ye did command to send unto me;
And since that I wrote in full secret wise
Unto your Grace from the university
Of Louvain, when God fortuned me by grace to see
Greater secrets and much more profit,
Which only to you I will disclosed to be:
That is to say, the great elixirs both red and white.
For like it you to trust that truly I have found
The perfect way of most secret alchemy,
Which I will never truly for merk ne [nor] for pound
Make common but to you, and that conditionally
That to yourself ye shall keep it full secretly,
And only use it as may be to God's pleasure,
Else in time coming, of God I should abye [I shall have to answer
    to God]
For my discovering of his secret treasure.

Therefore advise you well with good deliberation,
For of this secret shall know none other creature
But only you, as I make faithful protestation,
For all the time that I here in life endure:
Whereto I will your Lordship me to ensure,
To my desire in this by oath to agree,
Lest I should to me the wrath of God procure,
For my revealing his great gift and privitie.

And yet moreover I will your Highness to pardon me,
For openly with pen I will it never write,

But when that ye list [wish] by practice ye shall see;
By mouth also this precious secret most of delight,
How may be made elixirs red and white,
Plain unto your Highness it shall declared be,
And if it please you with easy expense and respite [sufficient time]
To help, I will them make by help of the Trinity.

But notwithstanding for peril that might befall,
Though I dare not here plainly the net unbind,
Yet in my writing I will not be so mystical,
But that ye may by study the knowledge find.

---

28 Alchemical processes described in symbolic language. Alfonso X of Castile: *Tesoro* (attributed, 13th century)

Our Hermes says that it is the sky
and earth: but others that it is a man and a woman
whose marriage usually creates
other puzzles which serve as a veil.
The lowest sphere showed in the vault
some of the names of water or of earth;
others refer to the cold which pens in the heat;
the wise had so much mistrust.

In my opinion, the ancient chaos
Was put together from four elements.
It was likened to this compound
When it was divided up to make
The sky and the earth so that it came to be
A fifth essence an essence of the whole;
For this matter is in such a state
Because it comes to compose everything.
In this matter, the four elements
Are not united in equal parts.
If one makes a move, the others do likewise,
Because they follow the lead of the first.
If such a thing makes itself equal with its individual parts,
In some kind of vegetable, animal, or mineral [form],
You can find something better
Because you will be the sort of person who went to the wise.

29 Alchemical processes described more clearly.
John of Rupescissa: *De consideratione quintae essentiae* (mid 14th century)

[*Catalan Franciscan, physician, and alchemist. He spent more than one period in prison for prophesying. His* De consideratione *is his principal work. It is in two parts. The first is a description of procedures to extract the fifth essence, the second lists and describes remedies for various diseases.*]

Note that antimony is called a 'stone'. If it is reduced to a fine powder and burned in a small dish over a fire, it turns red and is an extraordinary sight. God is witness that I shall now reveal to you a great secret which hitherto has been revealed to few people or none, and is the mystic secret [*arcanum*] of every natural philosopher. Reduce antimony to a powder to the point where you cannot feel it, and then put it in distilled vinegar of the best quality until the vinegar turns red. When you have done this, remove the coloured vinegar to another vessel and pour on top of it some fresh vinegar until it, too, has taken on colour over a moderate heat. Then take it off. Do this until the vinegar takes on no more colour; then put all the vinegar you have coloured in this way into a distillation vessel, and at first the vinegar will rise. Then you will see an absolutely extraordinary marvel, because through the beak of the alembic you will see as it were a thousand rivulets of the blessed mineral running down in reddish droplets, like blood. Keep this blessed liquid in a stout, closely sealed bottle because it is a treasure of which the whole world does not have an equal. See a miracle – such a great sweetness of antimony that it surpasses the sweetness of honey; and I say by the love of God that the human intellect could scarcely believe the power and strength of this water, or 'fifth essence' of antimony. Aristotle says that this is his 'lead' in his book, *The Secret of Secrets*. Believe me that there has never been a greater secret in nature. All humankind has laboured to sublimate the spirits of minerals and has never possessed the fifth essence of antimony I have just mentioned. I could never describe the half of this mystery in just a few words. It takes away the pain of wounds and effects marvellous cures. Its power is miraculously not subject to diminution and it is extremely useful. It needs to decay at the bottom of a sealed bottle for forty days, and then its mystery begins to work. Don't think what I have been saying is impossible. If you put carbonate of lead in distilled vinegar and boil them together for two hours, or until the vinegar evaporates and [the remaining mixture] has the consistency of oil, this is called 'the oil of Saturn' and has the sweetness of honey. That sweetness, however, is insipid in comparison with the sweetness of the fifth essence of antimony, which is like the sweetness of honey and sugar. Believe me, read the books of all the natural philosophers, look for their 'lead', and you will never find that it refers to the fifth essence [of antimony]; nor will you find the true art whereby anything other than quicksilver can, in the most extraordinary fashion, be turned to gold in the colour red. Therefore, praise be to God.

30 Use of the word 'Stone'. Roger Bacon: *Secretum secretorum* (13th century)

[*Franciscan scholar, c.1220–92.*]

'Stone' is understood metaphorically in the first place to refer to anything which acts as the starting-point for an alchemical operation. This can be mineral matter, such as sulphur and arsenic; but vegetable matter, such as fruit and the parts of trees and herbs, is better. Best of all is matter which comes from living creatures, such as blood, an egg, and hairs, and especially human parts: and among these, blood in which the eye picks out four humours, namely, phlegm, choler, blood, and black bile. The alchemist then looks for a way to separate these humours from each other, and to free each from any taint of the others; and after they have been reduced to their pure, simple states by means of different procedures, then they should be mixed together in a proportion which is both secret and very reliable. To these, quicksilver is added after it has been put through the death-process ('mortification') and sublimated several times. The same thing should be done with the calx or powder of a baser metal from which more noble metal will be made; and likewise the calx of a more noble metal. After this, they should be mixed together until they form a single body. This is then projected upon a baser metal which has been liquefied, and it becomes more noble.

31 The Stone. Avicenna: *De anima* (1021/4)

[*Avicenna, 980–1037 AD. Persian physician who wrote a philosophical and scientific encyclopaedia. His most influential work was his* Canon of Medicine, *widely translated and studied during the Middle Ages.*]

Take some 'stone' (which is not a stone and has none of the distinctive features of a stone). Divide it into four parts – air, fire, earth, and water. I am unable to discover that it can be done in any way other than the following. A human being lives, dies, and depends upon blood. Likewise the stone. Consequently they say that this stone is a living [*animalis*] stone, and therefore because there is no higher soul [*anima*] than a human being, they take the stone of a human.

32 Description of the Philosopher's Stone. John Lydgate: *Secrees of Old Philosoffres* (c.1450)

Anent the Stone of ancient philosophers of which they make most important mention, there is one (as Aristotle said) which excels all others – stone of stones, most important and very famous – and he wrote to King Alexander about it as follows …

First you must produce in a strange fashion division in the [basic] substance, separating water from air, and parting fire from air, each being preserved from corruption, as natural philosophers have instructed in the past and with whose recommendations one should not argue. Careful separation of water from air, air from fire, and fire from earth is what the art [of alchemy] has assumed will be done accurately without error or deception. Purify each element in its composition in relation to the part it clearly plays in the alchemical process, as the Art reminds us perfectly.

The Philosopher's Stone is sometimes citrine in colour, like the golden-haired sun beaming down as is his nature, who makes hearts very happy with more treasure than the King of India has [in the form] of precious stones made each in its own fitting way: the citrine colour for the bright sun, white for the moon which shines all night.[33]

The natural philosopher born in Paris, who wrote at length about this stone,[34] set great store on this process of separation and laid great emphasis upon it, so that the final perfected stage should last a long time, according to the purport of Aristotle's message – a stage which none but he could manage to undertake.

[33] I.e. the yellowish 'stone' makes gold, the white 'stone' makes silver.
[34] This person is not identifiable.

33 A medicine produced by alchemy. Ortulanus: *Practica vera alkimica* (1386)

[*The name also appears as 'Hortulanus'. His identity is uncertain. He has been identified with the Englishman, John Garland, 1202–52, but this is generally regarded as unlikely to be accurate. There is also a Hortulanus, c.1358, about whom nothing more is known.*]

Take rectified aqueous alcohol in whatever quantity you wish and put it, drop by drop, into what is left over from the perfected Stone – as much as can dissolve therein. In this solution will emerge burning or flaming golden sparks, and there will appear as many colours as anyone can imagine. When the colours have stopped appearing and the water clears, it will be golden or a kind of bright red, transparent and unclouded. This is perfected aqueous alcohol and a sound medicine for the body, a more valuable medicine than those of Galen, Avicenna, Hippocrates, and any other doctor, having the power to pluck out, uproot, purge, and expel all infirmities from the human body. Even if the infirmity has lasted for a hundred years, it will be completely cured in one month; and if it has lasted for fifty years, it will be completely cured within a fortnight. If some infirmity has lasted for twenty years, it will be completely cured within eight days; and if some infirmity has lasted in the human body for seven years, it will be cured within three days; and if some infirmity has lasted for one year, it will be cured in a single day. This is quite obviously the secret of secrets. Its power cannot be bought, and it is rightly called 'the blessed stone' because there has not been anything which Almighty God has given humankind, which is more precious.

Here is how the medicine should be taken. Take one draught of wine as strong as the patient's condition and appetite warrant, and put therein one drop of this aqueous alcohol – two, if the patient is very ill, but no more at one time. Warm it a little by the fire and the medicine will immediately begin to mix with the wine. Once the two are thoroughly mixed, give the draught to the patient, and he will begin to recover in the name of the Lord and will be well, by the grace of God. Do this every third or fourth day until the patient has recovered and is out of danger. The same medicine can be taken in any concoction the patient finds agreeable. In a case where the patient is weak and feverish and cannot drink wine, he may be given the medicine in any concoction by maintaining a conveniently appropriate dose in everything.

34 The importance of alchemy to physicians. Roger Bacon: *De erroribus medicorum* (13th century)

[*English Franciscan.*]

The fifth fault [among physicians] is their ignorance of alchemy and agriculture, because almost all herbal medicines are derived from these two branches of knowledge, as is perfectly obvious. They prescribe the wrong things particularly because of their ignorance of alchemy. Since the art of medicine presupposes that the working properties of medicines are accepted as valid without the presence of a material substance, and since on innumerable occasions this must happen, because the substances used are gross, earthy, and harmful, one cannot give a detailed description of them except by referring to the methods used in alchemy which is the only branch of knowledge which teaches us how to extract the working properties from anything. In things used for healing, solutions and separations of one thing must be produced from another, something which cannot happen without the power of alchemy which teaches us how to condense one thing out of another ...

Alchemy is useful for practical medicine, and its working is extremely useful for the theory of medicine, as well as in the highest degree necessary, because it defines the whole way things are produced from the elements via the simple and complex humours right up to the parts of animals, plants, and humankind ... Medicine, however, does not demonstrate this generative process but passes physicians over entirely to alchemy, as Avicenna makes clear in several passages, and as other writers on medicine do as well. Consequently, alchemy alone among the various branches of knowledge has dared to determine that (a) there are four elements, then (b) another four, and thirdly (c) four, making twelve in all, from which humankind and the whole lower world are composed. Therefore there are twelve material bodies with the potentiality to produce fixed types of things with a separate form of existence in this world. The natural philosopher does not explain them, but refers physicians to alchemy, as Avicenna makes clear at the beginning of his *Canon of Medicine* where he argues against Galen who says that only blood runs through the parts of the body which need nourishment; for he shows that other humours are necessary for many reasons, and after putting his case he underlines what he is saying by referring to his experience with alchemy, saying, 'I have also found that blood has been mixed with other humours which have a separate existence from it. When it is extracted and duly put into an *atuus* or *eges*, which are distilling vessels used in alchemical processes, you see that it is separated into one part which is like lye and is muddy and blackish, one part which is like the albumen of eggs and reminds one of phlegm, and a watery art which is pellucid. If there is too much of this part, it is expelled in the urine' ... .

For this and innumerable other reasons, then, alchemy is a necessary part of theoretical medicine, in that it investigates how things come into being and the special properties of their individual characters.

35 Some famous alchemists. Al-Nadim: *Kitab al-Fihrist* (987–8)

[*Abu 'l Faradj Muhammad ibn Abi Ya'kub Ishak al-Warrak al-Nadim al-Baghdadi, Arabic bibliographer.*]

Hermes Trismegistus. The people who practise alchemy (that is, who make gold and silver from other metals) say that the first to speak about the technique as a science was Hermes the Sage who originally came from Babylon and then settled in Egypt after the dispersal of peoples far from Babel. He was King of Egypt, a sage, and a philosopher. He successfully practised alchemy and wrote a number of books on the subject. He studied the properties and spiritual qualities of bodies and, thanks to his researches and labours, succeeded in building up the science of alchemy. He undertook the business of making talismans, and composed many treatises on the subject. Those who support the theory which attributes to alchemy a great antiquity, however, assert that this science existed thousands of years before Hermes.

Abu Bakr al-Razi, (i.e. Muhammad ibn Zakariyya) maintains it is not permissible to attach the name 'philosophical science' to any branch of knowledge which does not include alchemy, and that a scholar does not deserve to be called a natural philosopher unless he is well skilled in the Great Work; for he alone can do without anyone else, although everyone else needs him because of his knowledge and his position. Certain adepts in alchemy say that the work was revealed by God – may his name be glorified! – to a certain number of people who devoted themselves to the art. Others say that the revelation was made by Almighty God to Moses, son of Amram, and Aaron – peace be upon both of them! – and that the person who practised [the art] in their name was Karun. He accumulated a treasure of gold and silver but, at the request of Moses, was carried off by God who had noticed the arrogance and pride and wickedness which had inspired him to acquire and keep this wealth ... According to some people, [Hermes] was one of the seven guardians whose job it was to keep watch over the seven temples. He was in charge of the Temple of Mercury, from whom he took his name, because in Chaldaean 'Mercury' is expressed as 'Hermes'. Other people say that, for various reasons, he was carried off to Egypt and became King there. He had a number of children [*names given*] and was the foremost sage of his time. After his death he was buried in the building known in Memphis as the Abode of Hermes, and which the common people call 'the two pyramids', one being his tomb, the other his wife's. Certain authors claim that this second pyramid was that of his son who succeeded him after his death.

Khalid ibn Yazid. The person who first brought to the light of day the books of the ancients on alchemy, says Muhammad ibn Ishak, was Khalid ibn Yazid. He was a preacher, a poet, a man of eloquence, full of enthusiasm and discernment, and was the first to translate books on medicine, astrology, and alchemy. He had a generous disposition, and we are told that in reply to someone who said to him, 'You have devoted the greater part of your efforts to alchemical research,' Khalid replied, 'All my researches have no other goal but to enrich my friends and brothers. It was my ambition to be Caliph, but it was taken away from me and I have found consolation in seeking to reach the limits of the Work. I want to spare anyone who has known me for a single day, or whom I myself have known, the necessity of having to stand at the doorway of a prince's palace like a petitioner or a man overcome by fear.' They say (and God knows better than anyone if this is true) that Khalid was successful in his alchemical endeavours. He wrote a number of treatises and short works on this subject, and also a lot of verse. I have seen about five hundred pages filled with these verses, and I have also seen among his works his book on heat, the big and small treatises on balances, and the book of advice he wrote to his son about the Work.

Djabir ibn Haiyan. [*i.e. 'Geber' in the west*]. A person worthy of belief and a practitioner of alchemy told me that Djabir used to live in Bab Ec-Cham Street, in the area known as the Gold Quarter. He maintained that Djabir lived most often in Kufa because of that town's especially favourable climate, and that he made his elixir there; and when they demolished the portico in which they found a golden mortar worth about two hundred rotls, this same man told me that the place where they found it was where Djabir ibn Haiyan's house had stood, and that in the portico they found not only this mortar but a work-place for the processes of dissolution and conjunction. This happened during the reign of 'Izz al-Dawla. The vizier told me that it was he who had removed the mortar to keep it for himself. A number of scholars and important booksellers have told me that Djabir never actually existed. Others say that if he did exist, he never wrote any books other than *Summary of the Perfection of the Philosopher's Stone*, any other works carrying his name being attributed to him by their real authors. As far as I am concerned, a talented man who got down to work and took the trouble to write a volume of two thousand pages (never mind the physical fatigue attendant upon putting it down on paper), and then attributed it to someone else (whether that other person existed or not), would be a lunatic. It is something which no one with the slightest claim to learning will ever do or to which he will voluntarily agree. After all, what profit or advantage would he derive from doing so? Djabir, then, actually did exist. His identity is certain and well-known, and he is the author of a very large number of important works.

Alchemy. Muhammad ibn Ishaq says this: the books on this subject are very numerous, too numerous, in fact, for me to be able to count them all; but many of the authors have merely repeated the teachings of their predecessors. The Egyptians especially have a very large number scholars and writers on alchemy. The science originated in that country, and the monuments called 'pyramids' were simply alchemical laboratories.

36 An unfriendly portrait of an alchemist.
Geoffrey Chaucer: *The Canon's Yeoman's Prologue*, 64–130, adapted (1380s–90s)

[*English poet and diplomatist, c.1340–1400. His* Canterbury Tales, *from which the following extract is taken, was begun in the late 1380s.*]

[*A yeoman describes his master, a canon who is also an alchemist, to the landlord of the Tabard Inn in the London district of Southwark.*]

'My master has knowledge of such a subtle kind – but you can't blame his cunning on me: I just help him a little while he's working – that he could turn all this ground on which we've been riding, and from here to Canterbury, completely upside down and pave it with silver and gold.'

When the yeoman finished saying this, the landlord said, 'God bless you! I find it quite extraordinary that if your master has such lofty knowledge which ought to make people respect him, he pays so little attention to his personal dignity. His overcoat is not worth a farthing – and I am actually obliged to dress as he does – it is dirty and torn all over. Why is your master so slovenly when he has the power to buy better cloth, if he can do as you say? Answer me that, please!'

[*No, replies the yeoman, I shall keep it a secret.*] 'My opinion of him is that he is both ignorant and foolish. When a man has an over-great intelligence, he frequently misuses it. So does my master, and I am very sorry for it. God put it right! I can't tell you any more.'

'It's of no consequence, good yeoman,' said our landlord. 'But, since you know about your master's skill, please tell me how he lives, since he is so cunning and so subtle. If you are willing to tell me, where do you live?'

'In the suburbs of a town', he said, 'lurking in corners and blind alleys where this kind of robber, these thieves by nature, live in secret and in fright, like people who dare not show themselves in public. This is how we live, if I'm to tell you the truth.'

'Now', said the landlord, 'let me go on talking to you. Why is your face so discoloured?'

'God damn it, Peter, I am so used to blowing the fire that I believe it has changed my complexion. I don't usually look in a mirror. I work hard and learn how to multiply [turn base metal into gold]. We are always making mistakes and staring into the fire; but in spite of all that, we fail to achieve what we want and never bring our work to a successful conclusion. We give many people illusions, and borrow gold – perhaps a pound or two, or ten, or twelve, or much greater amounts – and make them imagine that, at the very least, we could make twenty pounds out of one. It's always a lie, but we always really hope we can do it, and we blunder about, trying to achieve it. But that kind of knowledge has eluded us so far, and we are not successful, although we had sworn the contrary; it rushed past, it slid away so fast. It will make us beggars in the end .... Yet they [the alchemists] never weary of the art, for to them it is apparently something bitter-sweet. Even if they had only a sheet to wrap themselves in at night, and a cloak to wear during the day, they would sell them and spend the money on this craft. They can't stop until they have nothing left. Wherever they go, people always recognise what they are by the smell of brimstone. They stink for all the world like a goat. The smell is so much like that of a ram in heat that even if someone is a mile away, he is contaminated by the smell. People can therefore recognise them by their stink and their threadbare clothes. If anyone asks them very quietly why they are so poorly dressed, they will whisper in his ear and say that if it was found out they were alchemists, people would kill them for it. This is how these people deceive simpletons.'

37 Impediments to an alchemist's being able to work.
Pseudo-Geber: *Summa Perfectionis* (adapted)
(early 14th century(?))

(Chapter 4). If someone does not possess a complete set of bodily organs, he will not be able to arrive at a completion of this work of his own accord. If, for example, he were blind or had had his hands and feet cut off, he would not be able to rely on help from his members and these things, which are his instruments performing the role of servants to nature, enable him to achieve something in this art. If the body of the alchemist is feeble and sickly, like the bodies of those suffering from fevers: or like those of lepers whose extremities fall off: or those on the verge of dying: or those of old men rendered decrepit by age: he will not arrive at the completion of the art. The operative is therefore hindered in his intention by these natural weaknesses of the body.

(Chapter 5). Anyone who does not possess natural intelligence and a spirit which thoroughly investigates natural principles, the foundations of nature, the ways in which she is designed and put together, and which can grasp the peculiar character of the way she operates, will not discover the real root of this most precious branch of knowledge. The same can be said of many people who are devoid of intelligence and have a closed mind when it comes to any careful investigation; of those who can scarcely understand everyday speech; and likewise of those who find difficulty in learning what any Tom, Dick, or Harry knows how to do. In addition to these, we also find many who have a spirit ready to believe any kind of fantasy. They believe they have discovered the truth, but what they have found is a complete figment of their imagination, irrational, full of error, and far removed from natural principles: because their brain, filled with many fumes and vapours, is unable to accept the true meaning of natural things. Then there are others who have a busy spirit which flits from belief to belief, and from fad to fad; and those who believe something on one occasion and want it without any basis in rational thinking at all, and then shortly afterwards believe something else and believe it just as irrationally. These people are so easily swayed that they can hardly finish even a very little of what they are aiming to do, but leave it half done. Likewise, there are those who cannot appreciate any truth which arises from natural things, any more than wild beasts can – people who are prisoners in their own heads, for example, or madmen, or children. Others despise alchemy and think there is no such thing; so alchemy despises them and drives them away from accomplishing anything of this most precious work. Then there are those who are slaves, devoting themselves to the service of money, who profess this extraordinary branch of knowledge, but are afraid to spend the necessary cash. Therefore, although they profess to be alchemists, and follow the trail in accordance with its rules, they do not gain any practical skill in the work because of their avarice.

(Chapter 6). We see certain people who are clever and intelligent and not in the least ignorant of how nature works; who are, as far as is possible, responsive to her principles and operations: and in whose case investigation of everything beneath the orbit of the moon, which is regulated by the movements and actions of nature, is not a matter of fantasy: ground down by the final stages of poverty because they have spent all their money and are obliged to defer [their pursuit of] this lofty discipline. In addition to these, there are also many others who are curious about it, but are held back by the various problems and anxieties of this world and devote themselves entirely to every type of worldly business. From people such as these, our precious discipline runs straight away.

---

38 English royal licences granted to practise alchemy. *Calendar of State Papers* (15th century)

(a) *Henry VI. 6 July 1444.* Whereas John Cobbe showed by a petition to the King that though he wished to operate on certain matters by the art of philosophy, to wit, to transmute imperfect metals from their proper sort into perfect gold or silver, in order to await or mature all experiments and examinations, such as any gold or silver growing in any mineral, yet his ill-wishers suppose him to work by unlawful art and disturb him in such experiments: the King wishing to know the conclusion of the work has granted licence to him to work and experiment therein, provided always that to do so be not contrary to law.

(b) *7 April 1446*. Licence for Edmund de Trafford, knight, and Thomas Assheton, knight, and their servants to pursue their art of transmutation of metals.

(c) *4 July 1446*. Licence for William Hurteles, Alexander Worsley, Thomas Bolton, and George Horneby to pursue their art of transmutation of metals.

(d) *30 April 1452*. Licence for life for John Mistelden to exercise his art of the transmutation of metals.

(e) *31 May 1456*. Licence for John Fauceby, John Kirkeby, and John Rayny to search the doctrines and writings of the wise ancients and to practise transmutation of metals, notwithstanding the statute of Henry IV; and protection for them in the premises.

(f) *3 September 1460*. Licence for William Sauvage, Hugh Hurdeleston, and Henry Hyne with their three servants to pursue their art of transmutation of metals, as Richard Trevys, doctor of theology, John Billok, and William Downes have had licence.

(g) *Edward IV. 21 October 1463*. Grant, during pleasure, to Henry Grey of Cotenore, knight, and his deputies and assigns of power and authority to labour, by the conning of philosophy, transmutation of metals with all other things requisite and necessary to the same at his own cost, so that he shall answer to the King if any profit grow.

(h) *7 December 1468*. Licence for Richard Carter to practise the art of alchemy with all kinds of metals and minerals for the space of two years in the King's manor of Woodstock.

(i) *18 June 1476*. Grant for four years to the King's servant David Beaupe and John Marchaunt that they may practise the faculty and science of philosophy and the turning of mercury into gold and silver.

39 An alchemist terrorised into making silver. *Calendar of Patent Rolls* (3 April 1337)

Commission of oyer and terminer to John de Pulteneye, mayor of London, Robert de Scardeburgh and William Scot, on complaint by Thomas de Eboraco that, whereas he by the science of alchymy had forged silver plates and had them proved by goldsmiths and others of the city of London, one Thomas Corp of London, 'spicer', and others plotting to disturb him maliciously took him by night at the said city and brought him to the house of the said Thomas Corp there, and made him bring with him an elixir and some other instruments wherewith he made such silver, and to compel him to teach them the art, imprisoned him there until through fear of death he forged silver by his art in their sight, and made two bonds to the said Thomas in £100 each, and carried away the elixir and instruments with other goods, and that they afterwards, by pretext of the bonds, although he was never bailiff of the said Thomas Corp or receiver of any of his moneys, before the mayor and sheriffs of the city they called him to account before auditors appointed for this for the sums in bonds and arrears and procured him to be adjudged to Newgate gaol until he satisfied him of these, whereby he has been long and still remains in the said gaol.

40 Alchemy regarded as fraudulent. Sebastian Brant: *Das Narrenschiff* (1494)

[*Sebastian Brant, 1457–1521.*]

No. 102. At this point I shall not forget the great swindle which is alchemy: the making of gold and silver already concealed in the stick [which stirs the pot]. It uses tricks and diddles people dreadfully. It demonstrates a 'proof', and then produces a serpent. Curiosity sends abroad many a person who had formerly lived contentedly without much money, and now throws his goods into a monkey-glass until they are burned to a cinder and turned to dust, so that he doesn't know who he is any more. Many are ruined thus; few become rich, for Aristotle says, 'The basic structure of a thing does not change.'

41 Fraudulent alchemists. *Calendar of Patent Rolls* (18 August 1452)

Henry VI. Commission to John Hewet, John Edmund, and John Assheby, appointing them to arrest all persons in the city or suburbs of London or the county of Middlesex or elsewhere, who, pretending themselves expert in the science of multiplying gold and silver, have approached simple persons and received from them on such false pretences sums of money and jewels of gold and silver, making no restitution thereof. Contrary to the statute of 5 Henry IV, with their instruments, and to bring them before the King or Council to answer touching the premises.

42 Papal prohibition against alchemy. John XXII: *Extravagantales decretales: De crimine falsi* (early 14th century)

[Pope John XXII, c.1244–1334. His pontificate began in 1316. French by birth, he was the second of the Avignon Popes. During his reign he was engaged in lengthy struggles with some of the Franciscans and with an anti-Pope, Nicholas V.]

Alchemists solemnly promise riches to the poor, and do not produce them. Likewise, thinking themselves so full of knowledge, they fall into a pit which they have dug; for there can be no doubt that people who profess this art of alchemy are deluding each other when they express astonishment at those aware of their ignorance and who have drawn attention to their self-delusion. When the real thing they have been looking for does not turn up, these people fix a day, exhaust their resources, and paint a false picture so that – unable by the very nature of things to produce real gold or silver – they talk up a transmutation and produce it that way. Sometimes their temerity reaches the point where they stamp real metals with the characters of public money, which look genuine enough, and this is how they deceive the unwitting public about the 'alchemical' fire of their furnace. Therefore, wishing to do away with these things in perpetuity, We confirm by this our decree, that whoever makes gold or silver of this kind; or has it made in obedience to his command; or hereafter knowingly provides for those who make it, during the time of its manufacture; or knowingly uses such silver or gold in business transactions: let them, as penance, be compelled to give an equivalent amount of gold or silver which will then publicly be disbursed to the poor, once it has been legally established that they have committed an offence in one of the foresaid ways. Those who continue, notwithstanding, to make alchemical gold or silver, or knowingly use it (as is said above), have been stained with the mark of perpetual disgrace. But if these offenders have not the wherewithal to discharge the foresaid monetary penance, a lenient judge will be able to use his discretion to commute this penance to another – imprisonment, for example, or something else according to the nature of the transaction, the differences between individuals, and other attendant circumstances. As for those who have rushed into the ignorance of this wretched activity with the result that not only do they sell coin, they also despise the natural precepts of proper conduct, exceed the bounds of the art, and violate the prohibitions laid down by law – that is to say, by knowingly striking or casting illegal coinage from alchemical gold and silver – these people. We order struck down by this censure, so that their goods may be confiscated and they themselves disgraced for ever. If the offenders are clerics, let them in addition to the foresaid penalties be deprived of the benefices they hold, and in every respect rendered disqualified from holding them.

Bibliography

Sources

Acta et processus canonizacionis beate Birgitte, ed. I. Collijn 3 vols (Uppsala 1924–7).
Ademar of Chabannes: *Chronicon*, ed. P. Bourgain, G. Pon, R. Landes in *Corpus Christianorum Continuatio Mediaevalis* Vol. 129 (Turnhout, Brepols 1999).
Aelfric: *Homily on the Octaves and Circumcision of Our Lord* in B. Thorpe (ed.): *The Homilies of the Anglo-Saxon Church*: Part 1, *The Sermones Catholici or Homilies of Aelfric* 2 vols (London 1844–6).
Albertus Magnus: *Speculum astronomiae* in *Opera Omnia* 38 vols, ed. A. Borguet, Vol. 10 (Paris 1891).
Alexander VI: *Decretal* in J. Hansen (ed.): *Quellen und Untersuchungen zur Geschichte des Hexenwahns und der Hexenverfolgung im Mittelalter* (Bonn 1901).
Alexander of Tralles: *De arte medicina*, ed. Th. Puschmann 2 vols (Vienna 1878–9).
Alfonso X of Castile and Leon: *Tesoro*. Text in R. Luanco: *La alchimia en España* 2 vols (Barcelona 1889) 2.179.
Alfonso de Madrigal Tostado de Rivera: *Libro intitulado Las catorze questiones del Tostado* (Burgos 1545).
Ambrosius de Vignate: *Tractatus de hereticis* in J. Hansen (ed.): *Quellen und Untersuchungen zur Geschichte des Hexenwahns und der Hexenverfolgung im Mittelalter* (Bonn 1901).
André de Fleury: *Vita Gauzlini*, ed. R.-H. Bautier & G. Labory (Editions du Centre National de la Recherche Scientifique, Paris 1969).
Andrew of Strumi: *Vita Sancti Joannis Gualberti* in Migne: *Patrologia Latina* 146.765–812.
Anon.: *Adjuration Against a Hail-Storm* in J. Grimm: *Deutsche Mythologie*, ed. E.H. Meyer 3 vols (Berlin 1875–8).
Anon.: *Alchimiae tractatus*, unpublished manuscript (fourteenth century), held by the University of St Andrews, Scotland.
Anon.: *Christ Before Pilate, The Dream of Pilate's Wife* in R. Beadle (ed.): *The York Plays* (Edward Arnold, London 1982).
Anon.: *Ovide moralisé*, ed. C. de Boer in *Verhandlingen der Koninklijke Akademie van Wetenschappen te Amsterdam* 1915–38.
Anon.: *Vita Sancti Roberti* in Martín del Rio: *Disquisitiones Magicae* (Louvain 1608), Book 2, question 28, section 3.

Anthoni de Balcebre: *Document de l'any 1424 relatiu a la bruixeria a la vall d'Àneu* in Cels Gomis i Serdañons (ed.): *La Bruixa Catalana* (Alta Fulla, Barcelona 1996).
Arnald of Villanova: *Opera Omnia* (Venice 1505).
Arnaldus of Bruxella: Text in W. J. Wilson, 'An alchemical manuscript by Arnaldus de Bruxella', *Osiris* 2 (1936).
Athelwold in W. de Gray Birch (ed.): *Cartularium Saxonicum* 4 vols (London 1885–99), vol. 3.
Avicenna: *De anima in Artis chemicae principes, Avicenna atque Geber* (Basel 1572).
——: *De congelatione et conglutinatione lapidum* ed. E.J. Holmyard & D.C. Mandeville (Paris 1922).
St Alcimus Ecdicius Avitus: *Poemata de Mosaicae historiae gestis* in Migne: *Patrologia Latina* 59.329-38.
Bacon Roger: *De erroribus medicorum* in *Opera hactenus inedita Rogeri Baconi* Vol. 9 ed. A. G. Little & E. Withington (Oxford 1928).
——: *Opus Maius*, ed. J. H. Bridges 2 vols (Oxford 1897).
——: *Secreta secretorum* in *Opera hactenus inedita Rogeri Baconi*, Vol. 5 ed. R. Steele (Oxford 1920).
——: *Speculum alchemiae* in *Alchemiae Gebri Arabis* (Bern 1545).
Balsamon Theodore: *In epistolam Sancti Basilii canonicam III* in Migne: *Patrologia Graeca* 138.800-4.
Barbour John: *The Brus*, ed. C. Innes (Aberdeen 1856).
Barsanuphios: *Correspondence* 3 vols in 5 (Editions du Cerf, Paris 1997–).
Beati Angelae Fulgimatis vita et opuscula (Foligno 1714).
Pseudo-Bede: *De mundi celestis terrestrisque constitutione*, ed. C. Burnett (Warburg Institute, London 1985).
Benedict XII: *Letter* in J. Hansen (ed.): *Quellen und Untersuchungen zur Geschichte des Hexenwals und der Hexenverfolgung im Mittelalter* (Bonn 1901).
Boccaccio Giovanni: *De genealogia deorum gentilium* (Paris 1511).
Brant Sebastian: *De monstroso ansere atque porcellis in villa Gugenheim* (Basel 1496).
——: *Das Narrenschiff*, ed. L. Geeraedts (Dortmund 1981).
Calendar of the Patent Rolls 1334–38 (London 1895); 1441–46 (London 1908); 1446–52 (London 1909); 1452–61 (London 1910); 1461–67 (London 1897); 1467–77 (London 1900).
Charlemagne: *Capitularia* in Etienne Baluze (ed.): *Capitularia Regum Francorum* 2 vols (Paris 1677).
Chaucer Geoffrey: *The Canon's Yeoman's Prologue* to *The Canterbury Tales* in *The Complete Works of Geoffrey Chaucer* ed. W.W. Skeat (Clarendon, Oxford, 1894).
Childeric: *Capitularia* in Etienne Baluze (ed.): *Capitularia Regum Francorum* 2 vols (Paris 1677).
Chindasvind: *Leges Visigothorum* in *Monumenta Germaniae Historica* Leges Section 1, Tome I ed. K. Zeumer (Hanover & Leipzig 1902).
Choniates Niketas: *Historia*, ed. J. A. von Dieten (de Gruyter, Berlin 1975).
Council of Auxerre in *Monumenta Germaniae Historica* Leges section 3: Concilia Vol. 1 ed. F. Maasson (Hanover 1893).

Council of Orléans in *Monumenta Germaniae Historica* Leges section 3: Concilia Vol. 1 ed. F. Maasson (Hanover 1893).
Council of Paris in *Monumenta Germaniae Historica* Concilia Vol. 2, part 2 (Hanover & Leipzig 1908).
Council of Worms in *Monumenta Germaniae Historica*: Concilia Vol. 4 (Hanover 1998).
Chronicum Scotorum, ed. W. M. Hennessy (London 1866).
Damian Peter: *Die Briefe des Petrus Damiani*, ed. K. Reindel 4 vols (Munich 1983–93).
David of Ganjak: *Penitential*, ed. and trans. J. F. Dowsett = *Corpus Scriptorum Christianorum Orientalium* Vols 216 & 217, *Scriptores Armeniaci* (Louvain 1961).
De gestis Herwardi Saxonis in *The Anglo-Norman Metrical Chronicle of Geoffrey Gaimar*, ed. T. Wright (London 1850).
De origine gigantum, text in *Arthurian Literature* 13 (1995), 93–114.
Dionysius Exiguus: *Canones* in A. Strewe (ed.): *Die Canonessammlung des Dionysius Exiguus in der ersten Redaktion* (Berlin 1931).
Eberhard of Bamberg: *Collectiones judiciorum Dei* in *Monumenta Germaniae Historica*, Leges section 5 (Hanover 1886).
Paulus Eck von Saltzbach: *Clavis philosophorum* in *Theatrum Chemicum* Vol. 4 (Strasborg 1659).
Enguerrand de Monstrelet: *Chroniques*, ed. J. A. Buchan Vol. 1 (Paris 1826).
Etienne de Bourbon: *Anecdotes historiques*, ed. A. Lecoy de la Marche (Paris 1877).
Ficino Marsilio: *De vita libri tres* in *Omnia Opera*, Vol. 2 (Paris 1641).
Fitzhugh Robert: *Memorandum* in A. Zellfelder: *England und das Basler Konzil* (Berlin 1913).
Geber: *Liber Fornacum* in *Alchemiae Gebri Arabis* (Bern 1545).
Gerson Jean: *De superstitiosa dierum observantia* in *Oeuvres complètes* 10 vols (Vol. 10, Paris 1997–).
Giovanni di m. Pedrino Depintore: *Cronica del suo tempo*, ed. G. Borghezio & M. Vattasso in *Studi e Testi* 50 (1929) and 62 (1934).
Giraldus Cambrensis: *Topographia Hiberniae* (Frankfurt 1603).
Glaber Rodulfus: *Historiae*, ed. J. France: *Rodulfi Glabri historiarum libri quinque* (Clarendon, Oxford 1989).
Grosseteste Robert: *Expositio* in *epistolam Sancti Pauli ad Galatas*, in *Corpus Christianorum Continuatio Mediaevalis* Vol. 130, ed. J. McEvoy (Brepols, Turnhout 1995).
Gui Bernard: *Practica inquisitionis heretice pravitatis*, ed. G. Mollat 2 vols (Paris 1926–7).
Guibert de Nogent: *Monodiae*, ed. E.-R. Labande under the title *Autobiographie* (Les Belles Lettres, Paris 1981).
Guillaume d'Auvergne: *De universo* in *Omnia Opera* (Venice 1591).
Heinrich von Gorkum: *De superstitionibus quibusdam casibus* (Esslingen c.1473).
Herard: *Capitula* in Etienne Baluze (ed.): *Capitularia Regum Francorum* 2 vols (Paris 1677).
Heribert: *Epistola de haereticis Petragoricis* in Migne: *Patrologia Latina* 181.1722.
Hermann of Carinthia: *De Essentiis* in C. Burnett (ed.): *Hermann of Carinthia, De Essentiis* (Brill Leiden, 1982).

Hieronymus Radiolensis: *Vita Sancti Joannis Gualberti* in Migne: *Patrologia Latina* 146.811–970.
Hugh of St Victor: *Didascalion*, ed. C. H. Buttimer (The Catholic University Press, Washington DC 1939).
St Isidore of Seville: *De natura rerum* and *Etymologiae* in *Opera omnia quae existant* (Paris 1601).
Italikos Michael: *Lettres et Discours*, ed. P. Gautier (Paris 1972).
Jacques du Clerc: *Mémoires*, in J. A. Buchon (ed.): *Chroniques d'Enguerrand de Monstrelet* Vol. 14 (Paris 1826).
John XXII: *Extravagantes Decretales: De crimine falsi* in *Liber sextus decretalium D. Bonifacii Papae VIII, Clementis Papae V constitutiones, Extravagantes tum viginti D. Ioannis Papae XXII, tum communes*, editio ultima (Leiden 1613).
——: *Letter* in J. Hansen (ed.): *Quellen und Untersuchungen zur Geschichte des Hexenwahns und der Hexenverfolgung im Mittelalter* (Bonn 1901).
St John of Damascus: *De fide orthodoxa* in Migne: *Patrologia Latina* 96.866–78.
John of Rupescissa: *De consideratione quintae essentiae* (Basel 1597).
Kedrenos George: *Compendium historiarum* in Migne: *Patrologia Graeca* Vol. 121.
Komnena Anna: *Alexias*, ed. D. R. Reinsch & A. Kambylis 2 vols (de Gruyter, Berlin 2001).
Laws of the Earliest English Kings, ed. F. L. Attenborough (Cambridge University Press 1922).
Leo IV: *Letter to the Bishops of Britain* in *Monumenta Germaniae Historica*, Epistolae Vol. 5 (Berlin 1899).
Lex Frisionum, ed. K. A. Eckhardt & A. Eckhardt in *Monumenta Germaniae Historica* Vol. 12 (Hanover 1982).
Lex Ribuaria in *Monumenta Germaniae Historica* Leges Section 1, Tome 3, part 2 (Hanover 1954).
Liutprand: *Laws* in *Monumenta Germaniae Historica* Leges Vol. 4 (Hanover 1868).
Lydgate John: *Secrees of Old Philosoffres*, ed. R. Steele (London 1894).
Maimonides: *Dalalat al-Ha'rin [Doctor Perplexorum]* (Sabbioneta 1553).
Marbodus: *Liber lapidum* in Migne: *Patrologia Latina* 171.1738-70.
Marie de France: *Les Fables*, ed. C. Brucker (Peeters, Paris/Louvain 1998).
Martin le Franc: *Le champion des dames* in M. Ostorero, A. Paravicini Bagliani, K. Utz Tremp (eds): *L'imaginaire du sabbat* (Lausanne 1999).
Molitor Ulrich: *De laniis et phitonicis mulieribus* (Strassburg c.1489).
Al-Nadim: *Kitab al-Fihrist* in M. Berthelot: *La Chimie au Moyen Age* Vol. 3 (Paris 1893, reprinted Ossnabrück/Amsterdam 1967).
Nicolas of Cusa: *Opera Omnia* Vol. 16. (1) ed. R. Haubst (Hamburg 1970).
——: *Dialogi de ludoglobi* (Basel 1565).
Nider Johannes: *Preceptorium divine legis* (Milan 1489).
Ortulanus: *Practica vera alkimica* in *Theatrum Chemicum* Vol. 4 (Strasborg 1659).
Pactus legis Salicae in *Monumenta Germaniae Historica* Leges section 1, Tome IV, part 1 (Hanover 1962).
Picatrix. See Pseudo al-Majriti.
Pietro d'Abano: *Pretiosa margarita novella* (Venice 1546).

Pseudo al-Majriti: *Ghayat al-hakim* [*Picatrix*], ed. D. Pingree (London, Warburg Institute 1986).
Pseudo-Geber: *Summa Perfectionis in Alchemiae Gebri Arabis* (Bern 1545).
Ripley George: *The Compound of Alchemy* in G. Ashmole (ed.): *Theatrum Chemicum Britannicum* (London 1652).
Rolandino da Padova: *Cronica in factis et circa facta Marche Trivixane* ed. A. Bardi (S. Lapi Città de Castello, 1903).
Rothair: *Edictus* in *Monumenta Germaniae Historica* Leges Vol. 4 (Hanover 1868).
Savonarola Girolamo: *Trattato contra li astrologi* in G. Garfagnini & E. Garin (eds): *Edizione nazionale delle opera di Girolamo Savonarola: Scritti Filosofici* Vol. 1 (Angelo Belardetti Editore, Rome 1982).
Scot Michael: *Liber phisionomie* (Paris c.1515).
Silvestris Bernardus: *Cosmographia*, ed. P. Dronke (Brill, Leiden 1978).
Sortes XII Patriarcharum, in T. C. Skeat: 'An early Mediaeval Book of Fate: the Sortes XII Patriarcharum', *Mediaeval and Renaissance Studies* 3 (1954),41–54.
Summa Parisiensis, ed. T. P. McLaughlin (Pontifical Institute of Mediaeval Studies, Toronto 1952).
Synod of Salamanca 1451 in *Synodicon Hispanum* Vol. 4 ed. A. Garcia y Garcia (Madrid 1987).
Thomas of Cantimpré: *Bonum universale de apibus* (Paris 1516).
Trial of Gilles de Rais, ed. L. Hernandez, *Le procès inquisitorial de Gilles de Rais* (Paris 1921).
Trial of St Jeanne d'Arc, ed. P. Champion: *Procès de condemnation de Jeanne d'Arc* 2 vols (Paris 1920–1).
Trithemius: *Beati Rabani Mauri Vita* in Migne: *Patrologia Latina* 107.91-3.
Villani Giovanni: *Croniche Fiorentini* in *Croniche di Giovanni, Matteo, e Filippo Villani* Vol. 1 (Trieste 1857).
Wynkyn de Worde: *The Myracles of Oure Lady*, ed. P. Whiteford (Heidelberg 1990).
Yonge James: *The Governance of Prynces* in R. Steele (ed.): *Three Prose Versions of the Secreta Secretorum* Part 1 (London 1898).

Secondary sources: select reading

Adamson P.: 'Abu Ma'sar, Al-Kindi, and the philosophical defence of astrology', *Recherches de théologie et philosophie médiévales* 69 (2002), 245–70.
Ankarloo B. & Clark S. (eds): *The Athlone History of Witchcraft and Magic in Europe* Vol. 3 *The Middle Ages* (Athlone Press, London 2002).
Bailey M. D.: 'The Mediaeval concept of the witches' Sabbath', *Exemplaria* 8 (1996), 419–39.
——: 'From sorcery to witchcraft: clerical conceptions of magic in the later Middle Ages', *Speculum* 76 (2001), 960–90.
——: *Battling Demons: Witchcraft, Heresy, and Reform in the Late Middle Ages* (Pennsylvania State University Press, University Park 2003).
Bartlett R.: *Trial by Fire and Water: The Mediaeval Judicial Ordeal* (Clarendon Press, Oxford 1986).
Bechtel G.: *La sorcière et l'Occident* (Plon, Paris 1997).

Bertelli S.: 'Un manoscritto di geomanzia in volgare della fine del secolo XII', *Studi di filologia italiana* 57 (1999), 5–32.
Bildhauer B. & Mulls R. (eds): *The Monstrous Middle Ages* (University of Wales, Cardiff 2003).
Blauert A.: *Frühe Hexenverfolgungen: Ketzer-, Zauberei- und Hexenprozesse des 15 Jahrhunderts* (Hamburg 1989).
Blöcker M.: 'Ein Zauberprozess im Jahe 1028', *Schweizerische Zeitschrift für Geschichte* 29 (1979), 533–55.
Boureau A.: 'Le sabbat et la question scolastique de la personne', in Jacques-Chaquin & Préaud: *Le sabbat des sorciers*, q.v., 33–46.
Brann N. L.: 'Alchemy and melancholy in Mediaeval and Renaissance thought', *Ambix* 32 (1985), 127–48.
——: *Trithemius and Magical Theology: A Chapter in the Controversy over Occult Studies in Early Modern Europe* (State University of New York Press; Albany 1999).
Broedel H. P.: *The Malleus Maleficarum and the Construction of Witchcraft: Theology and Popular Belief* (Manchester University Press 2003).
Brown P. (ed.): *The Interpretation of Dreams from Chaucer to Shakespeare* (Oxford University Press 1999).
Burland C. A.: *The Arts of the Alchemists* (Weidenfeld & Nicolson, London 1967).
Burnett C. (ed.): *Magic and Divination in the Middle Ages: Texts and Techniques in the Islamic and Christian Worlds* (Variorum, Aldershot 1996).
Butler E. M.: *The Myth of the Magus*, (Cambridge University Press 1979).
Bynum C. W.: *Metamorphoses and Identity* (Zone Books, New York 2001).
Caciola N.: 'Wraiths, revenants, and ritual in Mediaeval culture', *Past and Present* 152 (1996), 3–45.
——: *Discerning Spirits: Divine and Demonic Possession in the Middle Ages* (Cornell University Press, Ithaca 2003).
Cardini F.: 'La stregoneria e le sue radice mediterranee: indagine sui predicatori italiani nel xv secolo', in J. Hinojosa Montalvo & J. Pradells Nadal (eds): *En el umbral de la modernidad* (Generalitat Valenciana, Valencia 1994), 475–86.
Caroti S.: 'Nicole Oresme's polemic against astrology in his *Quodlibeta*', in P. Curry (ed.): *Astrology, Science, and Society: Historical Essays* (Boydell Press, Woodbridge 1987), 75–93.
Catani R.: 'Girolamo Savonarola and astrology', *The Italianist* 18 (1998), 71–90.
——: 'The polemics on astrology, 1489–1524', *Culture and Cosmos* 3 (1999), 16–30.
——: 'The danger of demons: the astrology of Marsilio Ficino', *Italian Studies* 55 (2000), 37–52.
Cohn N.: *Europe's Inner Demons: The Demonisation of Christians in Mediaeval Christendom*, revised ed. (Pimlico edition, London 1993).
Collard F.: 'Veneficiis vel maleficiis. Refléxion sur les relations entre le crime de poison et la sorcellerie dans l'Occident médiéval', *Le Moyen Age* 109 (2003), 9–57.
Cook J.: 'Nice young girls and wicked old witches: the "rightful" age of women in Middle English verse', in E. Mullally & J. Thomson (eds): *The Court and Cultural Diversity* (Boydell & Brewer, Woodbridge 1997), 219–28.
Couliano I. P.: 'Dr Faust, great sodomite and necromancer', *Revue de l'histoire des religions* 207 (1990), 261–88.

Draelants I., Tihon A., van den Abeele B. (eds): *Occident et Proche-Orient: Contacts scientifiques au temps des Croisades* (Brepols, Lausanne 2000).
Eade J. C.: *The Forgotten Sky: A Guide to Astrology in English Literature* (Clarendon, Oxford 1984).
Eamon W.: *Science and the Secrets of Nature: Books of Secrets in Mediaeval and Early Modern Culture* (Princeton University Press 1994).
Elliott D.: *Fallen Bodies: Pollution, Sexuality, and Demonology in the Middle Ages* (University of Pennsylvania Press, Philadelphia 1999).
Fabricius J.: *Alchemy: The Mediaeval Alchemists and their Royal Art* (Rosenkilde & Bagger, Copenhagen 1976).
Fahd T.: 'The dream in Mediaeval Islamic society', in G. E. von Grunebaum & R. Caillois (eds): *The Dream and Human Societies* (University of California Press, Berkeley 1966), 351–63.
Fanger C. (ed.): *Conjuring Spirits: Texts and Traditions of Mediaeval Ritual Magic* (Sutton, Stroud 1998).
Ferreiro A. (ed.): *The Devil, Heresy, and Witchcraft in the Middle Ages* (Brill, Leiden 1998).
Ferreiro J. A.: 'La escuela de nigromancia de Toledo', *Anuario des estudios medievales* 13 (1983), 205–68.
Flint V. I. J.: The *Rise of Magic in Early Mediaeval Europe* (Princeton University Press 1993).
Font J. Garcia: *Historia de la Alquimia en España* (Editora Nacional, Madrid 1976).
Fraioli D. A.: *Joan of Arc, The Early Debate* (Boydell Press, Woodbridge 2000).
Frijhoff W.: 'Sorcellerie et possession: du Moyen Âge aux lumières', *Revue d'histoire ecclésiastique* 95 (2000), 112–42.
Gaignebit C.: 'Discours de la sorcière de Saint-Julien-de-Lampon', in Jacques-Chaquin & Préaud: *Le sabbat des sorciers*, q.v., 47–53.
Gari Lacruz A.: 'La bruixerìa a través de les ordinacions d'Àneu', in J. I. Padilla I Lapuente (ed.): *L'Esperit d'Àneu; Llibre dels costume i ordinacions de les valls d'Àneu* (Esterri d'Àneu 1999), 47–56.
Gessmann G. W.: *Die Geheimsymbole der Alchymie, Arzneikunde und Astrologie des Mittelalters* (Berlin 1922, reprint Ulm-Donau 1959).
Gettings F.: *The Secret Zodiac: The Hidden Art in Mediaeval Astrology* (Routledge & Kegan Paul, London 1987).
Goldish M. (ed.): *Spirit Possession in Judaism: Cases and Contexts from the Middle Ages to the Present* (Wayne State University Press, Detroit 2003).
Greenfield R.: 'Sorcery and politics at the Byzantine Court in the twelfth century: interpretations of history', in R. Beaton & C. Roueché (eds): *The Making of Byzantine History* (Variorum, Aldershot 1993), 73–85.
Griffiths B.: *Aspects of Anglo-Saxon Magic* (Anglo-Saxon Books, Hockwold-cum-Wilton 1996).
Haas A. M.: 'Otherwordly journeys in the Middle Ages', in B. McGuire (ed.): *The Encyclopaedia of Apocalypticism* Vol. 2 *Apocalypticism in Western History and Culture* (Continuum, New York and London 2000), 442–66.
Harvey M.: 'Papal witchcraft: the charges against Benedict XIII', *Studies in Church History* 10 (1973), 109–16.
Hasse D. N.: *Avicenna's De Anima in the Latin West* (Warburg Institute, London 2000).

Head T.: 'Saints, heretics, and fire: finding meaning through the ordeal', in S. Farme & B. H. Rosenwein (eds): *Monks and Nuns, Saints and Outcasts* (Cornell University Press, Ithaca 2000), 220–38.

Hutton R.: *Witches, Druids, and King Arthur* (Hambledon & London, London & New York 2003).

Institoris H.: *Malleus Maleficarum, Der Hexenhammer* (Deutscher Taschenbuch Verlag, Munich 2001).

Jacques-Chaquin N. & Préaud M. (eds): *Le sabbat des sorciers xve–xviiie siècles* (Millon, Grenoble 1993).

Jolly K. L.: *Popular Religion in Late Saxon England: Elf Charms in Context* (University of North Carolina Press, Chapel Hill 1996).

——: 'Mediaeval magic: definitions, beliefs, practices', in Ankarloo & Clark: *Athlone History of Witchcraft and Magic in Europe*, q.v., 1–71.

Kennedy E. S.: *Astronomy and Astrology in the Mediaeval Islamic World* (Ashgate, Aldershot 1998).

Kieckhefer R.: *European Witch Trials: Their Foundations in Popular and Learned Culture, 1300–1500* (Routledge & Kegan Paul, London 1976).

——: *Magic in the Middle Ages* (Cambridge University Press 1989).

——: 'Erotic magic in Mediaeval Europe', in J. E. Salisbury (ed.): *Sex in the Middle Ages* (Garland, London & New York 1991), 30–55.

——: 'The specific rationality of Mediaeval magic', *American Historical Review* 99 (1994), 813–36.

——: *Forbidden Rites: A Necromancer's Manual of the Fifteenth Century* (Sutton, Stroud 1997).

King P. D.: *Law and Society in the Visigothic Kingdom* (Cambridge University Press 1972).

Kirsch I.: 'Demonology and the rise of science: an example of the misperception of historical data', *Journal of the History of the Behavioural Sciences* 14 (1978), 149–57.

Kitson A.: 'Chaucer's astrology', in A. Kitson (ed.): *History and Astrology: Clio and Urania Confer* (Unwin, London 1989), 60–88.

Lecouteux C.: 'Les maîtres du temps: tempestaires, obligateurs, défenseurs et autres', in J. Duclos & C. Thomasset (eds): *Le temps qu'il fait au Moyen-Âge*, (Presses de l'Université de Paris, Sorbonne 1998).

Lemay R.: 'The true place of astrology in Mediaeval science and philosophy: towards a definition', in P. Curry (ed.): *Astrology, Science, and Society: Historical Essays* (Boydell Press, Woodbridge 1987), 57–73.

Lemke G. H.: *Sonne, Mond und Sterne in der deutschen Literatur seit dem Mittelalter: ein Bildamplex im Spannungsfeld gesellschaftlichen Wendels* (Lang, Bern 1981).

Lesses R. M.: *Ritual Practices to Gain Power: Angels, Incantations, and Revelation in Early Jewish Mysticism* (Harvard University Press, Boston 1998).

Lewis S.: *Astrology and Juan de Mena's Laberinto de Fortuna* (Dept of Hispanic Studies, Queen Mary & Westfield College, London 1999).

Linden S. J.: *Darke Hierogliphicks: Alchemy in English Literature from Chaucer to the Renaissance* (University Press of Kentucky, Lexington 1996).

Longobardi M.: ' "Ignotosque deos ignoto carmine adorat": qualche osservazione sullo scongiuro', *Annali della Facoltà di lettere e filosofia dell'Università di Siena* 20 (1999), 41–76.

Lucas J.: *Astrology and Numerology in Mediaeval and Early Modern Catalonia* (Brill, Leiden 2003).
Maguire H. (ed.): *Byzantine Magic*, (Dumbarton Oaks Research Library and Collection, Washington DC 1995).
Maier E.: *Trente ans avec le diable: une nouvelle chasse aux sorciers sur la Riviera lémanique, 1477–1484* (Université de Lausanne, Lausanne 1996).
Marshall P.: *The Philosopher's Stone: A Quest for the Secrets of Alchemy* (Macmillan, London 2001).
Mathisen R. W.: 'Crossing the supernatural frontier in Western late antiquity', in R. W. Mathisen & H. S. Sivan (eds): *Shifting Frontiers in Late Antiquity* (Ashgate, Aldershot 1996), 309–20.
Maxwell-Stuart P. G.: *Wizards, A History* (Tempus, Stroud 2004).
Meier F.: 'Some aspects of inspiration by demons in Islam', in G. E. von Grunebaum & R. Caillois (eds): *The Dream and Human Societies* (University of California Press, Berkeley 1966), 421–9.
Micrologus: III *Le crisi dell'alchimia* (Brepols, Lausanne 1991).
Modestin G.: *Le diable chez l'évêque: chasse aux sorciers dans le diocèse de Lausanne, vers 1440* (Brepols, Lausanne 1999).
——: 'Der Teufel in der Landschaft. Zur Politik der Hexenverfolgungen im heutigen Kanton Freiburg von 1440–1470', *Freiburger Geschichtsblätter* 76 (1999), 81–122.
Moore R. I.: 'Between sanctity and superstition: saints and their miracles in the age of revolution', in M. Rubin (ed.): *The Works of Jacques le Goff and the Challenges of Mediaeval History* (Boydell Press, Woodbridge 1997), 55–67.
Mormando F.: *The Preacher's Demons: Bernardino of Siena and the Social Underworld of Early Renaissance Italy* (University of Chicago Press 1999).
Moulinier L. & Redon O.: 'L'inondation de 1333 à Florence. Récit et hypothèses de Giovanni Villani', *Médiévales* 36 (1999), 91–104.
Moyer A.: 'The astronomers' game: astrology and university culture in the fifteenth and sixteenth centuries', *Early Science and Medicine* 4 (1999), 228–50.
Muchembled R.: *A History of the Devil from the Middle Ages to the Present*, English trans (Polity Press, Cambridge 2003).
Newman W. R.: 'An overview of Roger Bacon's alchemy', in J. Hackett (ed.): *Roger Bacon and the Sciences* (Brill, Leiden 1997), 317–36.
North J. D.: 'Mediaeval concepts of celestial influence, a survey', in P. Curry (ed.): *Astrology, Science, and Society: Historical Essays* (Boydell Press, Woodbridge 1987), 5–17.
Ostorero M.: *Folâtrer avec les démons: Sabbat et chasse aux sorciers à Vevey, 1448*, (Brepols, Lausanne 1995).
Ostorero M., Paravicini Bagliani A., Utz Tremp K. (eds): *L'imaginaire du Sabbat* (Brepols, Lausanne 1999).
Page S.: *Astrology in Mediaeval Manuscripts* (University of Toronto Press 2002).
Pastore F.: *La Fabrica delle Streghe* (Campanotto Editore, Pasian di Prato 1997).
Patai R.: *The Jewish Alchemists* (Princeton University Press 1994).
Peters E.: *The Magician, the Witch, and the Law* (University of Pennsylvania Press, Philadelphia 1978).
——: 'The Mediaeval Church and state on superstition, magic, and witchcraft: from Augustine to the sixteenth century', in Ankarloo & Clark: *Athlone History of Witchcraft and Magic in Europe*, q.v., 175–245.

Pfister L.: *L'enfer sur terre: sorcellerie à Dommartin, 1498* (Brepols, Lausanne 1997).

Pingree D.: 'The diffusion of Arabic magical texts in Western Europe', in *La diffusione delle scienze islamiche nel medioevo europeo* (Warburg Institute, Rome 1987), 57–102.

Po-chia Hsia R.: 'Witchcraft, magic, and the Jews in late Mediaeval and early modern Germany', in J. Cohen (ed.): *From Witness to Witchcraft: Jews and Judaism in Mediaeval Christian Thought* (Harrassowitz Verlag, Wiesbaden 1996), 419–33.

Polo de Beaulieu M.-A.: 'De Beaucaire (1211) à Àlies (1323), les revenants et leurs révélations sur l'au-delà', in J.-L. Biget (ed.): *La mort et l'au-delà en France méridionale (xiie-xve siècle)* (Editions Privat, Toulouse 1998), 319–41.

Purkiss D.: *Troublesome Things: A History of Fairies and Fairy Stories* (Allen Lane, London 2000).

Raudvere C.: 'Trolldómr in early Mediaeval Scandinavia', in Ankarloo & Clark: *Athlone History of Witchcraft and Magic in Europe*, q.v., 75–171.

Read J.: 'Alchemy under James IV of Scotland', *Ambix* 2 (1938), 60–7.

———: *Prelude to Chemistry* (Bell, London 1939).

Riisøy A. I.: 'What's on the case list? Legal texts and felonies rediscovered', *Scandinavian Journal of History* 27 (2002), 77–90.

Roberts G.: *The Mirror of Alchemy: Alchemical Ideas and Images in Manuscripts and Books from Antiquity to the Seventeenth Century* (British Library, London 1994).

Russell J.: *The Evil Eye in Early Byzantine Society: Archaeological Evidence from Anemurium in Isauria* XVI. Internationaler Byzantinischen Kongress, Vienna 1981, Akten II/3, *JOB* 32/3 (1982).

Russell J. B.: *Witchcraft in the Middle Ages* (Cornell University Press, Ithaca 1972).

———: *Lucifer: The Devil in the Middle Ages* (Cornell University Press, Ithaca 1984).

Schmitt J. C.: *Ghosts in the Middle Ages: The Living and the Dead in Mediaeval Society* English trans (University of Chicago Press 1998).

Skinner S.: *Terrestrial Astrology: Divination by Geomancy* (Routledge & Keegan Paul, London 1980).

Smoller L. A.: *History, Prophecy, and the Stars: The Christian Astrology of Pierre d'Ailly, 1350–1420* (Princeton University Press 1994).

Stephens W.: *Demon Lovers: Witchcraft, Sex, and the Crisis of Belief* (University of Chicago Press 2002).

Straubhaar S. B.: 'Nasty, brutish, and large: cultural difference and otherness in the figuration of the Trollwomen of the Fornaldar sögur', *Scandinavian Studies* 73 (2001), 105–24.

Strobino S.: *Françoise sauvée des flammes? Une Valesienne accusée de sorcellerie au xve siècle* (Brepols, Lausanne 1996).

Sullivan M. A.: 'The witches of Dürer and Hans Baldung Grien', *Renaissance Quarterly* 53 (2000), 333–401.

Tester S. J.: *A History of Western Astrology* (Boydell Press, Woodbridge 1987).

Thorndike L.: *A History of Magic and Experimental Science* 8 vols (Vol. II *The First Thirteen Centuries*; Vols. III & IV *Fourteenth and Fifteenth Centuries* Columbia University Press, New York 1923–58).

Travaglia P.: *Magic, Causality, and Intentionality: The Doctrine of Rays in Al-Kindi* (Brepols, Lausanne 1999).

Tschacher W.: 'Der Flug durch die Luft zwischen Illusionstheorie und Realitätsbeweis: Studien zum sog. Kanon Episcopi und zum Hexenflug', *Zeitschrift der Savigny-Stiftung für Rechtsgeschichte (Kanonistische Abteilung)* 116/129 (1999), 225–76.

Valakoudi A. D.: 'Deisidaimonia and the role of the apotropaic magic amulets in the early Byzantine Empire', *Byzantion* 70 (2000), 182–210.

Vescovini G. F.: 'Peter of Abano and astrology', in P. Curry (ed.): *Astrology, Science and Society: Historical Essays* (Boydell Press, Woodbridge 1987), 19–39.

Waite G. K.: *Heresy, Magic, and Witchcraft in Early Modern Europe* (Palgrave, Basingstoke 2003).

Waxman S. M.: 'Chapters on magic in Spanish literature', *Revue hispanique* 38 (1916), 325–463.

Wetherbee W.: *The Cosmographia of Bernardus Silvestris* (Columbia University Press, New York 1973).

Williams S. J.: 'Roger Bacon and the Secret of Secrets', in J. Hackett (ed.): *Roger Bacon and the Sciences* (Brill, Leiden 1997), 365–93.

Wilson A.: *Plots and Powers: Magical Structures in Mediaeval Narrative* (University Press of Florida, Gainesville 2001).

Wilson S.: *The Magical Universe in Pre-Modern Europe* (Hambledon & London, London & New York 2000).

Wolpert W.: 'Fünhundert Jahre Kreuzwig in Ediger an der Mosel. Inquisitor Heinrich Institoris als Initiator', in E. Biesel (ed.): *Hexenglaube und Hexenprozesse im Raum Rhein-Mosel-Saar* (Spee, Trier 1996), 19–34.

Zambelli P.: *The* Speculum Astronomiae *and its Enigma* (Kluwer, Dordrecht 1992).

Index

Abu Ma'shar, 170, 185
aeromancy, 71, 79, 83
air, 13, 19, 20, 36, 72, 91, 94, 96, 218
Albumasar, 168–9
alchemist, 106, 194, 217, 223–5, 229
alchemy, 107, 193–4, 201, 214, 220–3 passim, 226, 227, 228
alembic, 195, 202, 216
amulet, 7, 72 note 4, 73, 79, 81, 99–100, 116, 117, 129, 140, 142, 143, 145, 152, 171
angels, 2, 3, 4, 14, 40, 41, 42, 53, 79, 85, 90–5 passim, 103, 130, 131, 132, 142, 145, 169, 175 note 5
Aquarius, 100, 165, 180, 181
Aquinas, St Thomas, 7, 8, 9, 81, 130, 154, 164
Aries, 101, 165, 180, 213
Aristotle, 35 note 14, 38, 71, 166, 179–80, 181, 185, 216, 218, 228
arsenic, 194, 199, 212, 213, 217
astrologer, 17, 78, 79, 163, 164, 166, 167–8, 179, 181–2, 184 note 15, 185–8 passim
astrology, 62, 72, 79, 82, 107, 141, 163–4, 174, 181, 185, 186, 188, 189, 191, 193, 222
augury, 72–5 passim, 79, 129, 138, 140, 142, 143, 173
Augustine of Hippo, St, 2, 7, 8, 9, 46, 47, 83, 130, 131, 141, 164
Avicenna, 39, 185, 219, 220

bile (yellow), 19
bile (black), 19, 58, 217
blood, 22, 23, 24, 26, 27, 34, 59, 71, 80, 99, 100, 109, 118, 126, 172, 176, 178, 181, 213, 216, 217, 218, 220–1
blood (humour), 19, 36, 101

calcination, 195, 201
Cancer (astrological sign), 16, 165, 180, 181

Capricorn, 100, 165, 180, 181, 213
ceration, 196–7
characters, 7, 79, 80, 81, 105, 107, 108, 110, 111, 116, 175 note 5, 185, 186
charms, 75, 110, 147, 149
chiromancy, 79
Church, 1, 3, 5, 6, 9, 24, 25, 80, 88, 105, 127, 141–4 passim, 147, 148, 166
Circe, 34
circle, 74, 85, 90–1, 93–7 passim, 105–9 passim, 111, 120, 186
coagulation, 196, 199, 200, 210
comet, 2, 26, 166
concoction, 199
confession (sacrament), 75, 76, 117, 119, 126, 127, 154, 166
conjuration, 94, 97, 106
cure, 2, 7, 8, 34, 35, 43, 59, 60, 73, 85–8 passim, 100, 101, 102, 107, 145, 146, 149, 216, 219

daemon, 7 note 3, 8, 183, 184 note 16
decoction, 197, 199, 200, 212
demon, 2, 3, 4, 9, 32, 41, 42, 53, 54–5, 56–8, 63, 71, 72, 83, 85, 101, 103–8 passim, 110, 111, 112, 118, 119, 129–33 passim, 138, 155, 177, 183, 186
demoniacs, 53–4, 56–8, 80, 102, 152
descension, 195, 207
Devil, 6, 7, 38, 39, 58, 64, 67, 74, 76, 78, 79, 80, 103, 105, 117, 120, 121, 124–7 passim, 129, 131, 132, 137, 141, 143–7 passim, 151, 153, 155, 157–9 passim
distillation, 195
divination/diviners, 8, 54, 61–4, 71, 74, 78, 80, 82 note 12, 83, 84, 85, 88, 105, 119, 129, 136–47 passim, 149 note 56, 150, 185, 187
dreams, 31, 47, 62, 78, 83, 104 note 29, 143, 145, 171, 174

Index

earth (element), 13, 19, 20, 36, 71, 200, 218
earthquake, 26, 28
eclipse, 21, 22, 78, 163, 166, 192, 193
elements, 13, 16, 19, 36, 153, 157, 158, 182, 192, 200, 215, 218, 220
elixir, 194, 196, 213, 214, 215, 222, 228
evil eye, 38, 39, 73
excommunication, 144, 146, 147, 148 note 55
exorcism, 56, 92–3, 142, 155

fairies, 43, 48, 88
fire, 13, 15, 16, 19, 20, 26, 36, 48–9, 71, 74, 92, 93, 96, 106, 107, 218
fixation, 196, 197, 198, 202, 210
fumigants/fumigation, 92, 93, 98 note 21, 99, 107, 183

Gemini, 31, 165, 180
geomancy, 71, 79, 83, 84, 85, 105, 106, 174
ghosts, 4, 33, 34, 50, 119, 150 note 57, 191
God, 2–4 passim, 6, 8, 9, 14–17 passim, 25, 26, 40–2 passim, 44, 55, 56, 63, 73–5 passim, 78, 79, 81, 87, 91, 94–7 passim, 101, 102, 103, 110, 111, 114, 115, 116, 121, 126, 129, 131, 132, 137, 140, 143, 150, 154, 155, 157–9 passim, 168, 213, 219, 221, 222
Gualbert, St Giovanni, 56–8, 59

hail, 28, 94, 99, 103, 138, 144, 153, 158
Hell, 4, 49, 55, 124
heresy, 2, 5, 6, 9, 59, 76, 78, 85, 133, 141, 142, 146, 172
horoscope, 72, 79, 163, 164, 167, 168, 177, 179, 187
Host, 75–6, 89, 126
humours, 19, 36, 171, 176, 177, 178, 180, 183, 217, 220
hydromancy, 71, 79, 83

idolatry, 8, 75, 80, 85, 114, 142, 146
illusion, 5, 64, 71, 78, 120, 132, 133, 141, 143, 151 156, 186
images (magical), 66, 67, 85, 87, 89, 90, 99, 182–4 passim

incantation, 7, 47, 56, 57, 58, 60, 66, 72, 79, 80, 81, 85, 88, 116, 119, 132, 138, 139, 140, 145, 148, 150, 152, 191
incubus, 32, 116, 131
invocation, 88, 96, 105–11 passim, 138, 185, 186

Jews, 5, 6, 24, 170, 171
Joan of Arc, St, 43
Jupiter (astrological sign), 17, 165, 169, 171–2, 177, 178, 180, 181, 184
Jupiter (tin), 195, 196

Kabbalah, 4, 40

lamp, 151
Leo, 101, 165, 166, 180, 181, 192
Libra, 100–1, 165, 179, 180, 181
ligature, 72, 80, 149, 160
lightning, 25, 26, 28, 29, 72
lots, 61, 63–4, 72, 79, 83, 85, 88, 129, 136, 140, 142–6 passim, 185

magic, 4, 6–9 passim, 34, 46, 53, 56, 64, 66, 67, 71, 72, 82, 86, 87, 98, 99, 101, 110–14 passim, 117, 130, 132–50 passim, 152, 154–6 passim, 160, 164, 182, 185, 186, 190
magician, 3, 31, 83, 87, 93, 97, 105, 112, 142, 143, 152, 182, 186, 190
Mars (astrological sign), 17, 165, 166, 172, 173, 175–6, 178, 179, 181, 182
Mars (iron), 195, 196, 201
Mass, 48, 59, 61, 64, 66, 89, 93, 126, 127, 145
mathematica, *see* astrology
Mercury (astrological sign), 17, 165, 173, 174–5, 178, 182
miracle, 2, 3, 20, 29, 46, 59–60, 186
mirror, 79, 83, 182
monks, 22, 49–50, 52, 111, 113, 142, 144, 150
monster, 31–2, 46, 193
Moon (astrological sign), 17–18, 21, 74, 75, 79, 91, 92, 93, 98, 99, 100, 163, 165, 166, 175, 177–8, 180–1, 182
Moon (silver), 201
Moses, 24, 94, 95, 98 note 23, 190, 221, 222

necromancer/necromancy, 71, 72, 80, 83, 85, 104–12 passim, 150, 171, 175

ointment, 126
ordeal, 64–5, 79

pact, 77, 80, 105, 109, 114, 130
pentagram, 91, 93, 96, 97
Philosopher's Stone, 194, 198, 212, 213, 217, 218, 219, 223
phlegm, 19, 36, 217, 221
phylacteries, *see* amulet
physiognomy, 36, 79
Pisces, 165, 180, 181
planets, 6, 14–18 passim, 91, 93, 163–6 passim, 169, 176–9 passim, 181, 184 note 18, 187, 189, 193
Plato, 14, 176, 185, 187
Pope, 22, 45, 48, 84, 144, 145, 148, 166, 229
portents, 27, 28, 30, 72, 136, 137
possession, *see* demoniacs
powder, 110, 121, 126, 216, 217
praestigia, 8, 71, 72, 151, 152, 185
priest, 25, 44–5, 57, 58, 59, 63, 64–5, 105, 107, 116, 120, 142, 145, 147, 154
prodigies, 23, 26, 31, 190
prophesiers, 116, 118–19, 136, 137, 139, 143
Ptolemy, 18, 78, 179, 181, 185
pyromancy, 71, 79, 83

quicksilver, 196–200 passim, 210, 212, 217

relics, 8, 20, 63, 64, 75, 81
ring, 42, 85, 110, 111, 112
ritual, 2, 85, 140

Sabbat, 120–1, 122–8, 133, 158 note 63
sacrifice, 104, 105, 107, 126, 138, 140, 158, 185, 186
Sagittarius, 102, 165, 180
saints, 3, 8, 27, 64, 75, 86, 108, 140, 155, 185, 186
Satan, 2, 6, 10, 42, 103, 108, 121, 156
Saturn (astrological sign), 165, 166, 171, 173, 176–7, 178, 181, 182, 217
Saturn (lead), 195, 196

scepticism, 5, 148–50
Scorpio, 102, 165, 180, 181
Scotland, 27, 46
sigil, 90, 100–2
sodomy, 104, 105, 126
Solomon, 90, 96, 97, 175 note 5
solution, 195–6, 202, 212, 219
sorcery, 75, 85, 88, 121, 154, 155
spirits, 2, 3, 4, 7, 8, 40, 42, 51, 53, 56, 62, 71, 72, 75, 77–82 passim, 85, 88, 90, 91, 94, 96, 97, 104, 105, 106, 113, 114, 116, 117, 130, 132, 152, 153, 155, 156, 173, 183
stars, 6, 13, 15, 16, 17, 20, 21, 22, 62, 82, 99, 164, 165, 169, 183, 189, 190
storm, 2, 25, 80, 103, 121, 138, 145, 153, 156, 157, 258
sublimation, 194, 201–2, 210, 211, 212, 216, 217
sulphur, 177, 197–202 passim, 212, 213, 217
Sun (astrological sign), 17, 91, 92, 100, 101, 102, 165, 173, 178, 182, 184, 213
Sun (planet), 21, 22, 79, 99, 100, 166, 192
superstition, 1, 2, 3, 8, 75, 80, 81, 88, 110, 148, 164; superstitious, 1, 4, 5, 7, 8, 77, 78, 81, 82, 88, 110, 111, 130, 145, 185
sympathy, 4, 6

Taurus, 101, 165, 179, 180
torture, 67, 76, 104, 121–4 passim, 127, 130, 133, 137, 138, 153
tricks, 8, 53, 86, 87, 103, 110, 143, 151, 152, 185, 228

vampire, 117–18
Venus (astrological sign), 17, 165, 169, 173–4, 176, 178, 179, 181
Venus (copper), 195, 196, 201
Virgin Mary, 28, 43, 57, 58, 86, 103, 108, 128, 129, 169, 170
Virgo, 102, 165, 180

water, 13, 15, 19, 20, 24, 36, 64–5, 71, 73, 80, 92, 93, 150, 151, 175, 195, 196, 200, 210, 213, 218

werewolf, 43–6
witch, 4, 66–7, 75, 114, 115, 117–20 passim, 122–5 passim, 128, 129, 135, 136, 144 note 52, 146, 147, 150 note 57, 153, 154, 158 notes 60, 61, and 63, 158, 159

witchcraft, 4, 103, 110, 115, 122, 124, 125, 141
wonders, 2, 3, 8, 104, 132

zodiac, 14, 16, 99, 163
Zoroaster, 71